REVENGE

LAURA BLUMENFELD holds a master's degree in international affairs from Columbia University, and has been a staff writer at the *Washington Post* since 1992. She has also written for the *New Yorker*, the *New York Times Magazine*, *Elle*, and the *Los Angeles Times*. She currently lives in New York City.

Critical acclaim for
REVENGE: A STORY OF HOPE

'Thorough, courageous, intelligent, well written'
Financial Times

'A mighty achievement. Blumenfeld's drive to understand revenge leads her towards an examination of the emotional converse: empathy, compassion'
Guardian

'Blumenfeld's real point is that what happens in conflict zones is always personal as well as political'
Observer

'Remarkable . . . The book is an astonishing rollercoaster chronicle of the path of revenge'
Jewish Chronicle

'There is a strange compulsion in the litany of hatred and revenge; Blumenfeld illuminates the bitter, secret places of the human psyche and demonstrates just why vendettas can carry on for centuries, in a horrible conflation of the personal and the political'
Good Book Guide

'An intrinsically dramatic narrative, one almost mythic in its contours . . . Blumenfeld has delivered a work of ambition and humanity'
Washington Post

'The writing is energetic and concise, the first paragraph hooks you immediately, and the concept is fascinating'
Boston Globe

REVENGE

A STORY OF HOPE

LAURA BLUMENFELD

PICADOR

First published 2002 by Simon and Schuster, Inc., New York, USA

First published in Great Britain 2002 by Picador

This edition published 2003 by Picador
an imprint of Pan Macmillan Ltd
Pan Macmillan, 20 New Wharf Road, London N1 9RR
Basingstoke and Oxford
Associated companies throughout the world
www.panmacmillan.com

ISBN 0 330 49360 4

3 5 7 9 8 6 4 2

A CIP catalogue record for this book is available from the British Library.

Printed and bound in Great Britain by
Mackays of Chatham plc, Chatham, Kent

For Paul Appleby and Zehava Ben Ovadiah

of Blessed Memory

CONTENTS

REVENGE

1

HEAT

JULY 1998. KALANDIA, WEST BANK

THE GUNMAN WAS NOT HOME. "Come in," his mother said. "Would you like some orange soda?" She smiled back at me, waving me out of the sun and through her front door. The knock must have shaken her out of a nap; she had shuffled out in slippers and a pink embroidered bathrobe. She drew me inside, into a dimly lit living room, the curtains closed against the heat. Children were tucked into every shadow, three small boys wedged in an armchair, a teenager straddling the arms of the couch, toddlers blinking up from the floor.

"That's him," the woman said, pointing over her grandchildren's heads. I followed her finger to the wall, to the shooter's photograph, saw his face for the first time, and sank into the couch. His mother sat down on the edge of the coffee table facing me, her shoulders forward, her feet squared with mine, six inches separating our knees. We looked at each other for a moment. Her features were faded, but her brown eyes glittered, the wrinkles flying out like sunrays. She leaned closer and passed a glass of cold soda to me. Her fingers slid along mine, moist and cool.

"He tried to kill someone," she said in an easy voice.

"Who?" I asked.

"Some Jew," said the twelve-year-old on my right, shrugging.

I turned to him. The boy smiled crookedly. "I don't know who. A Mossad agent."

He laughed and everyone laughed. I joined in too, as best as I could. After all these years, I had arrived unannounced on their doorstep on a fiery July afternoon, a stranger with a notebook, dressed in white. I was a newspaper reporter from America, had picked my way down to their home on the edge of a barren gorge, woke them from their sleep and asked to hear their story. There were eight people in the living room, then ten and then fourteen. Family members wandered out of bed, out of a maze of connecting apartments, to see what the noise was about, to meet the unexpected guest.

"I'm not sure he was a Mossad agent," said a man with a well-plowed brow, leaning against the far wall. "He was a person from the outside, the head of a municipality in New York. We heard he was doing something against Palestinians. Why else would they choose him to be shot?"

This was Saed, the shooter's oldest brother. He served in Yasir Arafat's security forces in Ramallah. He wore an olive-drab shirt and army pants, and had an eagle tattoo and a snakeskin scar etched below his collarbone.

I lifted my eyebrows, encouraging him from across the room.

"It happened inside the Old City, near the Western Wall," he said, coming closer. "He shot the man one time in the head."

"Why only once?" I asked.

"It was in the marketplace." He laughed through clenched teeth.

"After the shooting, he threw the gun in the air, and it fell in the marketplace," said his mother.

We all started to chuckle at the comic scene: one bullet, a cowering Jew, the gun pinwheeling out of reach. The mother, laughing, smacked my thigh.

THE SHOOTER, it seemed, had bad aim. He fired at the American man half an inch too high, missing his brain and sparing his life.

Some of his partners had more success. In all, twenty-five men belonged to the Jerusalem death gang, which police called "one of the most dangerous and well-organized terror cells in recent memory." They were Palestinians in their twenties and early thirties, many of them ex-cons, all of them members of a radical faction of the PLO, backed by Syria. Their leader had blown out his own eyes while wiring a bomb to a Palestinian informer's car.

The winter of 1986 had been a quiet time in Jerusalem. People walked through the Old City without fear. In March, that changed. The gang began gunning down tourists—American, German, British—point-blank, a single shot through the skull.

The American man was their first victim. Next, the gang killed an Israeli businesswoman. Her twenty-year-old daughter had just dropped her off at work at a building outside the Old City's Damascus Gate. The assassin followed the woman up the stairs to the third floor. He walked through her office door as she was settling into her chair, adjusting a green cushion to support her back. She wore a ribbon in her hair, and clips to sweep back her long, brown waves. Eight-thirty in the morning, and here was her first client. Wordlessly, he removed a Beretta from inside his shirt and reached across her desk, over the coffee creamer, over the desktop calendar. He lifted the pistol to her left cheek. She hit the white tile floor so hard it knocked out her teeth.

That same week, another gang member ambushed a German tourist. She and her husband were on a Holy Land tour. On the third day of their trip, they strolled through Jerusalem's walled Old City, down the Via Dolorosa, the route Jesus took to his crucifixion. The couple stopped, arm in arm, near the first station of the cross to read a sign about the condemnation of Jesus. Suddenly there was an explosion, and a burning trickle beneath the German woman's blouse. A bullet pierced her an inch to the right of her spine, flying out between two ribs. The couple twisted and saw a man with black, matted hair and wild eyes standing ten feet away. His finger was hooked through the trigger, ready to fire again. I'm going to die, the woman thought. She struggled to shift her body in front of her husband's, to shield him. They had two young girls at home in Munich. Her husband had to live.

Eleven days later a fourth gunman struck. He scouted the streets near the Old City for the perfect site: the Garden Tomb, a secluded park revered by Anglicans as the place where Jesus was buried. Outside the door to the tomb, he found a young man sitting next to his backpack.

"How you doing?" the gunman said in English.

"Good," the tourist said, looking up from under a fringe of curls. He was a boyish twenty-seven, with round cheeks and believing eyes. He was holding a Bible.

"You American?" the killer asked hopefully.

"No, I'm British," the tourist said, raising a water bottle to his mouth.

British was almost as good. The gunman let him swallow the water. As he watched him screw the cap on the bottle, he stepped forward, so close he could have shaken the tourist's hand. He felt for the gun on his hip instead. One bullet in the brain. An Anglican minister ran outside when he heard the shot. He found a young man, a boy, really, lying on his back, his eyes still, his lips moving, trembling with his last breath. There was something red on his cheek. Not a lot of blood, just a dab, smeared like a hurried kiss.

I HAD PIECED TOGETHER fragments of these stories before. But now, surrounded by the shooter's family, I was hearing about the attack on the American for the first time.

"He never talks about it, even now," the shooter's father said. The father had entered the room in a long, gray robe and sat down next to me. He smiled with the practiced reassurance of a man who had raised eight children.

"Maybe he was forced to do it," the mother said.

"No, he wasn't forced," the shooter's nephew cut in. "He did it willingly."

"He was proud, he was beaming." Another nephew.

"After the incident, he came home and ate a big meal," said the shooter's sister-in-law. "He said, 'Don't go to Jerusalem, there's been a shooting. The city isn't stable.' " She remembered serving him a plate of melon as they listened to the radio. They heard a report about an American tourist who was shot in the head.

Now she was serving me a plate of cubed watermelon.

"May God bless your hands," I said, the traditional Arab thanks to someone who gives you food.

"And your hands too," she replied, offering me a napkin and fork.

The mother sighed at the mention of God. "I pray five times a day for my son."

"Yes, she prays for God to take away all the Jews," said an uncle. "We call to God. We call to Allah. We call to Jesus." He threw up a hand. "Nobody helps."

I plugged my mouth with watermelon. I widened my eyes to look more understanding. The room was warm, but my hosts brought out trays of black tea. The ground-up leaves spiraled and settled at the bottom of my glass. I grasped the rim and brought the tea to my lips, blowing off ringlets of steam.

"Why did he do it?" I said gently. I sipped the hot liquid.

"No reason," the mother said, uncurling her fist to reveal an empty hand.

"He did his duty. Every Palestinian must do it," the father said. "Then there will be justice."

"Was it for your honor?" I said.

"Not for my honor, for the honor of our people," he said.

"We were all with him politically," said Saed, the shooter's oldest brother. "We all think it was worth it—his duty to get back all the cities taken by the Jews."

The family ideology decorated the living room walls: the emblem of Force 17, a crack Palestinian military unit; framed snapshots of Saed in uniform with Arafat, Abu Jihad, and other famous guerrilla leaders; and the centerpiece, over the doorway, an enlarged color portrait of the shooter himself.

"No justice comes from the Jews," Saed said. He pinched the

skin on his neck, twisting it right, then left. "My other brother was in the Popular Front for the Liberation of Palestine. The Jews deported him from Palestine to Jordan."

The deported brother, Imad, straggled in from his nap. He found an armchair and slouched into it. He lit a cigarette and reflexively tipped the pack toward me. This brother looked different from Saed, the officer. Imad's hair, mustache and goatee were dyed a burned orange. He had inherited his father's bony height and his mother's polished brown eyes. He wore a silky red and black shirt. Imad had returned in 1994 from twenty-five years of exile, after the Israelis and Palestinians signed a peace deal. The revolutionary now worked as a beautician.

"Anybody would do what my brother did under those circumstances," Imad said, squeezing his cigarette between his forefinger and his thumb. "If you pretend to be a Palestinian for five minutes, you'll feel what we feel."

"And what about the man he tried to kill?"

"It wasn't a personal vendetta," Imad said. "He didn't know the man. He did it so people would look at us. It was public relations."

As Imad spoke, smoke poured from his mouth. For a moment, he was a voice inside a cloud.

"I am a victim," he said.

A shot went off outside and I must have flinched.

"Don't worry," the father said with his reassuring smile. "It's not a gun. It's a wedding. Fireworks for the party."

Another sister-in-law brought out another tray of scalding tea. I had not seen her before. How many people were in this family? I started counting. Fifteen grandchildren blocked my exit to the door.

"Won't someone from the victim's family kill one of your people?" I said.

"No," said Imad. "There's no revenge." Smoke coiled around each syllable. "My brother never met the man personally. It's not a personal issue. Nothing personal, so no revenge."

The fan behind Imad was blowing his smoke onto me, mixing

it with his breath and his sweat. It was not an unpleasant smell, but it was strange, inhaling Imad. I drained my glass, burning my tongue. I looked at the clock behind him, a souvenir stamped "I ❤ Jerusalem" in English. I had been sitting with the shooter's family for over four hours. It was time to go.

Come back, visit soon, they insisted. I thanked them for their hospitality and promised that I would. They stood up and, one by one, offered me their hands—muscled housewife hands; gummy toddler fingers; bashful shakes from the girls; blanketing grips from the men; darting, palmy handshakes from the teenage boys. I looked into each person's eyes and felt my lips pull back in a smile.

Outside, more relatives waited and more handshakes. It was sundown on a Friday. The day was spent, burned out in the white hills above the gorge. Everything had turned a shamefaced pink. I walked up toward the main road, and after a minute, my cellular phone rang.

"Just wanted to see if you're OK." It was my husband.

"Yes, I'm just walking up the hill from their house," I said, breathing hard and I hung up.

Then I looked back. The family had gathered on the front steps, in the slanted pink light, arms and wrists and elbows all together, waving. There was Imad, his flaming curls sticking up behind the rest, waving good-bye. "My brother never met the man personally," Imad had said. "It's not a personal issue." I smiled and gave one last spirited wave before I disappeared around the corner. My limbs moved stiffly, as if I had been holding them for hours in an unnatural pose. I felt relief, and then I felt something else. Inside, a clamp came loose. All the swallowed heat rose from my stomach, stinging my chest and my neck. "Nothing personal," Imad had said, "so no revenge." The heat was rising in my face. It was personal. It was personal to me.

2

SHAME

LONG ISLAND, NEW YORK, SIX MONTHS EARLIER

SEVEN MORE HOURS until our honeymoon. Seven hours, and we would fly east, across the night and the black Atlantic, across Europe and another sea, and then circle down onto an orange-groved coast to live for our newlywed year.

I sat on the floor at my mother's house, two suitcases unzipped at my knees. My clothes lay heaped in a closet, stored between moves from my apartment in Washington to my husband's in New York City to our future place in Jerusalem. I stared into the empty suitcases, and I called my friend Rachel in Rhode Island.

"What things do I need?"

Rachel was an economics professor at Brown University and the child of excitable intellectuals. She had spent a lifetime soothing her parents. She calmed me too, chasing away my anxieties by making fun of me.

"What do you wear to get revenge?" Rachel said, mocking me. "Black. And red."

I hung up the phone and tossed in two boxes of blue pens. Then the telephone rang.

"Oh, hi, honey. Is your mother home?" It was a friend of my mother's, a voice graveled with good cheer and tinged with orange lipstick.

"So you're visiting Israel with your new husband," she said. "History is repeating itself. Just like when your mom went with your dad!" She laughed, making history sound so bright.

It was true, my parents had had an enchanted newlywed year abroad. My mother volunteered, teaching music to immigrant children. My father studied comparative religion at Hebrew University in Jerusalem. They hitchhiked with truckers to the Red Sea, tended a vineyard on a kibbutz, tasted their first pomegranate, their first falafel, tasted many things, my mother liked to say with a smile, for the first time. On their way home they stopped in Spain, saw a bullfight, went back to their hotel room and conceived my older brother.

Now they were divorced. "Mom?" I called down her hallway.

No answer, but I could hear a truck pulling into the driveway. My husband and I had ordered a houseful of furniture. We had no home, but we would have bookcases and a headboard for the home we would make one day. I said good-bye to my mother's friend and hurried out into the winter chill, still holding the telephone. The deliverymen lowered wooden crates onto the lawn. They pried open each crate with a satisfying crack.

The chairs were snapped in half; the round tabletop had split into six sharp pieces of pie; cabinet doors were ripped from their hinges; the glass panels had shattered. Every piece of our future home hatched from its crate damaged.

I dialed my husband at the apartment in Manhattan, crunching across the grass, slivers of glass sticking to my shoes.

"Our home is broken," I said, pausing for his reaction. *A broken home, see the omen?* But Baruch was not poetic. He was a federal prosecutor, a literal-minded lawyer, and he preferred to ignore me when I indulged in melodrama.

"Take pictures of everything," he said, unmoved. "We'll have to document this."

Then he went back to work, filling out a fifty-page application to become a judge. I went back to my work, plotting my own form of justice. It was late, the sun's chin had hit the ground and I could not find the poem. Twelve years had passed since I had written it. It was about my father, walking through the Arab marketplace. . . .

"Where's my little missy?" a voice sang out. The back door slammed. Clappity footsteps approached.

"Hi, sweety-pie dolly darling." My mother's head popped through my door, making me smile. She had that effect on people. She had grown up in Kansas City, a girl with a gap-toothed grin who had never lost her optimism. She had raised me and my brother and then went to law school. She married a businessman named Bernie, capped her teeth to match his and ran for Congress.

"Almost ready?" she said. Her cheeks were a windblown pink, like her sweater, making her look even cheerier than usual.

"I can't find one of my poems," I said.

"I have all your poems," she offered, turning, heels clacking down the tiles to her office. She walked ahead of me, radiating cool, sweet air. "They're in my file cabinet."

We flipped through the old, worn file and found the title "I Am His Daughter." The date: March 1986. I was at Harvard College, enrolled in a poetry-writing seminar taught by Seamus Heaney, the Nobel prize–winning Irish poet. The other students were much more sophisticated than I was. One classmate said that it seemed like I had arrived at college "after twelve years of nursery school." In a sense, I had. I had drunk wine once, had never crossed the line with boyfriends. I had puffed on cigarettes a couple of times, mostly in front of my mother. My home was a place where people got along. Neighborhood kids would gather at our house because while their parents yelled, mine sat around the dinner table, singing from the Rotary Club songbook.

Then I left for college and my mother left my father. Their marriage, a seemingly happy one for twenty-five years, ended. I wrote a poem in the voice of a bewildered child, called "When My Family Got Divorced." Later that semester, I wrote the poem "I Am

His Daughter." Heaney's assignment was to write about an event that had happened that week. I handed this in:

If you saw him walking
through the twisted canals
of the Arab market
last Friday night

If you are the one
watched his white yarmulke
glide along blackstone
alleys winding home
from the Western Wall

If you are the man
marked his head
float past the spiceman
rugdealer butcher
closing their shops

If you are the Arab
aimed in the near dark
grazing his temple
missing his life,
this hand will find you
I am his daughter.

It was not a great poem. "I don't think you've managed to get into the centre of your feelings and your own language yet," Heaney wrote on my final evaluation for the course. He gave me a B+.

I folded the sheet of paper into eighths and handed the square to my mother.

"I promised to find that guy," I said, a little amazed.

A look came over her face, as if she were wondering, Who is this girl?

"I wish you wouldn't do that," she said. She cleared her throat. This was either a serious or a frivolous conversation. She looked unsure, the pink in her cheeks receding. She had heard me talk about the man who had shot my father before, but had not taken it seriously. She could not imagine her daughter damming up that much anger. No one who knew me could.

"You know, he's a . . ." My mother paused, her lips rooting around, searching for the right words. Finally, "He's a bad dude."

And that was it. I left the subject alone, let her believe what she wanted to believe. There were twenty-five years between us, though we had grown up like sisters. We were confidantes and, sometimes, co-conspirators. Before I even understood what life was about, I understood that my mother and I were in it together. We had made plans, like schoolgirls who must never separate, to meet after we died, floating above our favorite hilltop.

Still, I said nothing more to her about the shooter. A woman who visited her marigolds in the backyard every morning, bending down to pat their heads, wishing them a happy day, had no place on a journey into revenge.

Not until I figured out how she could help.

Meanwhile, her housekeeper drove me to the station to catch a train into the city.

"Your mom and Bernie are a perfect match," she said, filling the car with the biting smell of alcohol. She was in the middle of her own divorce and was fighting over the children. "I can't believe your mom was married to someone else for twenty-five years."

"My father," I mouthed, grinding a paper cup into her floor mat with my shoe.

"You going to have kids?" she said. "Your mom was talking to me about it this morning. She says, 'Bring back a little Israeli citizen.' "

I ran from her car to make the train. When I arrived in Manhattan, I found Baruch in the living room in his underwear and an undershirt, stuffing a duffel bag with running socks.

Moments later, the doorman buzzed: "David Blumenfeld is

here." My father and his wife, Fran, had driven in from New Rochelle, a Westchester suburb, to take us to the airport. Fran taught high school science; he worked as an executive in a synagogue organization. They often dressed like twins—matching jeans and Hawaiian "Happily Mauied" T-shirts—but tonight, I noticed my dad had picked out a different outfit.

My father's hug was wide and warm. He took out a ten-dollar bill and gave it to me. "Give this to a beggar in Jerusalem." It was an old Jewish custom and a family tradition: send money with a loved one going on a trip, to give to charity. It protected the traveler by turning a journey into a good deed.

"Go, team, go!" my father said as Baruch struggled to cram the last few items into his bag. Baruch ended up putting them on, lumbering out to the Toyota in a T-shirt, a rugby shirt, a hooded sweatshirt, a leather bomber jacket and a lined trench coat. With the hood of the trunk roped and banging against Baruch's bicycle box, we left for Kennedy International Airport.

My father started to cough again.

"You should go to the doctor and check that cough," I said.

"Don't worry, Laura," Fran said. "I take very good care of him."

At the terminal, we pulled in behind my mother's car, white fumes snaking up from the tailpipe of her husband's Mercedes. Both of my parents wanted to see me off. She delivered my luggage; he delivered me.

"Hiya, Norma!" my father said, stepping toward her, grinning, as she got out of the car. His face looked young and hopeful, a snapshot from a long-ago family vacation—a man on a beach somewhere, framed by his two children, nuzzling his wife, grounded in the goodness of his home. My mother, my father had once told me, was always the most beautiful woman in the room. Suddenly I thought I understood why he chose a tweed blazer and a snug black turtleneck to drop off his daughter at the airport.

My mother smiled a tight hello. She crossed her arms and her ankles. He tried to catch her eye, but her eyes moved sideways. She never kissed him anymore, not even a formal peck. I winced. Did he feel humiliated, did anyone even notice? Baruch was grunting his bicycle out of the trunk. Fran, hands in her coat pockets, stood by on the curb.

"Be careful," my mother said, kissing me on the ear. Teary-eyed, she drove away.

The trickier good-bye was with my father. In some ways, this trip was all about him. I had told my father that I might look for the shooter, though I kept my intentions vague, partly because they were. I was heading off to start a new family; but first I had some unfinished business with my old family. There were things from the past that I had to set right before I could move forward.

As I walked down the airport corridor, I kept turning to look back. Ahead of me was Baruch, hurrying toward the gate, shrouded and bulked up in layers of clothes. Behind me, my father was growing smaller, his two arms above his head, waving me on. Finally, I disappeared around a corner. I stopped to peek around the bend one last time. My father, now the size of a burned match, was still standing there.

"IS IT OUR HONEYMOON YET?" I asked Baruch after we boarded the plane, dropping my head onto his shoulder. He rolled his eyes. When I was nervous, I reverted to a pesky kid sister, as if acting like the family baby would keep me safe. Who would hurt a round-eyed ninny? It was a trait that my friends found, at turns, endearing and irritating. Baruch's nickname for me was Kotzaleh, Hebrew for "little thorn"; when I told a friend at work, he said, "Yeah, well, what's the word for '*big* thorn'?" As soon as the "Fasten Seat Belt" sign blinked off, Baruch moved to the empty row ahead of us and stretched out. He began to snore.

I leaned my forehead against the seats in front of me. With one eye closed, I peered through the crack. So this man was my husband. It had taken Baruch twenty years to notice me. He had been my swimming counselor in summer camp when I was eleven, flat as a kick board and blind without glasses. Baruch was eighteen, the waterfront hunk. I remembered shivering in the green lake, doing a lopsided frog kick, consoling myself with blurry views of his ankles on the dock. Over the next two decades, I ran into him six times. The details varied, but my effect on him was the same: none.

When I finally caught his attention at age thirty-one, I was living in Washington, D.C., working as a feature writer for the *Washington Post,* covering national politics, lifestyle stories, occasionally traveling overseas for peace treaty signings or bombings. Our courtship was long-distance and brief. It still amazed me that we had married. He was a stranger. He was a dream. He was love, imagined. Now he would be real.

What will I do when I find the shooter? I jerked back from my peephole. The thought jumped out and startled me. *Shake him? For a minute I'll be close enough to his neck to smell him. Smells like clay. Neck is olive. He is wiry, short. He is young. That can't be true. He shot my father twelve years ago.*

How many times, over the years, had I pictured the scene? Usually around March 7, a date that I always noted, I imagined confronting the shooter. I would reach out through the darkness and grab his collar. I would shake him so hard, he would become someone else. It was feeble, but it was as close as I could come to hitting someone. He was a stranger. He was a nightmare. He was evil, imagined. Now he would be real.

This was not an all-consuming obsession, more like an old fracture that had never quite healed. In the past, when I traveled to Jerusalem to write stories for my newspaper, I had sometimes paused in the Arab marketplace, in the area where my father had been shot, and cast accusing looks. *Who hurt him?* Then the twinge would pass, and I would go back to work, writing the stories of other people's lives.

On a recent reporting trip to Jerusalem, though, I had happened to look up. In that spot, on an archway, sprayed in black paint, was the word REVENGE. It reminded me of the promise I had made in my poem. It was like being told, being awakened to a reality that I knew I would have to face one day. I did not know who the shooter was or where he lived. All I knew was that a finger out there had pulled the trigger on my father. What if I actually tracked him down?

EVEN THEN, sitting on the plane, I recognized the danger and the folly of taking a poem and turning it into life. *Am I really doing this?* My fantasy embarrassed me. During the twelve years since the shooting, I had told no one. It was one of those events that quietly informed my life. It was one thing to play it out in my mind, but in reality it did not make sense. Mostly, I felt grateful that he had survived. The bullet had skidded along the top of his head. It dug a furrow into his scalp, blazing a straight, flame-colored part through his hair. My father had saved the emergency room report from the Jerusalem hospital. I fished it out of my carry-on bag and read the neurosurgeon's notes carefully:

—51 y.o. male American tourist from NY tonight was injured after a gunshot in the old city.

—Fully conscious. A scratch in the vertex (longitudinal) 4 cm long. Neurologically intact.

—Wound was cleaned and adapted by steristrips.

—Skull x-rays—no fragments or fracture.

—Tetanus toxoid 0.5.

—Rest today.

—Clean wound after 5 days.

A flight attendant strode down the aisle, pursing her lips at my reading light. The rest of the cabin was dark. The other passengers were leaning against pillows and on each other's shoulders. I was sitting upright in a cone of light, puzzling over revenge. I looked through the crack between the seats. Baruch was still sleeping. I wished he would wake up.

Why would I dream about revenge? The answer, I suspected, had little to do with the size of the scratch. Other, subtler factors come into play with revenge, ones that I did not yet see. I was looking for the shooter, but I also was looking for some kind of wisdom. I was not acting rationally—but neither does half of the world. So much of life's turmoil comes from individuals or groups trying to settle a score. For seven years, from my perch at the *Post,* I had written about some dramatic examples: partisan vindictiveness in Congress; a bloody tit-for-tat in Northern Ireland; a memorial for a blood-libel pogrom in Poland. Now I wanted to break it down and study it. I wanted to master revenge.

That was why I felt like two people sharing one seat on the plane. One person sat up straight, anticipating the journey with enthusiasm. The other was hugging her knees, dreading what lay ahead. From the beginning the two worked against each other.

The journalist in me saw this as an opportunity for discovery. Reporting a book about revenge was an intellectual challenge, an exercise in empathy. I would talk to other people, ordinary and famous, and interview them to understand vengeance. Their stories would explore a shared taboo. Writing about them, I thought, would make me feel less alone. That part sounded respectable and easy.

The other person in me, the avenging child, knew that what was coming would be hard. I would lose all distance from my subject. Worse, I would become my subject. I would experiment on myself and record the results. I would try to answer the question, What happens when you make a revenge fantasy real? We all have dark thoughts; what if you pursued one of them? The outcome was unclear, the effort self-absorbed, the process full of ethical compromise. When I pictured telling anyone, I cringed. Instead, I told my colleagues that I was taking a leave of absence to research revenge. Only my family and my friend Rachel knew that I had written myself into the research.

I am not a large person, neither ideological nor heroic, yet for years I had been inhabited by a grandiose thought: my father's injury should not go unanswered. I knew that there was hatred and violence in the world. But the shooting was my first personal brush with evil. I was born to American parents who believed the world was good, who raised us in exquisite illusion. We were taught as children to respect the sanctity of the individual. The shooter blew a hole through that. He was more than just a man who had tried to kill my father. He became a symbol of terror. Terrorism, I believed, was not only about killing people; it was about dehumanizing them. I had to find a way to challenge the terrorist way of thinking. Confronting him was inevitable. Not with an act of violence—the revenge that I wanted was of a different kind, one that responded to the heart of the crime. So I set myself a goal that was outsized and naive, and most of all elusive: I wanted him to realize he was wrong.

MY FIRST INSIGHT into revenge came from my family. I asked my brother's wife, Michelle, a psychologist, "what triggers revenge?"

"Shame," Michelle said. "When people are humiliated, they feel like they have to get even."

Bruise a person's dignity, and revenge will repair it. If the offense is private, the punishment can be too. But if the humiliation is public, so is the revenge. In Europe, when two men dueled, they each fired just one shot. Even if both survived, they restored their reputations by the show of courage. Striking back publicly obliterates the insult, whether a person is the butt of an office joke or a head of state whose embassy has been bombed. Revenge erases that paralyzing moment of revealed weakness. It enhances honor, shifts dignity back into balance.

Shame was my first lesson in revenge. A Talmudic sage once said: "He who publicly shames a neighbor is as though he shed blood." Now I understood that shame, or the loss of honor, creates the need for revenge, sometimes even more than the actual offense. In Israel, for instance, a newspaper published a story about a thirteen-year-old girl from Nazareth who had been raped by her father. The abuse continued for four years with no reaction from the girl. Then one day the father showed up at her school.

"He came into the classroom, drunk, of course," the daughter said. She asked him to go home.

"Then he said to me, right in front of the teachers: 'Shut up. I screwed you and made you into garbage, and no one is going to want you now.' " From that day on, said the girl, "Whenever I would see him, revenge was the only thing on my mind. After he humiliated me at school, I took a knife from my uncle's house and dreamed of killing him."

Being raped was painful. Having it announced to her classmates was shameful.

Shame. In some tribal societies, it is the only lawful motive for homicide. Among the Druze, a religious community in northern Israel, Syria and Lebanon, men are expected to avenge their family honor by killing female relatives who disgrace them. Later, I came to know a Druze family torn apart by honor. Their story helped me understand the connection between revenge and shame.

IT BEGAN with a kiss. Every time Mahdi said good-bye to his sister, he would kiss her on the neck. One year separated them. Mahdi lived and worked at a packing house near the sea. Maytal, a high school senior, lived at home, in a village whose houses were built like bird nests in the cliffs above the plains of Galilee.

It was an idyllic setting, but Mahdi and Maytal Khatib found their home in Ein Al Assad revolting. Their mother had died of cancer. Their father had remarried a prickly younger woman who detested his children. The brother and sister hid out in the kitchen, two slight, inclining shadows frying potatoes and eggs for dinner. Maytal stood in for their mother, buying Mahdi a pair of black hiking boots. Mahdi stood in for their father, helping Maytal with homework at the computer.

"They were one soul, two bodies," an older sister said later.

Although, not quite. As a boy, Mahdi could escape their unhappy home. As a girl, Maytal was forbidden by Druze custom to leave home until marriage. If her virginity were lost, so was the family's honor. The men would be scorned, the younger sisters shunned.

One morning, Maytal argued with her stepmother about borrowing her sister's jeans. It was trivial, but for Maytal decisive. She wrote a letter to her brother:

> *Mahdi my love,*
>
> *I can't take it anymore. And so I've decided either to kill myself, or to leave home. Since suicide is taboo, completely forbidden, I've decided to leave home. I swear to you, on your life, I can't live in this house for a minute longer. Forgive me for this, I am begging you. Forgive me. Take care of my sisters and my father.*

By the time her note was discovered, she was dead.

Her escape lasted less than twelve hours. A friend helped her reach the nearest town. They called Maytal's uncle for help, but to Maytal's horror the uncle insisted on returning her home.

As Maytal dragged herself down the path to her house, her father barred the entrance. First Maytal had to prove she was a virgin. The friend who had helped her escape was a boy; rumors ricocheted around the village. At midnight the extended family squeezed into two cars in search of a doctor who could check her hymen. Maytal consented, but the doctor at the hospital refused to examine the girl without a police order. The police refused to order the exam because they said it was demeaning.

Everyone went home to bed. The next morning, Mahdi arrived to celebrate the Feast of the Sacrifice. When his father told him about Maytal, Mahdi's hands shook so badly he dropped his coffee cup on the floor. He kissed Maytal, as always, on her neck. He sat down in the living room, leaning his head against a chair, listening to his heart beat in his brain.

All around him, relatives argued Maytal's case.

"Your sister is clean. There's no reason to suspect her," an uncle said.

"It was a small mistake; these things happen," said a brother-in-law.

Mahdi could not speak. He looked gray, like a mop, soaked and twisted. He had absorbed one fact: his sister had left the house, left with a boy, and even if he was only a friend, Mahdi did not care. The rumors, true or not, shamed the family. Mahdi snapped up out of his chair.

Maytal, meanwhile, had withdrawn to rest before the holiday meal.

After fifteen minutes, a brother-in-law knocked on her door, calling Maytal to the feast. The door was locked. A man's voice answered from inside the room: "Just a minute."

It was Mahdi.

Five minutes later, the brother-in-law knocked again.

Mahdi replied, "Wait, I'm talking to Maytal."

He began the execution with his hands, pressing his thumbs into the hollow of her throat. After she passed out, he wrapped a computer mouse cord around her neck, pulling until the wire snapped. Maytal's face swelled. It turned a dusky blue. He was not sure if she was dead, so he looped a thicker computer cable around her neck like a noose and yanked with all his strength.

"For my honor," Mahdi sobbed hours later when he turned himself in. He threw his identity card on the police station floor, stomping with the black hiking boots that Maytal had bought for him. He took a pen and scrawled out a confession:

> I murdered her. Because she shamed me for the rest of my life and if I didn't murder her, I would die every day. Because every thing in life can be replaced, but if honor is lost, it never returns.

Afterward, he turned to the officer and said, "If it happened to you, what would you do? Wouldn't you do the same?"

In Mahdi's world, when a man is shamed, revenge follows. Killings to avenge family honor are so routine, they appear in the papers as news briefs, if at all. In cultures that value reputation and respect—in American street gangs, for example—revenge is expected for the most minor affronts, even for assault.

A point which brought me back to my own puzzle. Assault was what had happened to my father. By Mahdi's reasoning, or even by conventional psychology, shame was the force that was motivating me. Or was it? You could reason that my father being shot in the head was an attack on our family honor. Someone had disrespected us, took our family for fools. You might argue that I felt the shame of a crime victim—how could we have let our guard down?

That should have been right, but it felt wrong. There had to be more to it than that. I had spent a childhood in the suburbs, flapping around our living room in a pink tutu, not in one of Shakespeare's haunted castles, nor among the swaggering families of Icelandic revenge sagas. Even during the flight to Israel, I suspected something more complex was at work:

> "The insult you need to revenge is the one that attracts your most authentic fears and that inadvertently calls up your most hidden secrets."

The quote was copied into my notebook, the reference lost, the author wise. Something else was driving me. Something, if I was to believe the author, that touched upon my "most authentic fears." I was bad at introspection, clumsy about it. That is one of the benefits of being a journalist: you can explore other souls and shake off your own, connect with others and avoid yourself. If there was a hidden secret compelling me, I was not looking for it. It was not a priority. Action was.

THE PILOT ANNOUNCED that we would be landing soon. I pressed my forehead against the oval window, craning for a glimpse of Israel. A strip of Mediterranean coastline unrolled below, then fogged over from my breath against the glass. Maybe the beach beneath the wing was Ashkelon, where Samson, the biblical avenger, killed thirty Philistines for cheating him in a riddle contest. He stripped their lifeless bodies, shaming them, to cover up his own shame. "As they did to me, so I did to them," he said.

Then he slaughtered a thousand more Philistines, swinging the fresh jawbone of an ass. Samson was a model of revenge. He went down destroying everything and everyone around him. To this day, military strategists speak of the "Samson syndrome."

King David, another biblical hero, reigned several generations later. When David asked Saul if he could marry Saul's daughter, the prospective father-in-law said that he "desires no other bride price than the foreskins of a hundred Philistines as vengeance" on his enemies. David doubled the offer, hauling back a sack of two hundred foreskins. Saul, no romantic, had the skins counted.

That is the thing about Israel—no pot of gold, no fountain of youth, but heaps of heathen foreskins. It is an apt country to enroll in for lessons in revenge. Israel possesses an archaeology of revenge that layered all the way down to the beginning of time.

In the topsoil, the past one hundred years, Arabs and Jews have taken turns provoking each other. Burrow back through history to Genesis, to the earliest stories about the land, to Joseph and his brothers, to Jacob and Esau, to Ishmael and Isaac, who were all entangled in brotherly grudge matches. Dig a little deeper to Adam, who was buried, according to Christian and Jewish legend, in Jerusalem. Adam was not only the first human, but also, some Christians believe, the world's first instrument of revenge. Satan, bitter at being tossed out of heaven, vowed to tempt Adam and all his descendants to sin. Satan would use mankind to get even with God.

Satan, possible role model, I thought with a sly smile, feeling the plane's engines hum through the ashtrays into my elbows. The vibrations made my arms feel strong. But as we arced over the coastal plain toward the airport, I caught my face reflected in the window, reminding me of who I really was. The image thrown back at me splashed like cold water: the obedient brown eyes, the mouse-thin chin, the obvious absurdity of such a narrow face going after men with guns.

I looked up and saw that Baruch was awake. He had poked his head over the seatback and was staring down at me funnily. Maybe my eyes were red and bulgy from sitting up all night. Maybe it was the sight of his newlywed wife contorted over a notebook, scribbling.

I closed the notebook.

"Do you think I'll be pregnant on the flight home?"

"Hmmpff?" He pinched his nose and swallowed, trying to unclog his ears. "Who knows," he said, and turned around.

Men do not like being pressured, I reminded myself. That was my father's advice when I was dating. Now that I was married, my father had this advice: "Don't bug him too much."

Later, inside Ben Gurion Airport at passport control, I tried to act indifferent when Baruch joined a separate line.

"What is the purpose of your visit?" asked the Israeli immigration agent. She flipped through my blue passport, comparing my photograph with me.

I stood before her, hands at my sides, dressed for revenge. Black shoes, black socks, black pants, black T-shirt, black sweatshirt, black coat, black circles under my eyes. What if I told her the truth? It was Baruch's idea to spend our newlywed year in Israel. It was my idea to use it as an opportunity for a reckoning. I did not know where it would lead me.

"Umm," I faltered. "We're here for our honeymoon year."

"A year?" She handed back the passport and said with a conspiring wink, "Have a sweet year."

Outside the terminal, palm trees shuffled their fronds, reorganizing for the evening. The breeze carried a steamy, crawling feeling, alive like yeast in dough. We pulled off a few New York layers of clothes and loaded into a taxi. Our Israeli driver, a burly man, turned on the radio news: "The government said today it would protect the population from biological and chemical attacks. Gas mask distribution centers will be opening in major cities. . . ."

America was preparing to bomb Iraq, so Iraq was threatening to incinerate Israel. Saddam Hussein, Iraq's president, played by an important rule of revenge: If the true object of your anger is unassailable, reach for an achievable target. Israel, America's local ally, was the ideal dog to kick at home when the boss slammed Iraq at the office.

"This time Israel's going to finish Saddam off," the taxi driver said, disgusted. During the Gulf War, Iraq had hurtled missile after missile at Tel Aviv while Israeli generals strapped on gas masks and sat on their hands.

"It was terrible," the driver said. "Shameful."

At some point in every country and in every person's life, a choice presents itself that defines one's soul. You have been hurt. What will it be: Turn the other cheek, or an eye for an eye?

Both options were rooted in the Holy Land.

"You'll see," our driver sneered. His thick fingers throttled the gear stick, shifting for the steep, winding road to Jerusalem.

Torched military vehicles littered both sides of the highway. Their wheels and windows were gone, jagged reminders of the Arab ambushes during Israel's fight for independence. The taxi driver paid no attention to the wrecks lying among the evergreens. No one did after fifty years. Long ago the rust-colored ruins had merged with the hills, melting into the national subconscious, into the topsoil of revenge.

"This time," the driver said, hunching forward over the steering wheel, as if he were facing off with someone in the dark beyond his windshield. "This time will be different."

3

MEMORY

JERUSALEM

"WHAT DO YOU REMEMBER?" I asked. "What happened to you that night?"

"Well, the only thing is . . ." My father laughed nervously, looking down at his shoelaces as if he were feeling bashful. Maybe he was. My father was visiting Israel, attending a conference. I had brought him to the Old City this morning, to the Western Wall, to walk me through the details of the shooting. I had been living in Jerusalem for nearly a month, and had decided that before punishment, I needed to understand the crime.

We stood in the broad, white plaza below the Western Wall, the holiest place in the world for Jews. Israeli soldiers, their faces caked with mud, their green uniforms blackened with sweat, collapsed in piles next to their rifles. The soldiers had marched all night to the wall for their swearing-in ceremony. Closer to the wall, flocks of Hasids prayed. Their black-winged coats swooped and dipped in formation. Tourists jostled up to the limestone slabs, sticking handwritten notes into the crevices, as if it were a wishing well.

And yet for all its holiness, the wall was a sixty-foot pile of rocks. Spidery weeds and pigeons' nests sprouted from the cracks. The stones derived their magic from memories alone. They had been the retaining wall of the Holy Temple when Jewish kings ruled. Those days had ended thousands of years ago when conquerors turned the temple into rubble. Only the pocked stones survived, a reminder of the past and a promise for the future.

Like many tourists, my father found it meaningful to pray here. He had visited the wall the evening he was shot. I was eager to hear the details, but remembering made him uncomfortable, I thought. Maybe it was too horrible to believe that someone had wanted him to die.

"Yeah?" I said, waiting for his nervous laughter to pass.

"What I remember, the last time I was down here, not last summer, but the one before. I put a note in the wall, saying . . ." That shy smile again.

He hoped for divine vengeance.

". . . that I hope you marry well."

"Really." It came out sharper than I had intended.

"I swear. It said that everything in life is good for me, and now one important thing is left, that my daughter should have a husband, and he should be a good husband. I kind of felt like—"

"That was when I was dating that other guy."

"It's not that I had anything against him. I was just very worried about you meeting a nice groom. When I was up at the wall just now, I thanked God that He listened to my prayer."

"You like Baruch," I said. My father admired Baruch's father, a famous Talmud professor. Baruch's mother was the great-granddaughter of a Hasidic aristocrat, the Vishnitzer grand rabbi of Romania.

"I like him very much. He is a total answer to my prayer."

I was growing impatient. We were supposed to be taking a walking tour of revenge, and our conversation had slipped off the path, toward love.

We stood in silence for a while, then my father said, "This thing in 1986 is so far back, it's really a distant memory." He pressed his palm on the crown of his head, as if he could juice the memories. "It isn't in my mind."

Denial, I assumed, though it was his story.

"It was a Friday evening. I was with the Memorial Commission. We were visiting Israel's Holocaust museums. A couple of us came down to pray at the wall. They weren't religious people. They just wanted to be at the wall. They took a cab back. So I was left by myself to walk back."

My father, a Conservative rabbi by training, mixed religious tradition with modernity. He might play basketball on the Sabbath, but he would not drive. At the time of the shooting, he was working as executive director for the New York Holocaust Memorial Commission, planning a museum for New York City near the World Trade Center.

"It was twilight; it wasn't dark and it wasn't light," he said. "I was praying, next to the Vishnitzer Hasids in the corner. They were dancing all around and singing this song: 'The downtrodden put their trust in You . . .' " He hummed the melody.

The two of us began walking the route he took back to his hotel, uphill toward the Jaffa Gate, a main entrance to the city. Above us, on our right, six torches flamed, one for each million Jews killed during the Holocaust. The fires burned perpetually, lighting up the giant metal letters of one word: REMEMBER.

We turned, leaving the Jewish Quarter, entering a passage called the Street of the Chain, a crossroad of the bazaar. The atmosphere shifted from Jewish to Arab. Green graffiti spelled out the name of the Muslim god: ALLAH. Doorways were painted turquoise to chase away evil spirits.

"And you weren't scared?" I said.

"No, I had walked here a hundred times."

We climbed at my father's unhurried pace, the Arab market churning around us. Shopkeepers shook strings of olive-wood camels in tourists' faces. They thrust ram's horns at them, and plastic jeweled daggers. Boys played clay drums and reed flutes while riding on pushcarts stacked with spiced bread. The wind delivered potent whiffs of donkey droppings, fried chickpeas, damp goatskin, and dates so glossy and black they shone like giant beetles.

"Hello!" a teenager jumped out, fanning a deck of souvenir postcards. "Where is your home?"

"Thank you, no," I said, sidestepping his question.

My father continued, "Most of the shops were closed. It was dark and very quiet. There was a Hasidic boy and his father out in front of me. Behind me, women were speaking English, Christian tourists, maybe nuns."

"Is it at all weird coming back here?"

His ease surprised me.

"No, especially now I see all these Israeli soldiers patrolling."

We turned onto David Street, a narrow passage, with shops displaying a rainbow of pots brimming with henna, saffron and coriander.

"I passed the spice market; it was closed," my father said.

"Here." I stopped at the corner, reading the sign, "Butcher's Alley." I had seen my father's police testimony. The shooter lay in ambush down Butcher's Alley.

"No, not here. When I went to the police I was still confused. Now I remember exactly where it happened. See the stairs over there? I remember that overhang because something hit my head. It felt hot, like this." He flicked my scalp, as if he were shooting a marble. "I thought some kid on the roof dropped a firecracker on my head."

We threaded through the crowd up the long, wide stairs.

"This—is—the alley. This is it," he said, although he sounded hazy. "He was waiting for me and when he saw me, he shot, and dropped the gun. It was a Beretta. The gun was recovered. It was still hot. Now, you get over there . . ."

He wanted me to see how close the shooter had lurked. He backed up thirty feet on David Street, while I pretended to be the shooter, hiding in an alley. As my father approached, I drew my pointer and thumb as if they were a gun, closing one eye, training my fingertip on his fuzzy, light brown hair. What a difference half an inch makes, I thought. If the shooter had held his hand higher, if the wind had changed, the bullet would have killed my father. How easily the shooter had stripped my father of his humanity. The thought angered me and worse, it frightened me. In a world where people think and act that way, no one is safe. Terrorist attacks did not begin or end with my father.

Could I make my father human in the gunman's eyes? Only if I hid my identity from him. I would make myself invisible in order to be seen. He would come to know us and to recognize us—as long as he did not know who we were.

"As soon as it hit me," my father continued, still calm, "I looked up and saw these metal overhangs. And then I started bleeding. And suddenly I realized it was not a firecracker—"

"Did you fall over?"

"No, I was so shocked, I was afraid to fall. And I should have fallen because if the guy had taken a second shot I would have been dead."

"So you staggered? You did nothing? You just bent over?" I was agitated, strafing him with questions. As we continued to walk, I kept cutting him off.

"No, now, hold it. The blood was coming down my head and—"

"Did it get in your eyes?"

"No, no, no. It was dripping down my forehead and I knew that I was hit—"

"Bad?"

"I knew that I was shot. In the next second or two I'd know if I would live or die. And I looked up these stairs and I yelled—"

"In English?"

"In English and then Hebrew. 'Help! I've been wounded. Somebody shot me, help!' The Hasid and his kid turned and looked at me. They didn't do anything. Then I looked back and saw the Christian women and they just stood still."

I kept thinking that he should be angry. Instead, he sounded wistful. His cheeks, pillowy and generous, sagged.

"And these stores were open?" My voice cracked. How could it be that my father was so alone?

"No, these were closed. Until I got up to right—over—here. I remember it was a green door. There were three or four Arab men sitting here on stools and they didn't do anything, they just looked at me."

I noted the store's corner location.

"But did they see you were bleeding?"

"I was bleeding. I said, *'I'm bleeding.'* I was holding the blood on my head, trying to staunch the wound. And nothing. They just sat there like I didn't exist."

At that point, my father had remembered there was a police station at the top of the market, inside an old Ottoman prison. He felt a surge of adrenaline and stumbled up the stairs to the plaza, two hundred feet from the police station.

"I was very faint, dizzy, it must have been anxiety. I thought, If I fall here, no one will find me." Circling in his mind, like the black-hatted, dancing men, were the words from the Hasidic song that he had heard earlier at the wall: *The downtrodden put their trust in You . . .*

And then it was over. He tottered into the police station and lay down on a wooden bench. An ambulance flashed him away. By the next morning the ordeal was tidied into two columns on page four of the *New York Post:* TOP NY RABBI WOUNDED BY TERRORIST IN ISRAEL—"SAVED BY MIRACLE."

"But what about the shooter?" I asked as we passed through the ramparts at Jaffa Gate. Modern Jerusalem spread out beneath us. We ambled toward the reflected glare of the Hilton Hotel, through sooty bus fumes, along the rim of a construction pit.

"They rounded up people," he said. "I don't think they really knew who it was."

"Do you ever wonder who he was, or what he looked like, or where he was from? How did you picture him?"

"I don't picture him."

I looked at my father, surprised. How was it, then, that I had pictured him so many times?

LATER THAT DAY, my father suggested that we take a detour through the neighborhood where my parents had lived during their first year of marriage. He led me through a warren of shabby apartment buildings, past Dumpsters and stray cats licking empty yogurt containers.

"Here it is!" he called out. "Number seven Salant Street, our home when we were a newlywed couple like you." His pace quickened. "We didn't have any heat, but it was great."

My father walked ahead and swung open a rusted gate. "Look, look!" He was halfway down the path when I caught up with him. "Let me show you the apartment."

Every object his green eyes touched flashed back nearly forty years.

"That's the roof—we took home movies from there of schoolgirls running out for recess; and this tree—the doves would go *coo coo coo;* and the Ethiopian church across the street—the bells would ring; and on the first floor a woman would sing Arab songs all day long—I still love Arab music because of her."

He huffed up the stairs to the second-floor apartment. He knocked on a white, scuffed door.

An old man cracked the door, a slice just wide enough for his two narrowing eyes.

My father smiled sweetly. "Hellooo, can I peek in and look at the apartment?"

"No."

No had not occurred to my father. His smile wobbled.

"But this was my parents' first home," I said.

"Sorry, you can't come back."

Slam.

In those few minutes between the rusty gate and the door, memory embraced my father tighter than during our entire slog through the Arab bazaar.

"It's a treasure," he said back out on the sidewalk. His eyes were focused across the street, on some invisible honeymoon scene that was being projected for him like a drive-in movie on the wall of the Ethiopian church. "Treasure this time together."

"What time?" I said.

Baruch was about to leave Jerusalem. He was on sabbatical, officially, but the U.S. Attorney had recalled him to prosecute a fraud case in New York. He would be gone for several weeks, several months, as long as the trial lasted. And at that moment, he was having lunch with an old Israeli girlfriend, sucking on chicken bones, reminiscing about who knows what.

"You shouldn't be jealous," my father said. "Fran is never jealous and I see people I used to be involved with."

"Like who?"

"Mommy. And Fran isn't jealous. I mean, what could be worse than Mommy?"

Memories of her.

MEMORIES OF MY MOTHER followed us the next day on a tour of Bethlehem. Our bus stopped at Rachel's Tomb, the ancient burial place of Jacob's wife. My father looked past the tomb and marveled, "Mommy and I used to come here to buy oranges. They were so juicy and sweet. I look at the same places you look at—but I see things you don't see."

Outside the Tomb of the Matriarch, I picked up a small, rough stone to mail to Rhode Island, to my friend Rachel. For a year now, she and her husband had been trying to conceive. Rachel the Matriarch, who herself had trouble conceiving, was said to bless women with fertility. Rachel, an economist, was a rationalist, but here in the Holy Land, inanimate objects—a rock, a river, an olive tree—were vested with memory. And in this storied land, memory meant power.

After visiting the tomb, we boarded the bus. My father gripped my arm. "You see that guy over there in green?"

He gestured toward another American tourist, a short, white-haired rabbi mincing down the aisle.

"He shoved me aside when I was posing with the prime minister in 1969. I'll never forget it, that bum." His grip hurt my arm. His soft mouth hardened. "I'll never forgive him. I was young then and it was a big moment in my life. Today if he did it, I would shove him back, or worse."

Here was my father's defiance, the nostril-flaring that was missing in the Arab marketplace. Memories like these were the fuel of vengeance. They coursed so sharp and hot that they no longer belonged to the past, but to the present. If shame ignites revenge, memory keeps it burning.

That was my second lesson in revenge: the role of memory. It explains the saying, Forgive and forget. Or why vindictive types are said to have long memories. Even young, vindictive types. If a person is old enough to remember, he is old enough to feud. Soon after I arrived in Israel, I met a pair of eleven-year-old girls who had stored a wealth of grudges worthy of the Hatfields and the McCoys. Rotem and Hilah attended a public school in Pisgat Zeev, a suburb north of Jerusalem, but they reminded me of preteens everywhere.

The afternoon I met the girls, they were watching a school play in the auditorium, sitting eight seats apart. The assembly was called "Tolerance Yes, Violence No."

A narrator walked onto the stage and bowed. "Our play begins in Jerusalem many years ago, when the Jewish Holy Temple existed."

The drama was based on a Talmudic legend about two Jews who were feuding. One man threw a party. Through a mix-up in invitations, his enemy was invited.

"But you're my enemy!" the host said. "Get out."

The guest blanched. All of Jerusalem society was watching. "Please don't embarrass me. Let me stay and I'll pay for what I eat."

"No."

"I'll pay for half the cost of the party."

"No."

"Please, I'll pay for the entire party."

"No, no. Leave!"

He threw out the guest.

"What shame, what embarrassment." The man pulled at his hair. "I can't believe the other guests saw everything, and nobody came to help me." The actor pumped his eyebrows villainously. "I'll show *them.*"

The man falsely accused the Jews of planning a rebellion. The Roman emperor responded by flattening Jerusalem. He killed so many people, the blood rushing through the streets extinguished the fires.

At the end of the play, the narrator summed up: "And so, children, our Holy Temple was destroyed because of revenge."

"See," said Rotem and Hilah's teacher to the students. "People had the same problems thousands of years ago."

"I have an enemy," Rotem told me later, sitting in the playground. "It started in first grade. Hilah got the whole class to gang up on me. I cried every day and I decided to get even. All those years, I remembered what she did. In third grade, my moment arrived. I got ninety-nine percent of the class to ignore her for three months."

Then her face turned gloomy. "This year, she got everyone to boycott me. I invited the whole class to my birthday party. No one came."

After Rotem went inside, Hilah jogged out to the playground. "I had to get back at her. She made fun of my freckles. She told the whole class my parents' nickname for me—*Noosh-noosh.* I'll never forget it. I'm keeping the memories in a box, inside my heart. A black box full of all the bad things she did."

She cupped her hands, squaring an imaginary box.

"I'll remember her until the day I die." She peered into her hands. "I'll lie there, stooped over, with white hair and my cane. My friends and my grandchildren will be there. And I'll say, 'I hope even on this day, Rotem remembers all the bad things she did.' And I'll still have my freckles. And I won't ever, never forget."

Hilah kept a diary filled with references to "Rotem the repulsive." One recent entry:

> Today is Saturday. Don't ask what I saw yesterday, how the boys are afraid of bossy Rotem. Sure! Maybe in front of her they act nice, but behind her back everyone, I mean *everyone,* gossips about her, those chickens. A few days ago

> Rotem picked on me in class and I talked back to her and in the end I left the room crying. . . .

At age eleven, Hilah did what societies had been doing for thousands of years. She wrote it down. She preserved the curse, making it impossible to forget. After reading Hilah's diary, I started a file marked "Memory." I began collecting the ways that people cultivated memory and revenge:

• Albanians keep memories fresh by piling stones on the spot where a loved one has been killed. Passersby throw pebbles, leaves and grass onto the heap, reminding relatives of the need for revenge.

• Women in southern Greece sing vengeance lullabies to the sons of murder victims so that the infants will grow up and remember.

• In the Balkans, every generation of Serbs has studied the Battle of Kosovo Polje, inspiring centuries of atrocities. They remembered their 1389 defeat by the Turks as if it happened to them last Saturday.

• In Ireland, the bardic tradition has kept sectarian revenge at a froth since the Battle of the Boyne, in 1690. The narrated pain has been handed down as part of an Irishman's inheritance.

• The nomadic Bedouins exercise an oral tradition that is so reliable in transmitting cross-generational grudges, they have a saying: "If a man takes revenge after forty years, he was in a hurry."

Then there was David Chinitz, an American academic who played basketball in Jerusalem with my husband. His method for remembering revenge was similar to his method for grocery shopping.

"I keep a list. My father kept a list. For all I know, your father is on my father's list," David said. "An enemies list is a family tradition."

People keep lists, transmit family lore, living inside narratives of past animosities. They try to rewrite history by reliving it. They get stuck inside a story.

YITZHAK SHAMIR, one of Israel's toughest leaders, suckled his revenge stories as a child in Poland.

"Our Bible says an eye for an eye," he said.

Shamir, who had been prime minister during the 1991 Gulf War, met me in his office in Tel Aviv. An elfin man with a giant's hands, his head barely rose above the horizon of his desk. I asked him about vengeance. Instead of retreating into euphemisms like most people did, the white-haired man lit up as if I had recalled a favorite nursery rhyme. He balled a fist and banged out his words on the desk.

"Tooth for tooth, limb for limb, burn for burn. Those are the ABC's of retaliation."

The water in Shamir's glass jumped as he pounded.

"My childhood stories are the Bible stories I learned in Hebrew school—Moses saw an Egyptian master beating a Jewish slave," said Shamir. "What did he do?"

Shamir raised his fist. He lifted a bat-wing eyebrow.

"Killed him."

Thump.

"Simple."

Thump.

"Buried him in the sand. Blood for blood."

For Shamir, Exodus was more than a legend, it was a battle plan. In Israel's prestate days, when he fought in the Jewish underground, "We had unwritten rules, we paid them back for every death." A secular Jew, he did not live by the Bible, he lived in the Bible. Same ancient, sandy stage. New cast. The role of Egyptian overlords was performed by British Mandate officers and Palestinian nationalists. Shamir played the part of Moses.

"Without paying them blow for blow, Jews would cease to exist. It's been that way since Moses' time."

As prime minister, Shamir scoffed at compromise with the

Arabs. He departed from his stony script only once, during the Gulf War, when Iraq bombarded Israel.

"We should have fired back, we could have taken revenge. But we made a calculation. America said, 'We'll pay them back, not you.' "

Shamir's fists flattened out. He slipped lower in his chair, his jaw dipping below the desk's edge.

"I'm not the kind of guy who dreams, but I still feel like getting back at the Iraqis." He picked up a paper knife. "We'll get them when the time is right."

He perked up and skewered the air. "Their payback day is going to come."

Retribution adorned Shamir's office walls in paintings of Bible scenes: a robed Moses avenging Amalek, the nation that attacked the weakest of the Israelites; Samson, biceps swelling, cracking a lion's jaw as if it were a peanut shell.

In the Middle East, such figures do not remain submerged in the past. Legendary characters poke through the layers of time, inhabiting people like demons. The Egyptian soldier who assassinated Egypt's president Anwar el-Sadat shouted, "I have killed Pharaoh." Iraq's Saddam Hussein tried to double as Nebuchadnezzar, sovereign of Babylon, lord of the Middle East during the sixth century B.C. After Iraq's war with Iran, Saddam struck a coin with Nebuchadnezzar on one side, and his own face on the other. He threw up billboards of the two of them, clinched and grinning, like two politicians running on the same ticket.

DURING MY FATHER'S visit to Israel, Saddam was gripped by another delusion of ancient grandeur. He defied the United Nations' orders to allow arms inspections. He dared America to respond, and startled Israelis into war preparations.

The day my father and I set out for the police archives building, we walked along Jaffa Street, passing a furniture store that advertised an "End of the World" couch sale. People spilled out of pharmacies carrying bags of antibiotics. Overhead, a chartered plane circled the city seven times, while the mystics on board cursed Saddam, blasting ram horns and quoting from the Book of Joshua—the passage about the walls of Jericho being trumpeted flat by the Israelite commander.

Meanwhile, Israel's modern military commander conceded that he was lying awake nights.

"Our main concern is that Saddam may conclude his world is crumbling," said the defense minister, Yitzhak Mordechai. "He might think he has nothing left to lose and try to strike at Israel, like the blinded, captive Samson, who declared, 'Let me die with the Philistines.' "

It was the "Samson syndrome" that panicked people most. When my father and I arrived at the Jerusalem police station, the archives clerk was raising the volume on his radio for the news. Top story: fights had broken out at gas mask distribution centers.

The clerk eyed us with irritation. A bumbling American and his pushy daughter wanted files from a twelve-year-old case. They asked if the police had caught the assailant. Who he was. If he had confessed.

"Too late. We just destroyed all files from 1986, except for murders," he said, the thrill of refusal beading his eyes.

"They tried to kill me," my father said. "They shot me. It wasn't murder."

"I can see that," the clerk said with an arch look.

Heavily, he turned around and began to check the shelves. As he pecked through the stacks, we listened to the news: Hamas, a militant Islamic group, announced that it would kill Israelis in revenge for an American attack on Iraq.

The clerk returned to the counter. No records. As we left, he said to our backs, "Write a letter to the prosecutor's office. Ask if there was a trial."

We trudged out of the police station. "Why would they want to shoot me?" my father said, inspecting my face, scanning my features as if they were the pages from the missing file. "Because I was an American tourist? Because I was wearing a yarmulke?"

We walked back to Jaffa Street, to a hardware store, and lined up with the rest of Jerusalem to buy packing tape and plastic sheeting. The clear polyurethane, sold in rolls like plastic wrap, would seal windows and doors in case of a germ or a gas attack.

"I wasn't an Israeli. I wasn't a soldier. I wasn't their enemy trying to usurp their land. I'm an American." My father glanced at me. "You understand?"

I understood, but part of me did not care if they shot him for being a Jew, or for being a Westerner, or for wearing a blue suit, or for having earlobes that dangled. I never thought of the need for revenge in political, religious or ideological terms. The journalist in me was curious about the shooter's motives. The daughter in me was not. It did not matter why they had hurt him. It only mattered that they had.

He was the baby of his family, the son of Polish immigrants. He had grown up in Newark, New Jersey, playing stickball in the Avon Avenue school yard, and fishing tennis balls out of the sewers for his two big brothers. He went to college, thanks to a full scholarship. In rabbinical school, he cut theology classes to play touch football on Brighton Beach. He married a pretty swimming counselor he met at summer camp (the same camp where Baruch and I had met). He caught her attention by swinging like a monkey from a tree. My father was an ordinary man, not rich, powerful or politically important. There was no logic in assassinating him.

So did I understand? No, because as a daughter I could not understand. Understanding meant explaining, meant excusing, meant forgiving. And I would not forgive the shooter. I had too much to prove.

"Find the motive," my father said, poking a piece of the plastic sheeting with his thumb, testing it for thickness. "That's important for me."

We paid the sales clerk for six yards of plastic.

"Maybe I should stay," he said as he walked me home. He would be returning to New York in a couple of days. Flights from the country were booked with foreigners trying to get out before the bombing. "I hate to leave you. Maybe I should give you my seat on the plane."

WHEN WE ARRIVED at my apartment, he called a family meeting. We descended on Baruch the minute he rolled his bicycle through the front door, his face glistening from his basketball game. He unstrapped a bouquet of red poppies from the back of his bike, the same flowers my father used to bring my mother. I put them in a vase, hoping my father would not remember, knowing that he would.

The three of us gathered on the roof under a mild blue sky. We sat around a half-eaten, heart-shaped box of chocolates that my father had brought me as a Valentine's Day gift. Our house was built on a hillside in 1860 in Yemin Moshe, one of the first neighborhoods outside the Old City. The red-roofed houses and the stone windmill faced the Old City's turreted walls. Our apartment was not elegant. The flooring was loose, the bathtub leaked and gray mold marbled the ceilings. The view, though, was paradise.

To the left stood Jaffa Gate and the Tower of David, a bullet-shaped parapet rising from a medieval fortress. To the right, the Judean desert stretched, gritty and bleached, all the way to the cliffs of Jordan. Straight across the valley was Mount Zion, crowned by the Church of the Dormition, where, according to Byzantine legend, the Virgin Mary fell into eternal sleep. Next to it, in a chiseled building, was the room where Jesus held the Last Supper. Seven weeks later, on the same spot, the Holy Spirit descended on the disciples.

It was hard to imagine missiles crashing here and mushrooming poison gas while we were sitting on the roof, the birds fussing in a cypress tree, so close to the sky.

"Do you have a flashlight?" my father asked.

"Yes."

"A cell phone?"

"Yes."

My father's face was strained with tiny movements, calculations shuttling to and from the brain. The newspaper had published a list of items to stock, including canned tuna and antibiotics. My brother, a neurologist, had sent bottles of amoxicillin, doxycycline and ciprofloxacin, which my father had arranged on the windowsill like a spice rack. The antibiotics came with recipes, combinations of pills, depending on which germs were seeping under the door. A neighbor had lent me her spare gas mask.

"You should get a mask too," I said to Baruch. He was not leaving for America until the day after the UN's deadline with Iraq, when the bombing was likely to begin.

"Quit bugging me," Baruch said. He was bent over, watching an ant struggle to lift a crumb of chocolate.

"What'll I do if there's an air raid?" I said. "Wear a mask and watch you choke?"

"You have to get a mask," my father said. "I'll pay for it. I'm going to tell your parents. You have a responsibility to your wife and to your unborn children. You're not a single guy anymore." My father moved to the edge of his chair. "If you die, everyone will say, 'Baruch the schmuck,' not 'Baruch, the big, brave guy.' "

I tried to peek behind Baruch's blue sports sunglasses to see what he was thinking—*What kind of family did I marry into?*

"I know it's not cool to panic," my father said, sensing that bluster was not working. "Look at the Holocaust. Look what happened. Cool people waited until it was too late. The cautious ones got out early and survived."

We were cartoonish in our fears of reprisals. I wondered if it was just our family or the people in Israel. But then a friend from the *Post* newsroom in Washington called. He said, "If America bombs Iraq, there'll be twenty years of revenge. Terrorists will sneak into America plugged with tubes of anthrax. Our children in 2012 will be paying the price."

IT WAS A SEASON of vengeance, a time of tables turned. As the UN deadline loomed, so did Purim, a costume holiday that commemorates the Jews' rescue from a genocidal plot by the grand vizier of the

Persian empire. At the last moment, the vizier is hanged on the same gallows that he built for Jews. In celebrating this reversal of fortune on Purim, the world turns topsy-turvy. Schoolchildren take over the classrooms from their teachers. Tradition calls for getting so drunk, you cannot tell the hero of the story from the villain.

This year the holiday approached with a sobering twist. Fathers carried home cat masks in one hand, and gas masks in the other. Mothers bought holiday noisemakers while municipalities tested air raid sirens.

Just before the festival, before my father left Israel for New York, he received a fax from the Jerusalem district attorney's office. It was a response to his inquiry about the shooting.

"I got a chill up and down my spine," he said to me on the phone. "Whew. That's closure."

We decided to meet downtown to discuss the letter. Half an hour later in the cafe district, I found him in the brightness, leaning against a railing. My heart bumped sideways like a pendulum.

"Hi, Papa."

He gave me a hug. He felt inside his jacket pocket and pulled out the letter.

"I always thought they'd be free," he said. "I assumed they weren't caught. And if they were, they were traded in a prisoner exchange and were running around Lebanon or Iraq."

The letter, typed in English, was written by the first senior deputy to the district attorney of Jerusalem:

> *Dear Dr. Blumenfeld:*
>
> *I am pleased to inform you that charges were brought before the Military Court in Lod, against the terrorist group who took part in various crimes, including murders, in the Jerusalem area, including the crime involving yourself. The terrorists were sentenced as follows:*
>
> *(a) Omar (al) Khatib (born date 1963)—was sentenced to 25 years in prison (still in prison)*

(b) Ali Mislamani (born date 1957)—was sentenced to life imprisonment (still in prison)

(c) Ala-din Bazian—was sentenced to life imprisonment (still in prison)

I hope that this time you enjoyed your visit in Israel.

"Do you think they got the right people?" I said. "They often arrest the wrong people."

I had worked as a journalist long enough to know that Israel's government could play with the truth. They were trying to appease a pestering American, I thought. The men in the letter must have been arrested for some other crime. Or, if they had been involved in my father's shooting, they were released long ago.

"Why don't you find out," my father said halfheartedly. For him the case could rest.

He flew home as scheduled, carrying a plastic bag with a roll, two yogurts and some leftover noodle pudding. He wrapped his arms around me, crushing me against his chest.

"You're my little baby," he murmured into my curls. "Promise you'll buy more tuna."

I waited until he left to cry.

Four days later at dawn, I walked my husband out into the street, into the cold, stone-licked air. Goose bumps spread along my arms and legs, beneath the blue flannel nightgown I had been wearing since college.

Baruch stepped toward the airport shuttle, his backpack hooked over a shoulder. He was flying to New York to prepare for his trial. He would sleep at a friend's apartment, on a mattress on the floor. He kissed my forehead. I wished him good luck with getting his criminal. He wished me good luck with mine.

I went back to bed and sank my face into his pillow.

IN THE DAYS that followed, the war was canceled. A last-minute deal was reached. Fears of bombings and retaliatory anthrax evaporated. People joked that the poison-gas plastic sheeting would make good holiday condom costumes. Then, a few days later, Israeli troops shot three Palestinian construction workers at a roadblock. Riots broke out. Newspaper headlines fanned anxieties with: FEAR OF REVENGE ATTACKS.

I went to the funeral of the Palestinian workers in Dura, near the West Bank city of Hebron. Car antennas rippled with black flags and horns blared. Flaming tires choked intersections. The three victims were carried through the sun-washed streets, their bodies wrapped in gauze hardened with drops of blood.

"Blood! We want blood!" the crowd chanted. Loudspeakers played the sound of machine guns firing. "Revenge! Blow up buses in Tel Aviv!"

"There will, of course, be a massacre against the Jews," said Hijazi Amour, a Palestinian who stood beside me. He squinted into the sun and the acrid black smoke, watching the procession. "Our blood is not less valuable than theirs. It is not sheep's blood. We don't forget Kfar Kassem, and the Jerusalem mosque, and the Hebron mosque." Hijazi was listing the massacres of Palestinians.

After the funeral, I visited Kiryat Arba, a nearby Jewish settlement, where the Israelis recalled their own massacres.

"Every time there's a problem, we bring up 1928, when the Arabs slaughtered the Jews, and they bring up the Hebron mosque from 1994," said David Ramati, a Jewish settler. He tapped his right temple. "It's a mathematical equation."

Like the joke about the husband who grouses that his wife "doesn't get hysterical, she gets historical," both parties keep a running score of insults. Palestinians observe so many commemorative days that the regional security officer at the U.S. embassy complained that his calendar was inked over with "likely violence" days. Israelis, meanwhile, have established a cult of tombstones, naming cities, streets, street corners and benches on street corners after their fallen. Israelis celebrate Independence Day the day after Memorial Day, ritualizing the connection between identity and tragic memory.

The evening that the Palestinians buried their three men, Jews gathered to hear the Purim story from the biblical Book of Esther. I joined the people of Kiryat Arba in the synagogue, where men dressed as women, women dressed as devils, and children wearing jester hats listened to the story. Whenever the narrator sang out "Haman," the wicked vizier's name, the audience booed. The floor shook with stamping feet, with cake pans banging, plastic flutes tooting and above it all—a gong. The noise was so loud it transcended sound. It became an object, rattling along the spine like a stick.

In the Book of Exodus, God had ordered Israel to "blot out" the Amalekite nation, of which Haman was a descendant. Instead of drowning out his name, though, the din in the synagogue amplified it. Revenge, and all the attention it demanded, magnified rather than diminished the enemy. Who would remember the Amalekites today, if not for God reminding Jews to forget them?

"Haman came from the Amalekites," exclaimed Yoezer Ariel, a teacher hoisted onto the shoulders of his dancing students. "Today," Yoezer said, his stringy white beard flying like a kite tail, "Yasir Arafat continues in Haman's path."

For Yoezer, and other West Bank settlers, Palestinians were Amalekites. The Israeli-occupied West Bank was ancient Judea and Samaria. The land of Israel was a biblical pop-up book through which they tramped. God had commanded the Jews to remember, and to smite the Amalekites—man and woman, child and suckling, ox and sheep. In 1994, another settler from Kiryat Arba, a doctor named Baruch Goldstein, decided the commandment still applied.

On Purim morning in 1994, Goldstein pushed into Hebron's Tomb of the Patriarchs and fired 111 bullets into a crowd of praying Moslems. He murdered twenty-nine people before someone knocked him dead with a fire extinguisher.

The *Washington Post* had sent me to Israel to write about the massacre. In Hebron I met Moaz Jabari, an eleven-year-old boy, walking in his father's vineyard. He was looking for the twigs they had planted together the week before. There would be raisins, jelly and jam when the twigs grew fat, his father had told him. As the boy told me about his father, an intensity gathered around his eyes, the urgent look of one who has witnessed but is powerless to act.

He had been standing next to his father at the dawn service—shoes off, knees bent in prayer—when three bullets struck his father in the chest. All around him, bodies fell. The boy dragged himself over the prayer rug, which was slicked with blood. A purple stain ate across his father's good gray jacket. Moaz cried, "Daddy, speak." His father lay on his back, his eyes flickering. Moaz raced home from the mosque and shouted to his older brother, "Daddy needs blood!"

Moaz had told me his story in a high, stifled croak. At the end of my visit with his family, his big brother asked: "What will Moaz grow up to? All his life he'll think about his father, murdered before his eyes."

ON PURIM MORNING, exactly four years after the massacre, I walked back toward their vineyard on the eastern edge of Hebron. A narrow, gnarled valley separated their home from Jewish Kiryat Arba. Palestinian demonstrations raged around the house. The explosion of bullets could be heard above the music of the Purim parade.

"He suffers from a poverty of blood," Moaz's mother said, ushering me into the porch where we had sat four years before. Moaz, who had hoped to save his father with an infusion, now suffered from anemia.

In the nights following his father's death, Moaz roamed the vineyard in his sleep. Barefoot and in his pajamas, the eleven-year-old passed through the kitchen and picked up the thick, black-handled watermelon knife. He drifted out the back door. In the distance, he could see Baruch Goldstein crouching among the vines, carrying his deep-throated machine gun. Moaz had only a knife, but he was not afraid. He was going to surprise his father's killer from behind. Stab him three or four times to be sure.

The sleepwalking went on for weeks, driven by the itch of unfinished business. Moaz's strongest memory from the mosque was of his father lying on the prayer rug, his bloody right hand lifted and quivering. Moaz did not understand the gesture. Was he beckoning or was he urging him to flee? Was he asking him to get blood vengeance?

Memory kept the boy immersed in revenge, but it also connected him with what was lost. Every night, Moaz's mother and his sister watched him in the vineyard. One night, his mother woke him from his trance, held his trembling shoulders and told him, "Your father didn't die, he's alive in Paradise, sitting in a green place, dressed in white."

Shortly afterward, the boy began to write:

> I have been robbed of this word: Daddy. We lost him. We lost everything. Fathers protect their sons from evil. My memory is clear in my heart. I am begging all sons to take care of their fathers. We have to protect them as they protect us.

Moaz's mother read her son's words out loud. Then she returned the notebook to its top-shelf hiding spot. She had taken pages from him.

"He tried to write, but I prevented him," she said, licking her cracked, worried lips. "I don't want my children to be complicated from this."

The widow now had five sons and eight daughters to raise alone. There were things she had to do. During the first week of mourning, she washed her husband's blue blanket, drying it between the grapevines. If she was going to escape the memories, she had to wash away his scent.

Forgetting, even without forgiving, was their only chance for sanity, she said. The past might drive people, but it also drove them crazy. It drove them toward revenge.

The Moaz who came home from school the afternoon I visited was no longer the little boy with intense eyes. He was a fifteen-year-old high school student with a deepening voice and a broadening jaw.

"You are so kind," Moaz said to me, "not like the Jews."

"They're not all alike," his mother corrected him. "There are bad Jews and bad Arabs."

She told him to look ahead, not back. "I want you to think about the future." She wanted him to become what she and her husband had always planned: a doctor. What she prescribed for her son was functional amnesia, to forget in order to live.

FORGETTING WAS the way forward. I had seen this reaction in other people, whether they were unjustly fired from a job, or cheated on by a spouse, or defeated in a politically underhanded way. Rather than taking revenge, they followed, as my economist friend Rachel put it, the principle of maximization of expected utility: "What happened in the past—those are sunk costs. It's all about optimizing the future. How can I maximize the present value of my future stream of net benefits?"

The goal was to cut losses, and memory got in the way. I sometimes wondered if this was why my brother, Hal, did not share my obsession. Traditionally, the legal duty to avenge would have fallen on him. English law, I learned, stated as late as the seventeenth century: "The civile law denies the father's inheritance to the son which will not revenge the death of his father."

Instead, Hal skated serenely through life, married a smart beauty, had a baby girl. He taught at Yale Medical School, and spent his days peering into a microscope, puncturing brain cells with tiny glass needles. His Ph.D. thesis identified, of all things, the cellular mechanisms for memory.

Yet when I asked Hal about avenging our father, he shrugged and said, "I have no idea even when it was—what date it was, what year it was. The whole thing is so surreal."

Hal forgot things. He had a kind of adaptive dopiness.

I, on the other hand, woke up alone in Jerusalem on March 7, thinking that it was the anniversary of the shooting. Twelve years. Even my father was foggy when I asked him about March 7. He thought I was talking about his mother's birthday. Like many trauma victims eager to recover, he tried to forget.

Still lying in bed, I picked up a notebook and a pen from the floor:

> Easier to be happy if you forget. Like Mom. She isn't contemplative. Tap dances in the morning when she brushes her teeth, her slippers flapping on the bathroom tile. One time talking with Dad about childhood hurts, he said "just repress it." He was mistreated once as a kid, hinted at some dark misdeed. He blots out the memory and continues on his merry way.
>
> The opposite of revenge isn't forgiveness. It's shopping. It's being busy with the practical, shallow now.

I got out of bed. After lunch at a friend's house, I was tempted to bury myself beneath her quilt and nap, drifting into oblivion. Instead, I walked toward the Old City under the weak afternoon sun.

There were two hours left of daylight when I arrived at the Arab market. I would stay until dusk, the same hour as the shooting. I stepped from the Jaffa Gate plaza into the arcade. The stones were slippery and downward sloping, blurring past colors and noise. One breath might mix camel leather, singed coffee and honeyed sesame bars. Church bells and tour guide blather and chicken prattle collided in midair.

From my father's account, I knew where to stop: halfway down David Street, second alley, the corner souvenir store, where the shopkeepers had sat and watched my father beg for help.

I felt intimidated and unsure about what to do. The shopkeepers' sin was one of indifference. I stalled, stopping to ask other merchants if they remembered an American tourist shot here.

"It could've been something else passing his head, like a bird," said a shopkeeper with a ginger mustache. "I promise you, the man who told you this story creates big lies." He jingled the coins in his pocket.

"They would never shoot a tourist," his friend added, working over a wad of gum. He had sold trinkets in the market for thirty years. "They'd make sure he's a Jew before they hurt him."

The men were uneasy with my questions. The Arab market was crawling with undercover police, security agents and counterspies. It made people suspicious. The shopkeepers looked at each other, confirming what the other was thinking. I decided to move on.

The passage was tight with shoppers, bumping shoulders and swinging bags. I meandered toward the corner store and lingered outside. A boy, a shop clerk, was arranging a display of embroidered vests. He asked me what I wanted. The owner, I said. He brought me into the large, bright store, with jewelry cases and shelves striped with tablecloths. No other customers were in sight. He pointed to a man sitting at a desk in the back of the room.

His open collar flashed three gold chains. He had a head full of moussed, jet curls. He sat in front of a poster made up of twenty-nine pictures of himself, grinning.

"Hello," I said stiffly.

He looked at me like a rake might look at a pile of crispy leaves.

"How are you?" I said.

"Alive."

The answer startled me. His voice was so deep it seemed to come from his feet. He was smoking Marlboros, drinking black coffee in sharp, jerky sips. He jabbed at a calculator, adding up imaginary sales. I hesitated. Then I came closer, at five feet entering the perimeter of his cologne. He said his name was Taysir. Foreigners called him Tom. He patted the empty chair next to him and sent the boy to bring us tea.

Tom was thirty-six years old. He had inherited the shop and had worked there for twenty years.

"Friday evenings too?" I asked.

He nodded yes. I explained that I was a journalist writing a book, and was wondering about a shooting outside his store. It happened on a Friday evening, March 1986. An American tourist was wounded.

"Do you remember?"

"Maybe," he said coyly. I understood from his wink that he had been there that night.

Our drinks arrived on a copper tray. The sugary liquid glazed my mouth. I counted four more photographs of Tom on his desk, as I waited for him to say something else about the shooting.

"OK, you're not a killer, right?" he said. "But if I pushed you, maybe you will hit me. So you have to ask why someone wants to shoot someone. Why hate?"

I set my glass down on his desk. "And who do you hate?"

"I hate tour guides," Tom said.

His eyes narrowed until all that were left were lashes. "If I had a gun, I would shoot them. It's not fair. It's not legal."

From our seats, we could see tour groups babbling past on David Street, loaded with souvenirs. None of them entered Tom's shop. In 1987, the tour guides began demanding 40 percent commissions, Tom said. Any salesman who refused lost business. "I work seven days a week, I'm not working, I'm sitting. I read the newspaper, drink coffee." His syllables jumped, overcaffeinated. He strummed his fingers on the desk. "I see myself as useless. I am a failure. I have psychological problems."

Three German tourists trickled through the door. Tom did not bother to get up. A woman picked out a ring for two dollars.

Tom crumpled the bills and pitched them into his ashtray. "Memories are sometimes killing you, when you remember how you did two thousand dollars a day and now you make ten dollars. It makes you angry and stressed." He started smoking three packs daily and taking tranquilizers. "Playing cards is the only time when I forget."

If he could only get back—back in time, back to life before 1987. If he could only get back at *them*.

"I wish to kill the guides." He aimed his cigarette tip at me like a smoking barrel. "And then I arrest them."

A kind of nostalgia inspired Tom's revenge fantasies, as it does for many people. In his dreams, he would blast himself back to paradise, to the place where life was whole. That future Eden justified almost anything.

"I'm taking an M-16 and *pppppf!*" He sprayed a shelf of alabaster chessmen with imaginary bullets. "Just like that. And I am the laughing last man."

I wanted to hear more, but David Street was growing dark. I told Tom I had to go. I would be back.

"It's difficult to think. I don't know what to plan."

Neither did I. As I walked home across the valley in the fading light, I puzzled over what to do about Tom. I was satisfied that I had found the right shopkeeper. But he was so much younger, unhappier and loonier than I had imagined.

TEN NIGHTS LATER, I was lying in bed, staring across the bedroom at an old brass balance. The scale was tilted, the left pan heavier than the right. The imbalance bothered me. I climbed onto a chair, took it down and buried it in the closet. Revenge means restoring a kind of cosmic, primal balance. Tom had watched and done nothing to help my father; now I would watch Tom and do nothing. The analogy was imperfect, but it was a start, I told myself. I would think of something better later.

Later, thunder clapped me awake. Jerusalem was being pelted by a freak, spring storm. Snow erased the red roofs and bleached the pink geraniums. There was a squeaking sound, like bats at the window, as ice-covered leaves scratched the glass. The wind rattled the door handles, as if someone were testing the locks.

I reached for the phone next to the bed and dialed Baruch at the U.S. Attorney's office.

It was 4 P.M. in New York, and he was at his desk. When he heard my voice, he swiveled away from the FBI agents hustling in and out of the room. He was too busy to talk, he said in a muffled voice. The defense attorneys had a tape of the government's key witnesses, threatening the defendant: "I'm going to fucking kick your ass." The defense now claimed the case was a personal vendetta.

He hung up. I tried my mother.

"Hi, dolly sweety-pie!"

Already, I felt better. Her Kansas City accent made me smile.

"How you doing?" she chirped. She and Bernie were at their Florida vacation home overlooking a golf course. They were dripping across the white carpeting, after a whirl in the Jacuzzi. They were getting ready to hit balls on the driving range.

"I was just thinking about you," she said. "You got two wedding presents this week, a salad plate from Rene Sanchez and a soup bowl from Uncle Wilbert."

"Great," I said. A bolt of lightning crackled over Mount Zion. "Have you ever heard of snow with thunder and lightning?" I shivered. The gusts blew so hard it felt like the apartment was listing.

"In Jerusalem, anything is possible," she said. "I'm so excited that you're coming home. I miss you."

In a month, Baruch would deliver the opening for his trial. I was flying to New York to watch.

"I'm already nervous that Daddy's going to want to see me at the same time as you," I said.

"What are you doing for Passover?" The trial coincided with the holiday.

"Going to Daddy's," I said. "What are you doing?"

"I don't know."

"Come to Daddy's."

"Yeah?"

Surprisingly, she considered it.

"He wouldn't want us," she said. "I mean, he would want me but not Bernie, I guess. But Bernie wouldn't have to come."

"We should all be together," I said.

"But maybe we can't be together, and we have to just accept that."

I listened to the wind throw desert gravel at the windows. In the background, I could hear a second voice talking to my mother. Bernie was telling her about a cruise they were planning through the canals of Burgundy, France.

"Mom, hello?"

"Sorry," she said, coming back on the line. "Daddy tracked down those bad boys," she continued merrily.

At first I was not sure which "bad boys" she meant. Then I understood: the gunmen. The three names from the Jerusalem DA's letter.

"You talked to Daddy?" I said, my excitement peeking through.

"Are you trying to fix me up with him? Forget it. It isn't going to work." She said to Bernie, "OK—I'm coming. But you still need to put your shoes on." Then she said to me, "I gotta go 'cause Bernie is leaving me."

"What?"

"He's driving off in a golf cart. Gotta go."

I imagined them riding off together over the warm grass, their visors shielding their eyes from the sun. I opened a window and stuck my hand into the storm. Slivers of ice needled the black air. A neighbor's metal shutter was clanking against stone. There was another sound like glass shattering, like something breaking apart that could never be repaired.

Daddy tracked down those bad boys.

I slid under the blanket, remembering my father's face when he got the DA's letter. Both of us were stunned, my father happily so. I did not believe the letter, that his shooter was in jail. I could not believe that the Israelis had found the perpetrator of such a shadowy act. But I decided to play along, because I did not want my father to think that his assailants had escaped justice. Nor did I want him to worry about me. I tried to think of something positive to say.

"Mommy will be happy they're not loose and free."

He looked baffled. "Mommy?"

"Yeah, she was afraid I'd go running around looking for them."

For a moment he froze like a person pushed from a cliff, that cartoon moment in the air before you drop.

"Maybe now she'll believe it happened," he said, and then his face fell.

At the time of the shooting, my parents were still married. They were separated, although the divorce was not final. My mother had met Bernie and was with him at a resort in Hawaii. My father had called her to tell her he had been wounded.

"She put me down. She belittled it. I was so hurt. How can you be married for twenty-five years and not care if your husband was shot?"

The words seemed to push out of his mouth against his will. There was no pleasure in his pain, no self-righteous anger.

"Of everyone, she was the only one who didn't react with horror. We spoke on the phone for three or four minutes, and that was it. She didn't call back. That was it. Then she dances back to her swimming pool."

A crushed smile wavered on his lips. "Would she prefer it if I had died?"

The ache in his eyes was terrible. If no one cared, if no one remembered, if no one demanded justice, then the value of life was empty. It meant the people who were supposed to love you did not. It was like being left unburied. That is why men and women throughout history march to their deaths with a last plea to the living: *Remember.* That is why African tribesmen imagined that the ghosts of relatives haunted them, prodding them to avenge their deaths. And it is why clansmen in ancient Arabia believed the soul of a murdered man fluttered around his grave as an owl, crying with thirst until his family took revenge. Because there is something more frightening than being hurt. Being forgotten.

4

THE RULES

NEW YORK CITY

BARUCH ROLLED INTO THE COURTROOM pulling a cartload of evidence.

"He needs a haircut," Bernie said.

"No, he doesn't," said my father.

We were all squished together on a bench in the front row of the gallery—Bernie, my mother, me and my father—a motley cheerleading squad. After two years of trial preparation, six weeks of jury selection and three pretrial appeals, Baruch was about to open for the government at the federal courthouse in Manhattan. The government was trying Don King, America's top boxing promoter, on charges of defrauding an insurance company Lloyds of London.

Baruch's cart lurched and fifty pounds of criminal evidence rolled over his foot, leaving a gray wheel mark across his shoe. Baruch limped over to the prosecution table.

"I'm nervous," I said to my father. "Are you?"

"Yeah."

Ten feet away, King sat at the defense table, flanked by his seven attorneys, his bulk straining the pinstripes of his suit. He was sucking on a candy and sucking on his smile. Over the years, he had been tried for many crimes but had been convicted only once—for disciplining a man who owed him six hundred dollars by stomping him to death.

"The defense attorneys look happy," my father said.

"There are a lot of women on the jury," my mother said. "That's bad."

My parents were nudged up against me on either side, leaning across my shoulders to talk, their breath mixing like a cocktail. There was something unnerving about being in the middle. I remembered when I was little, waking up, afraid of the monster in my closet. I would climb in bed between my parents, careful not to let any part of me touch any part of them. Any contact, I imagined, and they would know what I was thinking.

What was I thinking? At the moment, about Baruch shirtless. How he lay in bed that morning in an exhausted sleep, purring like a jungle cat. My head had rested on his shoulder, his chest hairs tickling my nose. Usually, I loved to breathe him in. But on this visit to New York, my husband gave off the scent of a different man. He smelled like a man in a moldering raincoat running to catch a moving train. Like panic. On the surface, Baruch was as composed as ever. Inside, though, the strain of the trial had remixed his chemistry. Don King was on trial, but in a sense, so was the system Baruch served.

Baruch had been a prosecutor for thirteen years; recently he had applied to become a judge. He believed in the system, law and abundant order. It is the deal that every person strikes with society: I will give up pursuing vigilante justice, and you will protect me. In ancient Athens, civilization was said to flourish once the Furies, avenging spirits with snakes in their hair and whips in their hands, were subdued, once Athena institutionalized them under due process of law. Historians call it the cornerstone of civilization, the foundation of criminal law. The courts took over, monopolized revenge, sanitized it, moralized it and turned it into ritual. Revenge is subjective; justice is objective. Revenge is personal; justice is procedural. Due process harnesses the impulse toward revenge and strips it of hostility. It tames vengeance through the tedium of documents, testimony and cross-examination.

More important, the government has replaced the harmed party as the avenger. Retribution is no longer a private duty, but a public one. King's alleged crimes were not against Lloyds of London alone, but against the laws of the whole country, *the United States of America* v. *Don King.*

All the trappings of state sponsorship were on display in this arena of institutional revenge: the eagle symbol in the front of the courtroom; the American flag.

My mother, a tax attorney, leaned past me and whispered to my father, "You don't ever want anything that's important to you to be settled in a courtroom."

My father cocked his head.

"It's so arbitrary," she explained.

"It isn't real justice?" he said.

"It's horrible, people lie."

Baruch rose from the prosecution's table, his arms folded over a racing heart. He had practiced his opening statement, reciting it out loud while running around the reservoir in Central Park, while sudsing his hair in the shower, while riding home in empty subway cars after a late night's work. Now he walked to the jury box. He peered at the faces three rows deep.

"Ladies and gentlemen of the jury"—he took a breath like a diver on the edge of a board—"you can fight hard, but you have to fight fair." His voice rose. "That's boxing." His voice dipped. "That's life."

Baruch pointed at the defense table; he kept his eyes locked on the jurors.

"King, defendant Don King," Baruch said, "fought hard, to become rich and powerful in the world of boxing. But in this case, you will see he didn't fight fair. He stole three hundred and fifty thousand dollars through his company. How? Not with a gun or a knife, but with deception."

Baruch talked for nearly three hours, laying out the government's case in arid detail. Don King yawned. The jurors shifted in their chairs. The judge propped up the right side of his face as if it were a lean-to shack. He dozed.

"I'm about to conclude," Baruch said, his throat rasping dry. "You are hearing this evidence because we don't live in, pardon the pun, a 'kingdom.' And in our country, no man is above the law. Rich, powerful, poor, they're all the same. . . ."

"Not true," my mother said. In her spare time, she volunteered to represent people who could not afford a lawyer. "Not everybody is equal before the law, not if you have enough money to hire a team like Don King's. If King didn't have all that money, he'd be sitting in jail right now. Look at death row. It's the poor people who get executed."

When societies replaced private revenge with public justice, one goal was to equalize the weak and the strong. Left in private hands, revenge meant the stronger party escaped punishment. The law was supposed to remedy that.

Baruch finished and dropped into a chair, emptying a glass of water without stopping to breathe. King chortled, flashing a traffic jam of limousine teeth.

"Unbelievable," King said to a supporter. He shook his massive, tufted head, amused by the government's effort. "And they work hard, you know."

The judge called for a recess. As we walked out of the courtroom, my father held open the door for my mother, letting it go for Bernie.

I hugged Baruch, stroking the groove along his spine. "Were you nervous?"

"Did I look nervous?" He pulled back.

"No." The lining of his jacket was damp. "But were you?"

"How did I look?"

He looked as handsome and as unknown to me as ever. Our months of separation, while I was living in Washington, and now, in Jerusalem, had turned him into something of a theoretical husband.

A few days later, I came to court to say good-bye. The defense attorneys began their opening argument by attacking Baruch.

"There is an old saying," said the defense attorney. "Don't accept the message if you don't trust the messenger."

I thought it must feel terrible to be attacked like that. Before the trial, the defense had accused the government of being a "vindictive prosecutor." But Baruch shrugged it off as "nothing personal." Even so, sitting at the far end of the courtroom, Baruch looked much more vulnerable than the defense attorney, with his patrician chin and his senior-partner white hair. Baruch glanced at the jurors to see if anyone was watching. He checked to see that the judge's attention was elsewhere. Then he looked across the courtroom at me. His mouth opened for a silent "I." His tongue touched his teeth, "love." He rounded out a soundless "you."

That evening, from an airport pay phone, I called my friend Rachel. She let me ramble on about the trial, about the separation during our first year of marriage and the time it would take for the case to snail through the system.

"Wouldn't it be a lot easier if Lloyds of London just killed Don King?" she said.

Easier, I replied, laughing, and more cost-efficient. The justice in the courtroom might be legitimate; I was interested in its illegitimate brother. King's trial offered a glimpse of the rule of law. I needed to learn the rules of revenge. Before I found my father's assailant, I wanted to know what was appropriate, and what was recommended. I wanted to get revenge. I wanted to get it right. Was there an etiquette of revenge?

THE QUESTION brought me to Palermo, Sicily, cradle of the vendetta. If a system of private justice exists anywhere in the world, if there is a code of enforcement that shadows the government's, it is here.

On my first morning in Palermo, my translator pointed out the grand, gray building of the Palace of Justice.

"My husband is a prosecutor," I said offhandedly.

Her mouth pulled tight, like a drawstring bag. She looked at me with concern and then accusation. "Aren't you afraid for him?"

"It never occurred to me that it was dangerous."

She pointed to the guards slinging machine guns, blocking every entrance to the building. She noted the gated parking lot, filled with bulletproof cars. Judges and prosecutors were driven to work in them, she said, because so many had been blown up or shot. In recent years, security had improved, but not enough to make a prosecutor's work easy.

In Sicily, the Mafia never accepted a state monopoly on revenge. The opposite was true: The Mafia developed as an antistate in reaction to centuries of foreign domination. Members lived by a code based on the principle of *omertà,* the promise never to assist in the prosecution of crimes. In America, justice relied on confessions and testimony—on statements. The Mafia's system relied on silence.

The Mafia, like revenge, evokes mixed feelings. Revenge has been called an evil passion, a primitive, futile effort for the antisocial and the mentally ill. And yet it endures. More than that, it allures. It has a muscular, macho quality. In Sicily, even the clergy acknowledge this.

"You have to get revenge, otherwise you're a coward," Padre Ennio Pintacuda, a prominent Jesuit priest, told me. Mafia bosses had come to him to repent, but only when they were old, hairless and ready to die. "If you don't take revenge, you're like a woman."

"You're a man without honor," one of Pintacuda's bodyguards broke in. Several of the priests I met in Sicily employed bodyguards. "We spit on a man like this."

In countries where victims rely on the government for revenge, where civil servants like Baruch "whack" criminals for them, the state machinery, in effect, emasculates its citizens. That is why Mafia morality is so compelling. Mob bosses refuse to be emasculated. Vicariously, they make men out of us all.

There were no Mafia manuals, just a centuries-old oral tradition, so I traveled around the island, listening to Sicilians describe methods of revenge. They talked about "goating," a technique in which the victim's feet are bound with rope and tied to his throat. He is then dumped into the trunk of a car. If he moves, he strangles himself. A second method calls for building a bonfire with olive wood. The victim is handcuffed and grilled alive, like an animal on a spit. Another option is to lock him in a pigsty filled with hungry pigs.

During my visit, the most talked about revenge was the case of a twelve-year-old boy who had been kidnapped by a Mafia don when his father turned state's witness. The don kept the boy imprisoned in his villa for a year. Once the father's testimony led to a conviction, he had the boy choked to death. He dunked the body in an oil barrel filled with sulfuric acid, melting it like an ice cube in boiling water.

It was not the murders that empowered the Mafia, so much as the fear of being murdered. The Mafia's symbol is an octopus, a tentacled creature whose long, flexible arms reach into every pocket of society. To make the point, some hits are performed in daylight, in public, the message running red into the gutters: No one is beyond their reach. Especially if he refuses to follow the rules.

A man named Libero Grassi broke the rules when he refused to pay protection money. The evening I met his wife, Pina, she was alone in the family fabric store, closing the register. Seventy years old, she was a compact, placid woman, deeply tanned, with short, silver hair.

"The Mafia," she said, "is a secular church. It is here and it will always be here."

Whenever mobsters appeared at Libero Grassi's pajama factory asking for money, Libero said to his secretary, "Tell them I'm not here."

Then the phone calls began, the threats, the hang-ups. His watchdog was stolen and returned a month later.

"He looked like a skeleton," Pina recalled. "You would think the dog was Anne Frank. He was so weak, he couldn't even lift his leg to pee."

The tortured watchdog was signature Mafia, Pina said, like a noose in an envelope, or a goat head in the mail. They were warning Libero that if he disrespected them, they would take revenge.

Defiant, Libero became the first businessman to announce publicly that he was being squeezed. He went on national television and invited two thousand entrepreneurs to the town hall, asking them to join his fight. Twenty people showed up.

"He stood in front of the empty hall and told these frightened men, 'If there are a hundred of us, they can't kill us all.' Then they all took a step back."

Pina closed the shutters to her store and wearily turned her key in its lock. Outside, a violet umbrella of light was opening over Palermo. Women leaned out on their balconies, plucking laundry from the clotheslines. Along the street, men were lazing on wooden chairs, dicing up the news of the day. Their wives lowered wicker baskets to them, teetering with beer bottles. We drove through the dusk to her neighborhood, Quartiere Liberta, and parked. Toward the end, Pina said, Libero had changed his parking spot every day, hoping to avoid the inevitable.

At 7:25 A.M., on August 29, 1991, Pina saw her husband off to work. A minute later she heard gunshots. Shortly after, the doorbell rang.

"Is your husband home?" said a policeman with a solemn face.

Libero had made it around the corner, past the grocery store, almost as far as the barbershop. They brought him down with five bullets, four in the body, and one in the head, to seal it.

Now seven years later, Pina stood on the spot where her husband had met judge, jury and executioner, descending like sudden rain. A red stain covered the pavement, shaped like a puddle. Every year on the anniversary of her husband's murder, she spray-painted the sidewalk red.

"It's the simplest way to say, 'This is the blood of my husband,' " Pina said. Like Abel, the world's first murder victim, his innocent blood boiled in the earth.

But unintentionally, the widow's gesture serves the Mafia's interests too. The red paint warns: Hurt us, and we will hurt you back, and we always win. When a group has that much power, people stop calling it revenge; they call it punishment.

After hearing several more stories like Pina's it became clear that in Sicily, guns are the favored instruments of revenge. I knew nothing of guns. I never had touched a gun. Once, I tagged along with Baruch on a visit to the National Crime Lab in Jerusalem. I wandered downstairs to the ballistics unit, where I found a technician named Uri Argaman. Five hundred guns adorned his laboratory like wallpaper, a repeating pattern of rifles and pistols. I asked Uri to show me a Beretta, the gun the shooter had used against my father.

"A good, reliable pistol," Uri said, pulling a few off the wall. "This is a 7.65. This is a .22. This is a 9mm Parabellam, model 92."

He laid the gun on my palm. It felt cold and bony. I thought of the shooter holding it, weighing its heft, fingering the alternating smooth and ridged black metal. "Do terrorists like Berettas?"

"That's like asking if terrorists drive Fords," he said. "A typical terrorist gun is a Scorpion or Kalashnikov assault rifle."

I closed my fingers around the pistol, thinking about how different the shooter and I were. Bullets were his weapon. What was mine?

"The bullet flies out at a thousand feet per second," Uri said. "This is a magazine. Pull the slide back. Pull the trigger and fire."

I lifted the gun close to one eye, training it on the lightbulb on Uri's desk lamp. Ready, aim . . .

"Don't!" he said. It was a semiautomatic pistol; the slide would fly back into my face. "You'll take out your eye."

In Sicily, symmetry would demand that I shoot the shooter, or maybe his father. But I had to find another way, my way. There are as many ways to get revenge as there are to get someone to love you. What matters, in both instances, is to find the weak spot. That takes planning, and a certain knowledge of the person who is being targeted. It follows common sense: hit him where it hurts.

"It's a human reaction," said Fabio Fortuna, a twenty-seven-year-old Sicilian grocer. He was building a pyramid of tomatoes in a vegetable store in Corleone, home to one of the island's bloodiest crime families.

"It's not just me. It's not just us, living here," Fabio said. He held up a tomato, turning it into a globe. "Don't think that Corleone is another world." He rotated the tomato on its axis. Red, all around. "All the world is Corleone."

Fabio was right, with one small adjustment: all the world might dream of getting even, but in places like America the word *revenge* is a taboo. Revenge is one of those seedy impulses that upsets one's self-image as a civilized being. In America, even in death penalty cases, even when our military launches retaliatory strikes, we feel compelled to say, "We want justice, not revenge." To admit wanting revenge is to admit you have been crushed and need to be rebuilt. Few are comfortable admitting that, even to themselves.

In America I felt ashamed to tell anyone what I was doing. In Sicily, I felt part of an honored tradition.

When I visited Leoluca Orlando, the mayor of Palermo, I asked him about the Mafia's rules of revenge. He laughed.

"The rules?" he said, strutting belly first through the foyer of the mayor's mansion. "They have only one: the rule of self-interest. The goal is total physical and financial destruction."

Halfway into his sitting room, he turned to look at me. His eyes flicked up and down as if I were a befuddled traveler who had landed at the wrong airport. "Here we have no limits on revenge."

THE NEXT REVENGE CAPITAL I landed in had more explicit limits. There were so many, in fact, they had a rule book.

The *canon* was compiled by Leke Dukagjini, a fifteenth-century Albanian nobleman. Today, it is sold in kiosks in Albania's capital, Tirana, and can be found lying on top of the refrigerator in people's homes, as commonplace as the telephone book. In the *canon,* a word meaning "legal code," revenge is not a choice but a sacred duty. It is based on a curious alliance between the id and the superego. Acting out vindictive impulses is allowed—encouraged, demanded—as long as one follows the rules.

It took only a short time to understand why the *canon* thrives here. My driver and I were traveling one afternoon on the national highway, a two-lane asphalt strip rutted with craters. Our trip across the drained marshland was stop-and-go. Cars veered off and onto the road to buy gas, sold by peasants in soda bottles. There was a ten-minute delay when a donkey clomped into traffic and leisurely licked his behind. Then the driver ahead of us braked for a young man wearing a black tank top. He was shouldering a Kalashnikov rifle and leaned on the driver's window, discussing something with the passengers.

"What's the delay?" I asked.

"A robbery," my driver said sleepily.

The young man shifted his gun toward the passengers' faces. It left a red strap mark across his pointy shoulder blade.

"Five more minutes," the driver assured me, humming, as if the bandit were a local drawbridge.

Highway robbery is so common in Albania, few people drive after sunset. Even during the day, they travel in convoys. Almost everyone owns a weapon. More than half of the cars are stolen from Europe and smuggled across the border. Albanians drive sparkling Mercedes and BMWs, but have no regular running water or electricity.

"What are the jobs here?" I asked my translator.

"Drugs, prostitution, weapons trade," he said.

He was serious.

Albania is the poorest country in Europe and one of the most chaotic. Both the economy and the government had recently collapsed. As the central government failed to establish order, Albanians were drawn to the unofficial law spelled out in the *canon*.

I sat up at night in a hotel in Tirana reading the two-hundred-page English translation. I scoured chapter twenty-two, which dealt with murder, looking for anything that might be relevant to my father's case. One hundred and sixty-eight precepts outlined every variety of violence that triggered vengeance. They were organized under headings:

CXXIV: Blood
CXXV: Blood Follows the Finger
CXXVI: Blood Is Paid for With Blood

CXXVII: A Crime May Not Be Recompensed With Blood
CXXVIII: Blood Is Not Paid for With a Fine
CXXIX: Blood for Evil Acts

As daylight leaked into the crack between the curtain and the windowsill, I came across precept #906: "If I fire at someone and only graze his head . . ." The *canon* prescribed the revenge. My heart gave a small squeeze, an odd little squirt of hope. Here in Albania, in an arcane folk code, I had finally found kindred spirits. I had found the rule for avenging my father. The code even used "graze," the same word the New York newspapers had used to report the attack. The only problem was, I did not understand the precept. I needed an authority to explain it to me. I stashed my wallet and my wedding ring, and set out for the north.

In northern Albania, the Roman Catholic part of the country, the *canon*'s wild justice reigned. The mountainous terrain and isolated villages made it difficult for the government to penetrate. The folk code kept the peace, ordering men to walk at a distance of one rifle barrel length apart to avoid knocking against each other and starting a feud.

My translator and I traveled for hours. We rattled through the city of Lezhe, where cows stood on the sidewalks gnawing on watermelon rinds. We passed hayfields and bean fields and blackberry bushes. We drove until the black asphalt surrendered to a road the color and the texture of crushed bones. In Baldre, a village of 150 homes, we asked a farmer for Mark Pashko Malotaj, a *canon* expert. Mark was one of six members of the provincial Blood Feud Committee. The committee advised the twelve thousand inhabitants of the region on issues related to revenge. We found Mark at home, sitting at a wooden table with two other committee members, drinking Turkish coffee.

"You are now inside the *canon,*" Mark congratulated me. He flagged me into the seat opposite him. "We have been inside the *canon* for two thousand years. If France, England and America had the *canon,* they would be proud."

Mark was sixty-two years old, a retired farmer, with scant white hair and a chest so red that it turned his thin white shirt pink. His right eye wandered, as if he could look straight ahead and over his shoulder at once, inspecting those who came through his door. His living room was trimmed with Christian icons and angel prints. The icons prompted a question from me about the un-Christian character of the code.

"How does the *canon* fit in with 'Turn the other cheek'?"

Mark cupped a hand over his mouth to catch his laugh. The other men in the room tittered. "In Albania we have 'Don't hit my cheek because I'll kill you.' "

Mark's wife, a petite woman with a kerchief knotted under her chin, poured us glasses of raki, a potent local liquor. I already felt dizzy from reading the *canon* all night. My thoughts were leapfrogging from one precept to the next.

I understood from the text that if a man was shot, his male relatives were expected to "take their blood back." The role of female relatives was what interested me. There is a saying in Albania: "Men are born with rifles in their hands." There is another saying in Albania: "Women do not have rifles." Women serve the role of revenge cheerleaders, chanting funerary dirges, shaking the victim's blood-soaked clothes like macabre pompoms. They lacerate their own faces until they trickle red, boosting the men toward vengeance. Most cultures with codes of honor exclude women from revenge. The duty to avenge a father falls on the closest male relatives, often in the following order: son, brother, uncle, nephew, cousin.

I was not going to become an Albanian-style avenger, but I was curious to know how my claim would resolve itself here.

"Can a woman avenge the blood of, say, her father?"

Before I finished the sentence, the men's heads were wagging, no. Quickly, I added, "And she has only one brother. And her brother is . . ." Hal's gentle face genied up before my eyes.

. . . *retarded,* I started to say. "No, her brother is crippled. If he's crippled, can the sister avenge blood?"

The experts exchanged uncertain looks around the table. To my relief, they were considering it. Meanwhile, I was sorry that I had called my brother a cripple, but the truth was too embarrassing to explain. Hal was simply not confrontational enough for revenge. The last time I had seen him, he was up a tree.

During my visit to New York the week the King trial opened, Baruch and I had gone to my father's and Fran's house for Passover. Hal, his wife and their eighteen-month-old daughter, Eva, drove down from New Haven. An hour before the holiday meal, my mother called from Long Island.

"I wanted to call before you started," she said. "Would you have remembered to call?"

"Of course," I said.

"We just got out of the Jacuzzi." Her voice sounded small and pruney, as if it had shriveled in the bubbling hot jets. She was with Bernie at their Long Island house. My father's house, a modest split-level, more like the home we had grown up in, was bustling with holiday activity. Baruch was by the stove, sampling the turkey. Fran was snuggling with Hal's daughter on the couch, reading her the Passover story. My father was mopping the kitchen floor, singing opera like an actor in a spaghetti sauce commercial.

"I better go," I said.

"Well, I'm lonely." There was a tightening in her throat. "It's Daddy's year to have you."

My father looked up from his mop. "Who're you on the phone with?"

"Mommy."

"How is she?"

"I don't know." I put the phone in his hand. "Ask her."

"Hiya! I'm doing a 'sponga'!" He used the Hebrew slang for sponging the floor, a word they had learned their newlywed year in Jerusalem. "Why don't you come here tonight? You've got an hour, you still have time to get here."

I watched his ruddy, glowing face and I wondered, Was she stammering, was she giggling, was she chillingly formal—how was she telling him no? He hung up and looked at me, puzzled.

"Why isn't she coming?" he asked.

"It's Bernie. He doesn't feel comfortable."

"I knew it," he said, swishing the mop over the same clean spot.

The following afternoon my mother's car turned into the driveway.

"Hi, Fran," my mother said. "I like your hair." She turned to me. "Hi, my darling, precious girl." Then, with an embarrassed grin, "Hi, Dave."

Later, alone with my father, her grin fell away.

"This was the worst holiday of my life," she told him. "I was all alone."

Of course she had Bernie, but her father had died recently, and her only sister had succumbed to a brain tumor. She missed her family.

After a while, we walked her to her car. In the old days, my father would come up behind her and twirl her, kissing her loudly and hammishly on the lips. Now—shaking hands, patting shoulders—there was no right way. How do you say good-bye when you have said good-bye forever? I looked around the driveway to see if Hal was remembering, if he was watching the same sappy home movie inside his head. He was not there. I heard rustling and looked up. Hal was sitting on a branch among the budding leaves. As my parents fumbled through another parting, my thirty-six-year-old brother had climbed a maple tree.

"Be careful!" my mother called to him.

"Oh, let him be," my father said.

After my mother left, after Hal came down, I asked him why.

"It just seemed the thing to do," he said in his distracted way. "I knew it'd be awkward when Mommy and Daddy said good-bye."

That was Hal, climbing above the pain, while I burrowed into it. Hal would never get revenge because he rose above anguish. He lived beyond it, with the birds.

But that was too complicated a story to communicate through an Albanian translator, especially the part about the Jacuzzi and Passover. So sitting before the Blood Feud Committee, I said that, in this case, the brother was crippled. The men were talking it through, their opinions winging back and forth across the table. They kicked back glasses of the clear, piercing alcohol and stabbed their fingers into lines of the *canon.* Mark rolled cigarettes for everyone, spitting on the papers, sealing them with tobacco-stained fingertips.

"Yes," Mark said finally. "In this case, the father is shot, a daughter can revenge. But no one can kill her afterward. No one can touch the woman."

According to the *canon,* women are not counted as clansmen, therefore, "women do not incur blood."

"Sounds like a good deal," I said, skipping to the next question, eager to move on before Mark changed his mind. "Is prison relevant?"

Mark's eyelids fluttered with recognition. This one was easy.

"It doesn't matter if the man goes to prison," he said. The Albanian justice system is a nuisance, nothing more than a delay. "Prison isn't satisfying for the family. Someone will kill him after he serves the prison term."

In my father's case, whether or not the shooter was in prison, the question of timing troubled me. Twelve years had passed since the attack. I had vowed revenge in a poem long ago but, like most people, never acted on it, and like most people, I never expected to.

But now, before I disappeared into a new family—the one Baruch and I would make—I wanted to do one last thing for the old one. Had I waited too long to act? Was there a statute of limitations on revenge? Once again, I was curious to know if anything was written in the rules. In Saudi Arabia, tribal law called the period following a homicide the "boiling of blood." The dead man's family could take revenge with impunity for three and a third days. The Gilyak aborigines of Russia believed that the soul of a murdered man came back as a bird, pecking at his relatives to take revenge for up to three generations.

In Albania, the *canon* experts explained, the avenger had twenty-four hours to strike back and risk no counterattack. The avenger had one shot. If he missed, he could not shoot again. If he hit the man, he fired his weapon three times into the air, signaling an end to the killing. Few cycles resolved themselves that quickly, though. The longest one spooled on for 270 years. In fact, Mark said, pushing himself up from the table, his neighbor was involved in a blood grudge that was seventy-two years old.

We tramped down Mark's muddy path to visit Simon Dede Gjonaj. Simon, a sixty-three-year-old veterinarian, had four children and a sturdy wife. We found him sitting in the shade of his front yard, looking toward the mountains that capped his fields. Pouches hung like hammocks under his eyes. A sleeveless undershirt revealed the brown skin on his shoulders, cracked and baked like clay.

"At midnight, beyond the white fence, in the animal pen," Simon began his story, "my father shot a thief." The intruder was trying to steal a horse.

"One bullet in the heart," Simon said.

Afterward, his father had picked up the corpse, rinsed off the blood, dressed it in fresh clothes and returned it to the family. Simon's father, a young man then, understood the consequences. His family and the thief's were now "in blood."

"You cannot shoot a thief," Simon said. Sweat stubbled the skin above his upper lip. "A horse does not equal a man's life."

For the next twenty years, Simon's father and his family were forced to remain inside their home. He married and fathered Simon and his other children, never straying beyond the dappled garden where we now sat drinking raki. There are no time limits on Albanian feuds, but there are limits to the location: no man could be shot on his own property.

Taking asylum is like standing on base in a lethal game of tag. In ancient times, when revenge was in vogue, the practice existed everywhere. In many cultures, being asleep was a form of sanctuary, because the soul was thought to leave the body. In Greece, temples served as safe havens. In the Holy Land, a man who committed an accidental murder could flee to one of six cities of refuge. In tribal Afghanistan, a fugitive could find shelter in a mosque or in the shrine of a holy man. (Although, in modern Sicily, even the churches are not safe. Padre Paolo Turturro, a fifty-two-year-old priest in Palermo who preached against the Mafia, said a cadaver had been left at the back door of his church, pinned with a note: "For You." Turturro had been shot at three times, once during the Easter parade, emptying the town square of everyone except for the priest and a statue of Jesus Christ. Asked about the prescription for forgiveness in the New Testament's Book of Matthew, he said, "I don't turn the other cheek. I'm not stupid.")

In Albania, especially in the north, nearly every village had a family or two that were "locked in" asylum. In the Kashnjit area alone, fifty-five feuding families lived bolted inside their homes. Simon recalled growing up in the whitewashed house, his male relatives pasty, their beards long and their hair like gardens grown wild. All day they drifted from window to window, from the one large room downstairs, up the steep staircase, creaking across the slatted floors to two small bedrooms. Women were exempt from the threat of revenge. They worked in the fields, planting eggplants and peppers, and sold milk in town. Simon sometimes helped them. The rules excluded young boys and old men from feuds; like women, they did not count as "blood."

Then one day when Simon was around eight years old, he saw his father walk out the door and down to the road where the chickens left their three-toed prints in the mud. Communism had swept across Albania, suppressing the folk law, suspending blood vengeance. For the next forty-five years Simon's family could promenade through town. They forgot about their blood debt.

When Communist rule fell during the nineties, the old code was gradually resurrected. Simon and his brothers feared the horse thief's descendants would resume the feud. They did, recently, in a note that warned: "We have not forgotten our death."

That was when Mark and the Blood Feud Committee stepped in. In situations like Simon's, the committee tried to resolve the conflict within the framework of the *canon*.

"What if someone shot my father and he didn't die?" I asked, unaware that I had switched from the third person to the first.

Mark said that I would follow precept #906 of the code:

> If I fire at someone and only graze his head, I must still pay 3 purses for the wound.

What was a "purse"? And was not blood always paid for with blood?

Mark explained: "You could take three purses and forget it. Or if you want revenge, you could get it. It depends on you."

Three purses in the pre-Communist era, Mark said, meant fifteen large gold coins. Today that translated into roughly three million Albanian lek. Or, another revenge expert interjected, citing precept #892, if my father wanted, he could have fifty sheep and one fourth of an ox.

He and Mark began quibbling about farm animal inflation and the present value of sheep.

"Fifty sheep in Lek's time is not worth a hundred sheep today," Mark said, his red chest reddening further.

"No one cares about sheep anymore," said the other man. "All they want is money."

Talk of money offended Mark, a traditionalist. "If a man grazes your father's head and pays you, the feud is over," he said. That much was written in the Albanian code.

Albanian reality, however, was different.

"It's never settled with money," he said. "Because it's a shame to settle for money. I have never seen it settled without blood."

The three purses due to my father was known as blood money, a bloodless form of revenge. This form of compensation lies at the root of justice everywhere, payable in local currency: camels in the mountains of Yemen; reindeer and tea on the icy tundra. In some places, homicide was considered an economic crime against the victim's tribe. In Chad, the Mundang turned over the land upon which a man had been slain. Among the Anglo-Saxon tribes, the killer's clan took up a collection to pay wergild. In some societies, the murder weapon—a gun or a knife—is the down payment.

Revenge is quenched by compensating for the family's loss of manpower, sometimes literally. In Bedouin society, the closest female relative of the killer could be given to the victim's kinsmen. She regained her freedom when she bore a son who grew up and replaced the murdered man in battle. In Siberia, the killer's clan was expected to surrender a male relative. The male substituted for the dead man in every way, performing his work, raising his children, sleeping with his widow.

Today, even in the United States, the spirit of blood money lives on—neatened up and slowed down—in criminal and civil lawsuits. The federal government and most states permit courts to impose restitution as part of a criminal sentence or as a condition of probation. Civil court dockets are thick with personal-injury lawsuits. The difference is that, in America, if the injured party fails to win compensation, he cannot hack off the defendant's legs. There is, however, a country with a developed, authoritative system where the injured party can either accept damages or, if he chooses, inflict real damages, under the approving eyes of the judge. That was where I went next.

FOR MY VISA PHOTOGRAPH I bought a black scarf and wound it around my hair, ears, forehead, neck and chin. In the photograph I looked like a white wedge of nose parting black rayon curtains. I applied for a second, clean U.S. passport, free of entry stamps from Israel. The Islamic Republic of Iran would not have a sense of humor, I guessed, about an American Jewish woman from Jerusalem touring the countryside, seeking pointers on revenge. (When I told my father about the trip, he e-mailed me: *Laura, This is your father speaking. DO NOT GO TO IRAN! I don't care how much it helps your research—you have a responsibility to yourself and to others not to put yourself "in harm's way." Love and kisses, Dad.*)

Even before I boarded the flight from Amman, Jordan, there were signs that Iran took its theocracy seriously. Men removed their neckties, symbols of the secular West. Women, who had arrived at the airport in tight jeans and heels, changed into shapeless, ankle-length robes and flat shoes. They shed makeup and jewelry and covered their hair with scarves. My guidebook warned that tourists caught drinking alcohol, flirting or wearing shorts in public would be arrested.

During the two weeks that I traveled in Iran, I wore the black robe and black scarf, known as a *hijab,* always, even inside stuffy office buildings and overheated restaurants. "No *Hijab,* No Service" read the sign on the door to Iran's version of McDonald's, where Persia Cola and nonalcoholic Mullah Brew Beer were served. Once, when a bellhop knocked on my hotel room door, I accidentally opened it with my head uncovered. My black robe was closed, all twelve buttons fastened, from my shins to my Adam's apple, but my flattened curls were exposed. The bellhop's eyes bulged with embarrassment and curiosity, as if I had greeted him topless.

Since the Islamic Revolution in 1979, Iran has been guided by the teachings of Mohammed, the prophet of Islam. The government abolished all sections of the legal code that did not conform with the Koran. It purged secular influences from society, especially those from the United States, known as the Great Satan.

"You'd better pretend you're asleep," my Iranian translator said as our car rolled toward the holy city of Qom. We had been driving south from the Iranian capital, Teheran. We scrolled past eighty miles of repeating scenery, yellow scrub and salt flats, land whose color had been sapped like an overboiled tea bag. As we approached the tollbooth at the end of the highway, she rested a hand on my shoulder and pushed me down, out of view.

"They don't like foreigners here," she said.

Slumped against the car door, a scarf pulled halfway over my eyes, I got my first glimpse of this center of Shiite Islam. Brilliantly painted billboards soared over dull, parched buildings, depicting soldiers with bloody head wounds and one-legged veterans stooped on crutches. Political banners decorated traffic circles. One pictured axes chopping down a tree festooned with British and American flags. Above it all towered the bearded, glowering face of His Holiness Grand Ayatollah Hajj Sayyed Ruhollah Musavi Khomeini, leader of the Revolution. It was in Qom that Khomeini's Islamic revolutionary militia defeated the Iranian army.

Khomeini had trained here, at the country's largest theological college. Under his direction in 1983, the government rewrote the penal code and launched a Koranic system of retribution.

Qom's streets were crowded with seminarians, men in turbans and brown gowns that ballooned around them in a dry wind. Women sheathed themselves in an extra layer of modesty, a black cloak called the chador that fit like a tent over the body, the women's heads serving as a kind of tent pole. They held the two sides of the fabric together with their teeth, keeping the tent flaps closed.

Our car stopped in front of a yellow brick building trimmed with aqua glaze. I slipped on my borrowed chador. We walked through an arched entrance to the Golpaygani Seminary. Above us, tiled in black-and-white letters, were the words: "There is no God but Allah."

"No women allowed," a cleric said, standing inside the archway. My translator ignored him; I scuttled along behind her. In the courtyard, men sat cross-legged on the ground, debating the texts before them. They stared, surprised, as we left our shoes outside, next to theirs, and entered the seminary building. I padded up three flights of stairs to the ayatollah's office passing through blue and green squares of light shafting through the stained-glass windows. The air smelled stony, like that of a cave or a basement, though we were high up, overlooking the courtyard.

Ayatollah Ali Korani was fifty-one years old. He had a white turban, a white collarless shirt, a white beard and a high, egg-white forehead. He was a creamy man who exuded mildness. He handed me a card with his title: head of the Islamic Law Center at the Center of Islamic Learning. He tipped his head sideways as if to say our encounter would be pleasant.

"I heard you have a slogan about God on your money," he said.

I found a five-dollar bill in my purse and showed him the green letters printed on the back: "In God We Trust."

"This is a very good slogan you have," he said.

Outside, in the courtyard, loudspeakers broadcast the noon call to prayer. Students streamed toward the mosque. The speakers boomed, "God is great."

"Just like on your dollar bills," he said, delighted.

He launched into a comparison of his religion and what he presumed to be mine, Christianity. The Koran endorsed retribution, he said, but it also mentioned forgiveness twenty times. The differences between our religions, he said, were minor: "Jesus says if someone beats you, let him beat your other cheek. We say, beat him as he beat you."

In a short time, I felt comfortable with the ayatollah. I decided to begin my inquiry where I had left off in Albania with the Blood Feud Committee, with the subject of blood money.

"Let's say someone tries to kill someone, shoots him, say, and he doesn't die. Is there blood money?"

"All injuries have blood money, even one scratch."

"A 'scratch'?" That was the word from my father's hospital report. Islam considered a scratch actionable? "So, say a Muslim shoots another Muslim and it scratches his head."

"It depends. Is the scratch deep or shallow?"

"It causes a ridge but doesn't penetrate the skull."

"It depends. If it's a woman, and her hair was destroyed, then it's very important and very expensive." The ayatollah's response was Talmudic, his calculations complex. At the computer center across the hall, his pupils had filled a CD ROM with fourteen thousand questions about blood money.

"This person injured, he's a man," I said. "He went to the hospital. No brain damage."

He thought for a moment. "I can't tell you, exactly; we have more than thirty types of blood money for the head. The doctor has to say what kind of injury it is."

Head wounds are assessed according to the severity and the likelihood of permanent damage. Generally, a flesh wound is worth one fourth of an injury that strikes the bone. Death is a simpler calculation—in the time of early Islam, one hundred camels. The camels had to be female, paid in the following denominations: 25 one-year-olds, 25 two-year-olds, 25 three-year-olds, and 25 four-years-olds. Among the nomads of Islam, every male tribesman donated a camel to the victim's family for up to seven generations. They called this restitution "the camel of sleep," because it guaranteed sleep without fear. Today, in Iran, death demands roughly $10,000. For each lesser injury, there is a minutely prescribed scale. Half the total sum for the loss of a limb, one third for one eye, one quarter for a hand, one twentieth for a tooth.

"What if the shooter is a Muslim and the victim is a non-Muslim?" I asked.

"Half price," the ayatollah said pleasantly. "Don't laugh. In non-Islamic countries they don't give Muslims any blood money."

The blood money Muslims award to non-Muslims varies according to juristic schools. It is usually one half, though some rate Jews and Christians as worth one third, and Zoroastrians one fifth.

"If a non-Muslim wants to retaliate instead," I said, "does he have to inflict one half of the injury?"

This was where all my questions had been leading, to the problem of proportionality: How much revenge could we get?

"Non-Muslims only get blood money. They're not allowed to retaliate."

"Why not?"

"At least we pay you. Other religions wouldn't give you anything. If Black Muslims retaliated against Americans, there'd be no Americans left in the world."

Many Islamic jurists prohibit physical revenge when the victim and the victimizer are of a different gender, status or religion.

"You should thank God, at least you get blood money," he said.

What would I do with blood money? In the margin of my notebook, I had worked out the sum:

—no perm. damage

—shooter was Muslim

—victim an infidel

—heir of victim pressing claim, female

After all the deductions, according to the Mohammedian sliding scale, our family was entitled to one ninth of one camel. That might be a hoof and enough fur to sew a glove. And that was assuming that the shooter would pay. What Palestinian nationalist would compensate a Jew from New York strolling through the Arab marketplace? Blood money keeps a victim passive. It is a form of satisfaction one has to wait for and hope to be given. Revenge, on the other hand, is something one can take.

I thanked the ayatollah and did what Baruch might do when a district court judge ruled against him: I appealed. This expert was only an ayatollah. Next, I would meet with a grand ayatollah.

Grand Ayatollah Abdul Karim Musavi Ardebily had been Iran's chief of the judiciary. For eight years under Khomeini, he had headed the first Islamic Justice Department. He reviewed the religious laws and helped reinstitute them. Now he ran a school in Qom, where students packed its white marble hall. His disciples sat cross-legged on orange blankets and leaned against red pillows spread out over twelve Tabriz rugs. The grand ayatollah taught from the front of the hall, enthroned on the room's only chair.

Before his bodyguards let me enter his study, they took my camera and snapped a photograph of me. If my camera were a concealed weapon, they would find out by firing it. Momentarily disoriented by blue flashing dots, I tripped over my chador, through his doorway.

Grandpa?

Seated with one wrinkled hand on his desk, the grand ayatollah looked like my father's deceased father, a rabbi from Poland. The black knee-length frock coat, the thick glasses, the gray beard, the broad nose dotted with pores—the only difference between the men was in their hats. My grandfather wore a black homburg; this man wore a black turban, a sign that he was a descendant of the prophet Mohammed.

The furrow between his brows and the bustle of his aides told me that I would have to be brief. In my effort to load my questions with detail, they sprang out hopelessly coiled.

"If a man shoots, skims his head, he doesn't kill the man. He bled, he went to the hospital, it didn't enter his brain. If he's not a Muslim, it's half?"

Incredibly, he understood. "Sometimes non-Muslims can get the full blood money."

"What if a Palestinian shoots a Jew?"

This burbled out. Both of us breathed, startled. We checked each other's eyes, as if to ask, What was that funny sound? In Islamic Iran, there was no more hated nation than Israel. Not only had I uttered the word *Jew,* but I had inquired what revenge was within a Jew's rights.

The grand ayatollah's mouth opened, then it closed. Then he said sternly, "No Palestinians can give blood money or be revenged, because they're at war with the Jews."

The pinch in his brows deepened. This was not my Polish grandfather. I had plunged down the wrong alley, and the only choice was to keep on running. I hoped that if I asked the questions quickly enough, they might blur by unnoticed.

"But what if he was just walking down the street in, say, Jerusalem?"

"If the Jew was born in Jerusalem, he is a native, he gets blood money. But if it's a Jew from another country, occupying the Palestinian's house, then no blood money. Nothing."

"What if he's a tourist?" It was my last *what if.*

"Tourists can get blood money and revenge as long as they're not trying to occupy the Palestinian's house. They are entitled to retaliation. It's in Islamic law."

Suddenly the alley opened onto a vista. "Can the Jewish tourist retaliate and shoot and wound the Palestinian?" I asked.

"If he was only a tourist, not coming to hurt anyone, not to occupy the land, not to attack anyone, he can retaliate by shooting."

He quirked an eyebrow at me. It rose and fell, in my mind, with the thud of a gavel. The grand ayatollah had reversed the lower ayatollah. By his supreme authority, my father, my family, could get revenge.

"So could the Jew have the shooter just stand there"—I tried to flatten my smile—"and take a shot at the shooter?" I was repeating myself, but still, I was incredulous.

Yes, he said, but the Jew had to be sure not to injure the shooter "one millimeter more than the Palestinian hurt him." Otherwise, the balance of pain would be upset again, and the Palestinian could strike back. This was one of the problems with revenge: It often exceeded the original offense. The desert elders had tried to set limits: "One grave opposite one grave."

The effort to achieve proportionality has animated justice nearly four thousand years. In ancient Babylonia, the Code of Hammurabi said, "An eye for an eye, a broken bone for a broken bone, a tooth for a tooth." The law of retaliation, or lex talionis, documented in the Law of the Twelve Tables in 450 B.C., also called for equality of punishment and crime.

Every person who hopes to even a score has to answer this question: How much revenge is enough? The most honest reply I ever heard came from Leah Rabin, the widow of assassinated Israeli prime minister Yitzhak Rabin. "None," she told me, her green eyes hard as marbles. "Because there's not enough revenge in the entire world."

Iran, meanwhile, following Islamic law, also addresses this question of balance. The prophet Mohammed proclaimed: "If ye take vengeance, take it only in the measure that vengeance was taken from you."

This is not easy with nonfatal injuries like my father's. The Iranian clerics struggle today with the same technical problems that the rabbis of the Babylonian Talmud wrestled with in 200 A.D.: "Suppose the eye of one person was big and the eye of the other person was small. How, then, could you apply the principle of 'eye for eye' . . . ? How would you handle a situation in which a blind man put out someone's eye, or a cripple cut off someone's hand, or a lame person broke someone's leg?" The rabbis decided that "an eye for an eye" meant monetary compensation rather than physical punishment.

In Iran, the grand ayatollah sitting before me had presided over a case in which a man had thrown acid in the face of his beautiful, young wife. The wife took him to court. The husband offered to pay $7,000 in blood money.

"I want his eyes," the wife said, rejecting the money. "I want to blind him as he blinded me."

The grand ayatollah tried to work out a compromise. He told her she was cruel. She said her husband was more cruel. After days of haggling, the blinded wife accepted a deal: take the full blood money, poke out only one eye. In the presence of the grand ayatollah, she felt for her husband's face, her fingers striking the air like a piano player at the keys. The woman's relatives guided her wrists, helping her find her husband's eye socket. She used a metal spoon to dig.

"Is this justice?" I asked.

"Well," the grand ayatollah said, winking his right eye, then his left. "The husband was happy he got a discount."

Three aides and two bodyguards rushed into the study. Our meeting was over. I rode back to Teheran, content, staring out the window at the hypnotic, barren landscape. But when I reached the hotel I realized my success with the grand ayatollah was meaningless. It was an intellectual victory at best. The grand ayatollah said that I could shoot the shooter. That might be interesting to imagine, but it was far from my heart's true goal.

A ringing filled my hotel room, the jarring trill of a foreign phone.

"Hi, dolly!"

It was my mother, calling from Long Island.

"Do you think I'm overly involved with you?" she said.

"No." I pulled off my black head scarf. "What are you talking about?"

"I was just listening to a radio program about mothers who are overly involved with their kids."

Maybe she was, but I liked it. She brightened the dreariest of moments. The night I had landed in New York for Baruch's trial, she stood under the "International Arrivals" sign wearing a clown nose and waving two American flags.

"Which coat do you want?" she had said, holding up two black jackets that she had bought for us to wear like twins.

We drove to Manhattan, to the apartment where Baruch was staying. I thanked her for delivering me. "I'd have gone to pick you up on the moon," she said.

Now, hearing her voice tinny and echoing on the long-distance line, sitting in my hotel room in southwest Asia, where I could not find the lever to flush the toilet, I thought: Well, this is the moon.

"What are you doing?" my mother asked.

"Learning about blood money."

"What's blood money?" she said, pronouncing *blood* as if it were a foreign word.

"It's when someone gives you lots of nice things so you don't get revenge on them," I said.

"Sounds like a better plan than killing people."

For my mother, revenge had been cleansed, scrubbed of its messy intensity. Translated into money, it became rational and tangible. She was right, in theory; blood money was "a better plan." Mohammed himself said that blood money ransoms the death of a believer. But written prescriptions like blood money, like turning the other cheek, often fall apart in reality. The afternoon I met Nahid Najibpoor, a forty-one-year-old woman living in Teheran, the arguments favoring blood money crumbled.

Nahid had no furniture, so we sat facing each other on her blue rug. Above us a photograph of a girl stared out from the wall, wrapped in a black satin ribbon. The girl had a stranded gaze, like a shipwrecked passenger watching the horizon. Nahid began talking, slowly at first, the pauses filled with the stutter of the clock's second hand. In the corner of the room, a wicker basket creaked.

Nahid glanced at it. "That's probably the ghost of Arian."

Arian had been a quiet child. She had cradled her dolls and sung, "Baby, don't cry." She had wispy brown hair, soft like the fur on a kitten's belly. Nahid had loved to comb it, to smooth it into a neat, side part.

After Nahid's divorce, Islamic law had granted her custody for the first seven years. But on Arian's seventh birthday, an Islamic judge ordered her to move in with her father. Eighteen months later Arian was dead. The girl's body had absorbed so many blows, they filled pages of a hospital log: a fractured skull, broken arms, brown welts on her back, cigarette burns on her hands, fork tine burns on her legs, black-and-blue fingernails, broken teeth, gashed nose, dilated liver, torn-out hair. She was acutely malnourished, weighed thirty-five pounds. She died with dried blood on her lips, her mouth cracked open.

The chief suspects were Arian's father, and his son from another marriage, Ramtin.

"I thought God would give me the power to burn the father with my eyes," Nahid said, her voice trembling.

There was a trial, but Islamic law virtually prohibits a father's conviction for his child's death. The eighteen-year-old Ramtin was tried and found guilty of murder. In other countries the judge would then sentence the defendant. That was not how justice worked in Iran.

A judge from the Public Court of Teheran described the sentencing process to me: "At the end of a trial, the killers are in handcuffs and they ask the victim's family for clemency. Sometimes they fall on their knees. They kiss the hands and the feet of the family. They quote the Koran, swear on the life of the prophets that they are sorry. They beg and they weep and cry. It can get pretty loud."

If the victim's family chooses forgiveness, the killer pays them blood money and he goes to jail. Nahid chose the second option.

"I said, 'I don't forgive. I want the highest punishment.' "

"What does that mean?" I asked.

"Execution."

"And what did the judge say?"

"I can have it."

In Iran, the relatives of murder victims impose the death penalty.

The practice is based on passages in the Koran, including the Cow, Surah II: 178, "O ye who believe! Retaliation is prescribed for you in the matter of the murdered; the freeman for the freeman, and the slave for the slave, and the female for the female." Ancient vengeance rites and state law are so tightly braided, they are one.

For Nahid, though, there was a catch. The killer was male. The victim was female. If the victim had been a boy, the court would have hanged Ramtin as soon as Nahid demanded it: a life for a life. But a girl's life is worth half that of a boy's. The relatives of a female murder victim can have the male killer executed only if they make up the difference in the prices of blood. Nahid could have her vengeance if she could afford it.

"Do you have the money?" I asked.

"Unfortunately, no. Six thousand dollars is not a small amount in our country. He'll be in jail until he dies, but that's not enough. Any mother would feel this way."

Nahid's friends urged her to forgive Ramtin, to accept compensation. Nahid refused. She believed Ramtin was guilty, along with his father. Restitution would not work because what had been lost could never be restored. "I'm not going to sell the blood of Arian to anyone," she said.

Her disdain for blood money was not unusual. Some Holocaust survivors refused to accept German reparations. So did some Korean women who were offered compensation by the Japanese for being forced into prostitution during World War II. They claimed that blood money commodicized pain. Rather than restoring honor, it humiliated them further. Not only were they hurt, but that hurt could be bought. The infinity of anguish could be measured; owned.

Nahid did not know how, but someday, she would raise enough money to finance her revenge. At night, after she turned out the light, she stared at the ceiling and rehearsed the scene:

"We're approaching sunset; my whole body is shaking with the excitement and terror. The way it works, I'll be asked three times if I forgive him. I say, three times, no. We're in the prison yard. I see

Ramtin on the chair, the rope. He's blindfolded. I will say, 'No, no, no, I do not forgive you.' I'll be the one to pull out the chair. And he will hang. And this is the moment I will be purified."

In America, victims' relatives are sometimes allowed to witness executions. In Iran, victims' rights extend beyond that. Relatives can participate in the act, squeeze the trigger, pull out the chair.

"But it won't bring anybody back," I said meekly, offering, for argument's sake, one view of death penalty opponents: Why redress a death with another?

"It's a good lesson for our society and for other Ramtins," Nahid said, offering the classic argument of deterrence.

I left Nahid's apartment shaken by her story, sorry for her and embarrassed for myself. Like many of the avengers I had met, her circumstances and her suffering were many orders of magnitude worse than mine. And as I often did, I considered giving up. I had so much to be grateful for. I ought to go home and live a normal life.

At moments like these, and there were many, the person who legitimized my impulse toward revenge was the man who was the least impulsive about justice—my letter-of-the-law husband.

"He wanted to kill your father. He tried to kill your father. He shot him in the head," Baruch said over the phone from New York. "It was only the luckiest fortuity that the shot was a quarter of an inch off. The difference between him and someone who kills your father, from a moral point of view, is zero."

Afternoon in the Middle East was morning in New York. I could hear his spoon clinking against his cereal bowl, his chair scraping back as he started to pace.

"In either case—whether he succeeded or not—he planned the shooting, he obtained the gun, he lay in wait, he anticipated the opportunity, he sighted your dad, he pulled out the gun, he shot with intent to kill."

Baruch might be barefoot, unshaven and wearing shorts, but in his mind he was striding before a jury. What mattered was intent not outcome, he said.

"If revenge stems from an actual loss, then it's true, you don't have the same need for revenge. But if revenge stems from a moral outrage inflicted on you and your family, then the need for revenge is the same."

"OK," I said, still baffled.

His voice softened as if he were reaching out, cupping my chin. "Besides, revenge isn't rational."

That much I knew. I had told myself that I was learning the rules of revenge. In fact, I was hiding out in the rules. I was scared, I was stalling. I was studying the what, where, when and how, when all I really needed was the who. If I could find the shooter, put a face on his hissing shadow, instinct would guide me, no matter what the Mafia or the mullahs ruled. The prosecutor had made a fine case to convict. It was time to go out and hunt the shooter.

5

PREDATOR AND PREY

JERUSALEM

RACHEL WAS AT my door, her mouth slack, her eyes bleary, looking like she had been standing inside a great bronze bell.

"I have huge news," I said, hustling my friend inside. Rachel and her husband, David, were in Jerusalem delivering a series of lectures at Hebrew University.

She flopped onto the couch. Her fingers spread like a net over her stomach.

"You're pregnant?"

"That's not funny." I had not seen Baruch for months, not since my visit to New York. "I don't consider that a joke."

"You're impo—"

I cut her off. "They're out."

"Oh my God," she said. My father's shooter and his accomplices were not in jail.

Rachel turned onto her side. Her eyelids blinked rapidly, a sign that she was calculating something. "Well, this gives you a different option."

"Option?" I stood over Rachel. The shooter was free, within

reach, and Rachel was calling revenge an option? "Not an option, an imperative."

I was scolding myself more than her. Until then, the shooter had been a refrain in a poem. Now that there was a chance that I would actually meet him, I felt trapped by my own fantasy. I had written myself into a story that I could not control. Instead, I lectured Rachel. "This is what I came here for, this is what it's all about, the whole purpose of every—"

"Do you have any crackers?" Rachel rolled off the couch. She swayed toward the kitchen, her hands dragging along the walls.

Rachel's baby was the size of a plum pit, as big as the "magic stone" I took from the Matriarch's Tomb in Bethlehem. After so much waiting, planning and dreaming, she and David had finally conceived.

"I can't believe how nauseous I am," she said, her head inside the refrigerator, looking for something bland. "I guess that's what revenge is all about: frustration."

She was trying to help me, but the truth was, we could not relate to each other. She was preoccupied with creation: one and one is three. I was preoccupied with destruction: one and one leaves one. We walked around Jerusalem, talking past each other, our senses bent toward a purpose, misshapen and distorted. Rachel felt like the volume had been turned up in her nose; everything smelled so loud it hurt.

"It's as if I'm at a buffet," she said, "and I'm opening silver chafing dishes, and they're all filled with fetid, putrid, grilled, fried vomit."

Meanwhile, I was indulging in my own strange food fantasies. One afternoon, I sat at my kitchen table and wrote:

> Revenge is not a hunger. It's a craving. Can live without it but it gnaws at you. One specific thing will satisfy your hunger. Not a steak, but a steak sliced on a wooden board, strips two inches long, dripping, leaking pink juices. It's fussy and particular.

Looking back at the passage, I wondered where that image came from. I do not even like steak. But now, for the first time since I had arrived in Jerusalem, the craving had a chance of being satisfied. A Palestinian translator had checked the names on the DA's letter to my father. All three men had been imprisoned for attacking tourists in 1986, but they had been freed as part of the 1993 Oslo peace accord. Not only that, but all three lived outside Jerusalem, one of them in Kalandia, three miles south of Ramallah.

Rachel went back to her apartment to be sick. I went to the gym to swim. Every day I worked out, trying to make myself strong. Not that I expected to be chasing mustachioed villains down canyon walls, but as with most aspects of my revenge, the membrane dividing fantasy and reality was porous. One identity seeped into the other, mixing me up inside—part journalist, part lonely girl, part cartoon avenger—until they were hard to separate. It was hard to know how far I would go. *Am I really doing this?* Even I was confused. *Is this really real?*

In the locker room at the gym, I pulled on a bathing suit and caught a glimpse of my thighs in the mirror. *Hal.* They were starting to look like my brother's runner legs. The soft tissue had hardened, new contours had appeared. I tensed my muscles and punched them, testing their strength. A comic image, even to me.

As I headed outside to the swimming pool, an old seminary friend of my father's sloshed out of the shallow end, his jowls wet and friendly. He asked, "How's married life?"—a question that I always ducked. Then he asked about my work, and I told him the half-truth I told everyone: I was researching the topic of revenge.

"Revenge?" he sputtered. "What kind of family do you come from, anyway?"

It was a good question, the only question, I now see, that mattered to me. I twisted the fringe on my towel and said, "Well, you know my father."

His smile was strained. "Yeah, but your father's a sweet guy. A little girl like you," he said, wagging a finger, "should be writing love poems in her newlywed year, not revenge." He beetled off to the men's locker room.

So much for looking formidable. I splashed into the pool and swam the crawl, hard. *A "little girl" like me would get eaten in the jungle.*

In the jungle the roles are explicit, predators and prey. Aggressors and victims. No animal can hope for a mediating agent to swoop in and order a predator to retreat. When attacked, attacking back is not an option but an imperative. There are no emotionally charged, ethically laden terms like *revenge.* There is only self-preservation.

The more I listened to people's revenge stories, though, the more I realized the same might be true for human beings. Even in civilized societies, with their emphasis on order, there are no institutions or individuals that guarantee fair play. There are courts, of course, and teachers, parents, governing agencies, the United Nations and other nominal referees. But those referees often fall short. Inside anarchy, disputes resolve themselves to the rhythms of jungle justice: reprisal means survival. Revenge is Darwinian.

This idea, however unoriginal, captivated me that summer as I looked for the shooter. I divided the world into predators and prey. People who crumpled when attacked marked themselves as prey and would be abused again. The second type of person responded with action, turning his pain inside out, changing it into fury. In Hebrew the word for revenge, *nekamah,* is linked to the verb *kum,* which, fittingly, means "rising." During my visit to New York, Hal's toddler, Eva, missed a step and hit her head. She curled up, crying. Her mother took Eva's hand and hit the floor with it: "Bad floor. Powm, powm!" Eva stopped crying. It was as if her pain had traveled from the bump on her head down into the floor. Now the floor was the victim. She had inverted her identity, a prey rising—*nekamah*—to become a predator. There is no more basic form of self-assertion.

That was the kind of story that interested me that summer. I was a little crazy, and a lot scared. That somehow made me fiercer, or pretend that I was fiercer, than I ever had been before. June came in cool and settled down with a purpose. The sky was stuck on blue. The sun sought out living things and chased them under rocks and down snake holes. The petunias on our roof struggled as the ground dried up and cracked at the roots. I sank my fingers into our geranium pots and wondered why the earth here was eternally thirsty, why the ground was so greedy.

Nights, around 4 A.M., I would wake to the Islamic call to prayer, a groan that rolled like fog under our balcony doors. This was the best time to phone Baruch at the office in New York, as he was finishing preparing witnesses. He would tell me about his latest round in court. I would tell him about my latest round of interviews. We talked, sometimes for as long as an hour, chasing away night thoughts. We hung up wishing each other good morning and good night, the church bells ringing across the valley on Mount Zion.

During the day, I scratched around, searching for predator-prey wisdom. I was looking for the hawks and the realists, for unsentimental people who believed that the balance of good and bad in life tipped toward the bad. For them, revenge was driven by fear, not hate. It was a calculated response to their version of reality. Revenge did not reflect who they were so much as the world they saw around them.

"IN MY WORLD, if I'm helpless, I'm dead," Smitt told me the first time we met outside the methadone clinic in Jerusalem. "If someone crosses me? I don't forgive. Then everyone will beat me up, or grab my share of the loot. Revenge is the law of the outlaws."

Smitt was a burglar who slipped through the fissures in rich people's homes. On the job, he wore black gloves and Adidas sneakers, the brand with the quietest soles to creep across floors. He went worming for gold chains in people's coffee tins. He found engagement rings hidden in sugar bowls. He tied up businessmen in their boxer shorts, pressed a knife against the necklaced throats of their wives. He was pragmatic about his work; it was a job, no hard feelings. Aside from robbing people, he was a nice guy.

Outside the methadone clinic, we found a shady curb. On the sidewalk around us, other addicts lounged, sipping orange liquid from plastic shot glasses. The methadone, Smitt said, went down "like a tablespoon of horseradish snuffed up the nose." The men grimaced from the bitterness.

One of them noticed me talking with Smitt.

"Hey, lady," he said, snickering. "What are you—Smitt's stewardess for when he's flying high?"

I explained that I was studying the origins of revenge.

"Oh, that's easy," he said with a bored wave. "We all want revenge on our parents."

Smitt and I sat side by side, our knees bumping together, so the others would not overhear us. He was of Turkish origin, lithe and narrow. His biceps jumped with a faceless lion, a tattoo left unfinished, thanks to an early prison release. He was born in 1954, he said, although he was not sure how old that made him. He had been jailed ten times, then lost count of that, too. Drugs had a way of blurring everything, leaving one focal point: his fix.

"My world is a jungle," Smitt said. He had grown up in a gang in Jerusalem. "When we'd go and rumble with chains we'd say we're the fearless tigers, strong as horses and healthy as bears. And they're the rabbits, the yelping puppies."

His real name was Israel Siman-Tov. When he was born, his father was so drunk, he accidentally registered the birth under the same name as his older son's. Both brothers became addicts. One overdosed, *Israel Siman-Tov* etched on a tombstone. The other one, Smitt, supported his habit by robbing houses. The night before we met, Smitt had stayed up until 5 A.M. smoking cocaine. His skin had the yellowish-green tinge of a dying plant. He was cold, hot, goose-bumped and sweating, though he was gracious and willing to counsel me.

Over the years, Smitt had gathered a string of stories about his justice system. For him, revenge and justice were synonyms. When one of his burglar partners was caught pocketing the loot, Smitt put him on trial. A park bench substituted for a judge's bench. A pistol-whipping doubled as the strike of the gavel. Smitt raised objections to the defense by spitting on him. The stories unspooled—treacherous ex-wives, gunslinging brothers-in-law—until I decided that I could confide in him. It felt good to tell someone the truth.

"What if I wanted to get revenge?" I watched his face, expecting some part of it to react.

"What did someone do to you?"

"Injured my dad. Shot, but not killed."

He did not flinch. "Don't injure him back. It's not worth it."

"But you said," it came out with a trace of a whine, "you said you have to get revenge, otherwise people will think you're weak."

"Either you let it go, or you kill him."

"Why?"

"Because after that he'll come back looking for you." There was stealth in his voice, a measured sense of what you could and could not get away with. Once, Smitt said, he beat a man who owed him $300 with a wooden plank. A few weeks later, the man broke into Smitt's parents' apartment and stole a cherished necklace his mother had brought with her from Turkey as a child.

This taught him: If you leave a wounded animal, it will heal. And then it will come after you.

That, Smitt said, was the worst kind of revenge. Demi-revenge. It reminded me of something Niccolò Machiavelli advised in the sixteenth century: "Men should either be treated generously or destroyed, because they take revenge for slight injuries, for heavy ones they cannot."

The risk of counterattack exists as long as one leaves his enemy, or his enemy's kinsmen, strong enough to fight back. Attack, counterattack, and before long it spins into a cycle of vengeance. This is as true for two political candidates running attack ads as it is for two nations launching missiles. In the weeks that I was sifting through these ideas, India exploded five nuclear bombs. Two weeks later, Pakistan, India's rival, replied with five underground nuclear tests. "Today we have settled a score," Pakistan's prime minister said in a nationally broadcast speech. In Africa, Ethiopia bombed an Eritrean airport, claiming Eritrea had attacked them. The Eritreans, in turn, said Ethiopia had attacked them first.

Who started it? No one can remember, no one will admit it. Each side takes its turn, first as predator, then as prey. And what was once a strategy for survival becomes self-defeating. Revenge, which is supposed to strengthen a group, bounces back and threatens it with extinction.

And yet. There I was, alone with my thoughts, shambling forward that summer. Even though Smitt had warned me, even though I had written clearheaded newspaper stories about cycles of vengeance—from the brawls of ex-lovers to partisan payback in congressional confirmation hearings—all I could think was how I needed to prove that my family was strong.

When I went for my daily swim, I moved through the water, drawing quick, guttural breaths, pushing myself into a kind of hyperventilated intensity. *Predator or prey. What kind of family do I come from, anyway?*

"You hit me!" a woman yelled.

She grabbed me and yanked me back toward the wall. She was a large woman with a hard, carved nose. She and a friend were swimming in the wrong direction, pushing me into the ropes. After a few laps, I swam between them, and, I banged her. Not completely by accident. Jungle justice.

"You hit me!"

"I didn't mean to," I said, unconvincingly.

"You shouldn't hit," the woman said, the veins in her eyes zigzagging like striking bolts.

"Well," I said, rising up on my toes. "Then don't invade my lane."

Both of us seemed surprised by my response. I was a short, begoggled woman, borrowing lines from a gangster, or a defensive linebacker.

But the strange thing was, it worked. I went from prey to predator. The woman retreated, her chlorinated eyes pink as a rabbit's, as she climbed out of the pool.

"I was getting out, anyway," she snuffled.

I went back to my crawl, smug that I had won. Instead of swimming smoothly, though, my legs wobbled like jellyfish tentacles. It occurred to me that I had just been mean.

I tried to assure myself that hitting back served a pedagogical function: *that woman needed to learn*.

I had picked up this tip from businessmen in Tel Aviv. Their high-rise boardrooms were a long way from the curb outside the methadone clinic. Yet when I asked business executives about revenge, their answers resembled Smitt's: revenge is necessary for deterrence.

"You feel rage and you have to respond, otherwise it'll happen again and again," said Yossi Vardi, the father of Israel's Internet trade. Rather than being about the past, he said, revenge was forward-looking. "Getting even is a management tool. You use it both ways, as reward and punishment."

He said, "You teach them a lesson." One of the many justifications of revenge. But what lesson is taught? Does the other person learn, or does he retreat unthinkingly, or does he subvert the lesson and strike back? Does revenge prevent future offenses, or does it encourage them? I knew, however pedantic it sounded, that I wanted to teach the shooter a lesson. I had a specific message in mind, but I had to get close to him first. As I swam my laps, I floated various plans.

THAT EVENING, the Palestinian translator called. She was helping me find the three men named in the DA's letter. I wanted to interview them, I said. I did not tell her why.

"I couldn't locate a number for this guy Bazian," she said.

I knew from newspaper archives that Ala-din Bazian was the leader of a Jerusalem death gang. He had been in and out of jail, and had served three years for rigging a bomb to a Palestinian informer's car, a bungled assassination that blinded him. A year after he was released, he was rearrested for ordering the shooting death of a German tourist. In 1985, he was released again in a prisoner exchange.

Soon after, he recruited members of the Jerusalem gang. I called Bazian "the mastermind," the one who ordered members to kill.

"I could go down to his house and check if he's there," the translator offered.

"Why don't I go with you?"

We agreed to meet the following day at 2 P.M. on the road to Ramallah, a Palestinian city that most Jews were afraid to drive through. I tried to sound nonchalant, as if it were just another rendezvous with a translator.

"You sound out of breath," she said. "Were you running for the phone?"

"Yeah," I lied. "I couldn't find the phone."

I WENT TO BED that night thinking about the shooter's face. In the past, he was always down an alley, erased by shadows. Now pictures of his face, his many possible faces, flashed outside the window, against the illuminated Old City walls. They were fragments: white stubble on tan skin. A narrow nose balancing gold glasses. Eyebrows curving like a pair of basalt arches. I drifted into a shallow sleep, never quite submerging.

At 5 A.M. I surfaced and reached for the phone. Still feeling the images lapping against me, I dialed Baruch in New York. He was having a hard time with the trial, he said. The defense insisted that the government witness was trying to get revenge on Don King.

When he finished, I said, "I'm going to the mastermind's house today."

"Oh, yeah?" he murmured. "OK, I gotta go."

"Did you hear what I said?"

"No, sorry, I'm fading. I'm exhausted."

He apologized. And he apologized for postponing his return to Jerusalem by another month. The trial was dragging on. Baruch had suggested that I stay in Israel during the trial. He would be working all the time. More than once, I had whimpered about missing him, but the truth was, part of me was relieved. The isolation meant that I could uncork my anger and get drunk on the vapors.

"I'm ashamed of how we're living, so apart. Why did you even marry me?" I said. There was a fight inside of me this morning, kicking to get out.

"Every soldier needs a wife at home to write to," he said.

"I'm not a wife at home." I swung my legs out of bed and stood up. "I'm fighting too."

"OK, then." His humor held. "Every soldier on the front needs a wife on another front to write to."

I hung up thinking that Baruch would never understand. His identity was molded by the Department of Justice; mine was allied with its competition. The weakness of my system was the strength of his. The strength of my system was the weakness of his. Revenge is emotionally out of control; justice is emotionally unsatisfying.

For Baruch, for most people, justice and revenge are mutually exclusive. But I considered the division false. Revenge has no clear borders. Justice shades into punishment, into retribution, into reprisal, into retaliation, into counterstrikes, into getting even, into vendetta, into vengeance, into revenge. Social scientists have fixed the limits of it. But I thought defining revenge was like defining love: it is a force so overpowering people spend their lives denying it. They call it other things.

THE DAY I LEFT FOR Ramallah looking for the shooter, I called the twinge in my belly what it was—the need to get even.

Some time earlier I had a conversation with Israel's military chief of staff, and I asked him: What is the difference between retaliation and revenge?

"It depends which side you're standing on," replied Amnon Lipkin-Shahak with an ironic glint. "Everyone describes it how they want."

"When we do it, it's retaliation. When they do it, it's revenge," said Uzi Dayan, a top general, who had passed by the door. Dayan was talking about raids along Lebanon's border.

We were inside the Kirya, Israel's military headquarters in Tel Aviv, tucked behind layers of concrete perimeter walls, electronic gates and security checkpoints. Shahak himself was a broad, commanding man, hard-packed into a green uniform. In photographs, his light blue eyes radiated an artless bliss. In person, the innocence in his eyes was gone. They glowed like nightscopes sweeping the underbrush, seeking out what was hidden.

I had come to talk with Shahak about suicide bombings, to ask him how they fit into the cycle of violence. Islamic extremists were strapping dynamite to their chests, wading into Israeli vegetable markets, a shopping mall, a cafe district, a public bus at rush hour. In dozens of attacks, they had killed hundreds of people.

I told Shahak what Sheik Ahmad Yassin had told me. He was the spiritual leader of Hamas, an Islamic group based in Gaza that rejected peace with Israel. Sixty-one years old, a gnarled man in a wheelchair, Yassin lit the bombers' ideological fuse.

"First of all, these are not suicide missions," the sheik had said in his high, phlegmy voice. "We are protecting ourselves." They were following, he believed, the laws of jungle justice: revenge as self-preservation. "If the Jews attack and kill our civilians, we'll kill their civilians too. From the first drop of blood the bomber spills on the ground, he goes to Paradise. The Jewish victims immediately go to hell."

I also told Shahak about a twenty-one-year-old man I had met in Gaza named Abdallah Yosef Abu Sakran. Abdallah was a failed suicide bomber. He had been arrested the day before he was scheduled to blow himself up, and was being held in a Palestinian Authority prison. I interviewed him in the office of the prison's chief interrogator. He entered the room and flashed a stack of white teeth that, I imagined, would shatter in a bomb blast. To assemble a portrait of the suicide bomber was to disassemble him. His black hair—it would smolder. His thick neck—it would snap. His pug nose, his delicate ears—they would melt in the flames.

He said he wanted to kill Jews to avenge the slaying of another Hamas operative, who had been killed by a booby-trapped telephone. No one claimed responsibility, but Israeli intelligence was suspected.

As I described this to the Israeli chief of staff, he listened politely. But when I reached the part about the bomber avenging the Hamas operative, the Israeli general snorted.

"Hamas sends bombers just to avenge his blood? I'm sure not." Hamas had been planning terrorist attacks long before, Shahak said. By portraying themselves as victims, Hamas was inverting reality. They were predators dressing as prey to rationalize killing women and children. It was not revenge, Shahak said. It was a pretext.

The tendency to claim victim status to justify the next attack is one of the problems with revenge. Was the suicide bomber really avenging a wrong or was he rationalizing aggression? Is revenge an obligation or an excuse? In many conflicts—from hair-pulling between siblings to world war—all sides cite defense as the reason for offense. Palestinians and Jews alike present themselves as victims, with a history of degradation and displacement. Both sides see themselves as endangered, and therefore justified in striking back.

"Let's take the case of 'the engineer.' Oh, wait, we never admitted it," Shahak said, referring to Israel's assassination of the Hamas bomber. "So let's talk about it theoretically. Those on the other side say, What's the point of killing him? It's a circle we'll never escape."

But there was a point, Shahak said. "When I kill terrorists, those I hurt won't hurt again." He had been part of a squad that attacked the Lebanon headquarters of the Palestinian group that had massacred Israeli athletes at the 1972 Munich Olympics.

"There was a need to hurt back, but not just an eye for an eye. There was some feeling of closing the circle. Every person has only two eyes. After two eyes—it's over."

And as for both Israel's and Hamas's claims to be acting defensively, Shahak rejected the comparison.

"Hamas targets civilians. Israel never acted against civilians. The state doesn't work that way. That's the difference between us."

From that comment tumbled the clumsiest follow-up question I ever pitched: "So if someone shot my dad?"

The chief of staff assumed my question was hypothetical. He

drew a trench down the middle of his desk, digging with the outer edge of his palm, dividing his desk into us versus them.

"First thing you try to do is shoot him before he shoots your father." This was classic Israeli military strategy, and it had more than doubled the state's territory in war. The preemptive attack, offense as defense. "If you can prevent him from shooting in the first place, you save your father. That's best."

As he finished his sentence, his eyes, those eerie nightscopes with their light blue glow, must have detected something that made him pause. Maybe I was gripping my pen too tight, my fingers turning red and white. Maybe I was grinding my teeth, and he caught the anxious slide. Shahak folded his arms over the formidable territory of his stomach. He lowered his voice, a soldier well practiced at ambush.

"Your father . . ." He paused. "Was he a citizen of Israel?"

"A tourist."

My mouth felt dry. If I was going to pursue private justice against an Arab gunman, why was I informing Israel's highest-ranking military officer? Besides, I realized, I would come off, at best, as nutty. Maybe he had picked up the false, flat notes in my voice. Maybe he had seen through the phony journalistic distance. Whatever it was, I could see the suspicion swirling in his eyes like gasoline in water. Which explained his sudden shift in tone.

"It's not important if he was here as a tourist." The trench on his desk suddenly vanished. He slid his date book in front of him, redrawing his borders from us versus them to me versus you.

"They shot him," Shahak continued. "Because they thought he was an Israeli. The *state,"* he hammered that word, "is responsible to find the terrorist and act against him in court."

Or maybe he could smell that something was wrong. I sniffed—something reeked, and I realized that it was me. Stinking with anxiety. I had read once that men had weaker senses of smell than women. I hoped that it was true.

"You don't have the ability to respond, anyway," the chief of staff said, drawing himself up in his chair. "You couldn't even find him."

Neither of us addressed whether my scenario was real. He seemed to be thinking it through out loud. Who was this woman? Why was she playing games with a man who commanded a nuclear arsenal? Shahak was wary, then preachy, then, finally, dismissive.

"You don't have the intelligence or the resources," he said with a snigger. He was relaxing now, his arms unfolding, the defensive shield down.

"What are you going to do"—his eyes were incandescent with irony—"go to Ramallah and catch him?"

"Ha!" He spanked his desk. *"Ramallah!"*

THE MORNING I SET OUT, I called Rachel at her apartment in Jerusalem.

"So are you coming to the university for lunch today?" she asked.

"No, I'm going to Ramallah."

"What're you going to Ramallah for?"

"I'm going to find the people who tried to kill my dad," I said, aware that I sounded overwrought. "Do you want to come over?"

"Oh. Big day," she said. "I can't, I have a meeting at ten with the department chairman."

How would I fill the hours until 2 P.M.? I went up to the roof and watered the geranium pots until they spilled over. The blood of a man, I brooded, would not quench this thirsty earth, not even for one day. I packed my purse: two plums for quick sugar and a fresh notebook so no notes would give me away. I picked out a pink-and-white-striped shirt for innocence.

I stepped out of the shower and wiped the steam from the bathroom mirror. Did I look like my father? More than anything, I had to keep my identity a secret. The gunmen I would meet might have seen newspaper photographs of my dad. Local papers had published a picture of him on the front page. It had been taken in the hospital, as he told reporters what had happened. His eyes look dazed, his bottom lip drooped. His hair looped onto his forehead, a loose collection of light brown curls. I had my father's hair. Was that enough to give me away? Was I my father's girl?

I looked at my mirror image. The face was my mother's. I was a "photocopy," people would remark when they first met us. In truth, I was more of a smudgy reproduction, the same lines as my mother, but slightly off. My face was more like a Polish Jew's. And on this day, looking like a Jew was a problem.

The mirror steamed over again. I left the bathroom and began rummaging through my desk. I reread my college poem: . . . *this hand will find you/I am his daughter.* I rolled my eyes at the audacious college kid.

I leafed through a file of clippings I had gathered at the *Jerusalem Post* archives. I wanted to review the context of the shooting. It was before the *intifada,* the Palestinian uprising of 1987. My father's shooting took place at a time when a gun attack was big news. The Abu Musa faction of the PLO decided to shoot foreign tourists in Jerusalem. Abu Musa was a radical Palestinian based in Syria, who mutinied against Yasir Arafat because he thought Arafat was too moderate. Abu Musa's representative in Jerusalem was Bazian, the blind mastermind.

The attacks started with my father. Five weeks later, the mastermind's gang shot and killed the fifty-nine-year-old Israeli woman in her office in Jerusalem. The same day's papers announced: U.S. REVEALS WORLDWIDE LIBYAN TERROR PLAN. Ronald Reagan sent thirty-three fighter jets to bomb Libya in retaliation for Libya's involvement in the bombing of a Berlin disco that killed two American soldiers.

Following the U.S. assault, three Britons traveling abroad died in what were described as revenge killings. An Irish woman was caught trying to board a plane in London, unwittingly carrying a twelve-pound bomb that her fiancé, an Arab, had given to her. In Jerusalem, the mastermind's men shot and wounded a forty-two-year-old German tourist. Was it revenge? Some claimed the attacks were reprisals for the U.S. raid. Others said the terrorists were looking for an excuse.

President Reagan told reporters that the latest outbreak of terrorism was "another example of the fact that terrorism is something that we have to deal with, once and for all." British prime minister Margaret Thatcher, who aided the U.S. raid, spoke in terms of predator and prey: "If you let the threat of further terrorism prevent you from fighting against it, then the terrorist has won."

Following Thatcher's comments, the Associated Press reported: "Thirteen terrorist groups held a secret conference in Damascus last week and decided to escalate attacks against U.S. interests to avenge the air strikes on Libya." One of the terrorists at the conference was Abu Musa. His foot soldiers in Jerusalem, led by the mastermind, attacked for the fourth time. The next day's headline: YOUNG ENGLISH TOURIST SLAIN AT GARDEN TOMB.

At the time, Gary Sick, a member of the National Security Council staff during the Iranian hostage crisis (and later my professor at Columbia's graduate School of International Affairs), wrote an op-ed piece for the *New York Times* arguing that retaliation against Libya was misguided:

> "Most Americans exult at sending a 'message' to Colonel Qaddafi. That is the terror trap: succumbing to our own sense of outrage, we do ourselves more damage than the terrorists could ever hope to accomplish by themselves. The Middle East policies of three previous administrations have been discarded almost casually in favor of a policy of military retribution."

Then, as always, the world was grappling with the choice: Turn the other cheek, or an eye for an eye?

The tension between the two is ageless. As I sat at my desk I could see, through the window on my right, on Mount Zion, the site of the Last Supper, where Jesus told his disciples, "A new commandment I give unto you, That ye love one another; as I have loved you, that ye also love one another." Through the window on my left, six hundred yards to the north, rose the Tower of David, where Pontius Pilate condemned Jesus in the Hall of Judgment.

On the right, forgiveness. On the left, condemnation. Which way should one look?

ON MY WAY OUT THE FRONT DOOR, I passed a baby picture of my father. He was propped inside the arms of a black, overstuffed chair. He was looking up toward something bright, a window, or maybe a lamp, oblivious to the darkness that embraced him.

Happy Father's Day.

I reminded myself to call him later.

Outside, I flagged a taxi and asked the driver to take me to Damascus Gate, a quarter of a revolution around the Old City's ramparts.

"Where?!" the Israeli driver said, as if he had not heard me. "They stab a Jew there every Sunday." Few people from the western, Jewish half of the city crossed into the heart of Arab, east Jerusalem.

"Damascus Gate," I said, my voice cementing.

We drove toward the Old City, hot air rushing through the windows. The sky was pale blue, tinged brown along the horizon. In the distance the wind was stirring up sand, carrying grit in from the east. It crunched between my teeth and stung my eyes. The desert was visiting the city today.

At Damascus Gate, I got out and joined eight Palestinian men and one woman as we boarded a van to Ramallah. I examined the men and tried to imagine each one as the shooter. One was too old, one too young, one was missing half of his right thumb. The van drove along a road that skirted the Green Line, the border between Israeli and Arab land until the 1967 war, when Israel swept over the line into the eastern half of the city. The barbed wire was gone, but an invisible border remained, dividing the two Jerusalems.

Our van continued north onto a narrowing, deteriorating road. As we approached the army checkpoint, Jewish apartment blocks gave way to Arab stone homes. Sidewalks disappeared, eaten away by sandy shoulders. Hebrew signs surrendered to Arabic billboards. The land opened up to craggy hills and olive trees.

My plan, to the extent that I had one, was this: I would make myself blank. A white screen. I would let the mastermind project himself onto me. Today I would not take revenge; I would take his story. Then he would tell me about the other two men on the list. When I found the shooter, I would listen to him too. I would be a journalist, a spectator, a role that I relished for the immaculate blankness of it. I would observe, and act later.

Up ahead, at a roadblock manned by Israeli soldiers, a white flag with a blue Jewish star waved good-bye in the breeze. A few minutes later, Palestinian soldiers. The van rolled through Al-Bireh checkpoint, where we crossed into Palestinian territory. I got out, met my translator. We asked an Arab taxi driver to take us to Bazian's—the mastermind's—house.

Maybe I won't be able to take it. Maybe I should just go crazy and smack the mastermind and be over with it. . . .

We stopped at a lumberyard and asked a man for directions. He pointed down an unpaved road that bordered Atarot Airport. The wheels spit gravel as the taxi sped along the airport fence. We stopped in front of a small house at a dead end. A freckled boy ran to meet our car. I was in the backseat trying not to squirm.

"Are those Jews?" the boy said, eyeing me and the Palestinian translator hard.

"Not Jews," the Palestinian driver said. "Arabs."

The boy, no more than four years old, looked at us again. He nodded toward me. "She's a Jew."

"Arab, Arab!" the driver said, swatting at the boy. "She's not a Jew."

The boy backed away as I climbed out of the car. I stepped around him and approached his front door.

THREE HOURS LATER, I was knocking on Rachel's door. This time I was the one who looked like I had emerged from the inside of a gonged bell.

"Oh, good," Rachel said, pulling me into her kitchen. "You didn't call, so I was worrying—my fluffy little friend."

"Listen to this," said her husband, David, who was reading *What to Expect When You're Expecting:* " 'All my pregnant friends say that they had an increased desire for sex early in pregnancy—some had orgasms and multiple orgasms for the first time. How come I feel so unsexy?' "

I threw Rachel a look. "Multiple orgasms?"

"Yeah, that's when you barf and have an orgasm at the same time." She slumped into a chair.

David closed the book. "This whole pregnancy thing is weird."

"It's invasive," said Rachel. "It takes up all of you." She swallowed like she was trying to figure out what she just ate. "Imagine something kicking inside you."

Inside me, the thing that kicked had nails.

David knew all my secrets through osmosis from Rachel. He usually offered advice, though not this time. "I don't want to give you suggestions about how to get revenge," he said. "What if his buddies come after you?"

Rachel and I walked to my apartment. The sidewalks exhaled the heat they had drawn in from the day. The air was seasoned with rosemary, the spiny leaves chewed over by the sun.

"Well," I said tentatively. "What do you think happened?"

Her eyes blinked rapidly: "You found one of the guys, and you went in, and he was telling you his history, and you were—"

"What did he look like?"

"Ugly, young and rough, kind of orangish skin. And his mother was very nice and giving you drinks. It was dirty on the floor and there were snotty kids and a dog. And they have a picture of the Dome of Rock on the door and the mommy wears a big dress and has a big belly and a flat face, very hardened hands and slippers that flip-flop, and she keeps serving lots of drinks. . . ."

As I listened to her sketch the scene, I tried to shake the real images out of my head.

". . . the boy, the terrorist guy, he's wearing those acid-washed jeans," Rachel continued. "And he's kind of proud of what he did. You were taking notes, but your eyes are darting around the room, and you're wondering what's really in his heart."

She paused for a breath. "How am I doing?"

"A lot of that's true," I said, impressed and bothered that something so important to me could be so predictable. "Except for one big thing.

"He's in jail." I turned to her.

"Ooops," Rachel said.

"The translator made a mistake," I said.

The three convicts were still serving time, just as the government's letter had claimed.

If my search beforehand had been questionable, now it seemed pointless. The gunmen had been punished. I would go home to America, to a saner place.

We walked in silence through a tree tunnel of braided olive branches. Below us, the valley of Gehenah spread out peaceful and green. In ancient times, the valley erupted with smoke and greasy flames, with the wildcat cries of child sacrifice. Parents appealed to the pagan gods by sacrificing their children. They hoped it might bring them better lives. *Gehenah,* the biblical word for hell.

"It's over," I said as we entered my house.

"You're overreacting, I'm sure." Rachel stretched out on my couch. A look of amusement spread across her face. "Tell me what happened."

I sat at Rachel's feet, leaning back on my hands, my palms absorbing the stone floor's cool solace.

"I introduced myself as Laura. No last name. Which was good because as soon as I got to their living room, I saw a gold frame on the table. A picture of the mastermind from an English newspaper. The caption had my father's name: '. . . the victims, including Rabbi David L. Blumenfeld . . .' "

As Rachel listened, I disgorged the story, the facts coming in slivered details and choppy impressions. I was eager to get it out of me, to separate myself from what I had seen.

"My children are my revenge," the mastermind's mother had said. Thirteen children. Each new baby meant another soldier to redeem Palestine. Her eldest son, now forty-eight, sat across from her. I explained to him that I was a journalist writing a book about revenge, that I was interviewing Israelis and Palestinians.

"We can never have peace," he said. "It's written in all religions that blood will run to our ankles." The family was not religious, but this was one belief they embraced.

His sentences rolled out flat and factual: "My brother killed people he should have killed; the targets were spies. The British tourist—they said he was a British tourist, but he was a highly ranked person in his country. The PLO sent their names from abroad, and my brother organized the killings. It was sort of legal to kill them."

"How so?" I asked. I tried to imagine my father as a CIA agent, my father with his face as open as a daisy, wearing a trench coat, talking into his watch.

"When the foreigners come here and get involved, they get what they deserve." His words were so frank, so unapologetic, there was nothing left in his expression to interpret. "It was revenge," he said, "for the land."

Looking back, I am not sure how I sat through this visit. How I ate their honeyed cakes and drank their creamy mocha. How I complimented the satin pumps that the teenage daughter had bought for her upcoming wedding. How I admired the high ceilings when they showed me the mastermind's empty rooms. I had trouble concentrating. The news that the mastermind was in jail had caught me unprepared.

I asked, "Aren't you worried about your family because of the people your brother killed? Someone might want revenge."

"No," the brother said. "Westerners don't get revenge for their families, only for selfish reasons. They don't have family ties like us. In America, when someone's killed the only people who care are the police and the insurance company."

"So, you're never afraid one of the relatives of victims would hunt you down?"

The brother said, "If he decided to get revenge—if he could get to here, to my house and find me—I would do a *sulha.*"

"Really?" That surprised me. A *sulha* was an Arab reconciliation ceremony.

"No, I'm kidding. No *sulha.* There's no *sulha* for political killings." The brother laughed derisively. What a gullible journalist.

That was all I could relate to Rachel. I wanted to forget that they existed. They were caricatures, and Rachel had evoked them, more or less, without even meeting them. I took out a photograph of the mastermind that they had given to me.

"He looks like . . . a terrorist." Rachel laughed. "The beard unevenly grown, the scary, dark parka. His lips and nose are big and ugly. He has creepy features, a shifty mustache. He looks like he's trying to look cool and tough, like, 'I'm a motorcycle guy, or a cowboy.' But he's already a terrorist killer."

I turned the picture facedown on the coffee table so I would not have to look. "His family asked me to contact a humanitarian organization in America to help get him out of jail. They said, 'He's blind, he only gave orders to kill. He didn't actually kill.' They want me to bring him wraparound sunglasses from America."

"And you pulled out your pistol and said, 'Oh, yeah?' "

What I did was even more pathetic. At one point, I excused myself to go to the bathroom. Impulsively, I took a wad of tissues from the back of their toilet and stuffed it into my purse, as if I were some kind of warrior, bagging a scalp. Also, while we walked past the mastermind's dining room table, I wrote my father's initials in the thick, white dust: *D.B. We were here, and the mastermind was not.*

Before I left, the brother invited me to join them on their next visit to the mastermind.

"But I can't touch him because of the barricade," I told Rachel. Mesh wire separated the prisoners from their guests. The most I could do was to poke my fingers through and touch his fingertips.

"Well," Rachel said. "You don't want physical contact, anyway."

"How do you know? Yes, I do, that's the point."

"You're planning to hurt someone?" Doubt ridged her forehead.

"My dream was always to shake the shooter by the collar."

"Ideas are so much stronger than blows," Rachel said. "He didn't take your father away. He didn't cripple him. It was the intent and evil with which he shot at him. Other than the memory, he didn't take something from you on a tangible level, only on a psychological level. The revenge should be on an emotional level."

"But I can't hurt him with words because he's not sorry. So how am I going to get revenge?"

"You're not going to get revenge from him," she said with authority. "Whatever happens is going to have to happen in your head."

Rachel's idea of action was an epiphany.

"It's rare that a person's feeling of revenge is actually played out," she said. "The fantasy usually transmutes itself into something else."

"You mean"—the words weaseled out—"like becoming an economics professor?"

Cheap shot. I knew that Rachel was driven, not drawn, into academia. She had grown up listening to her Eastern European father, a professor, denigrate her housewife mother. Rachel's way of showing him, of avenging her mother, was to become a professor herself.

"Yeah, you protect yourself. Take a lesson from it," she said. "The truth is, really, your revenge is for what?"

Her lashes fluttered over irises so dark they were inseparable from her pupils. "You believed in the world that your American, camp sports-counselor parents created for you. I picture your dad standing on the dock at camp saying, 'Go, team, go!' And your mom's from *Kansas.* They told you Mommy and Daddy are happy and love each other, and they love little Laura and little Hal. Everyone is safe and brave and swims laps and has happy endings."

"So what?"

"For me the lake in camp was dark and murky and full of death. My parents told me seething, uprooted, European peasant stories, where the goose bites your head off and you die." Rachel sat upright. "Are you angry at the people for attacking your father, or that terrorists who hurt people exist in general?"

"Both. And not only that. I wanted them to know . . ." My throat tightened. "I can't say it, I'm too embarrassed. I can't even look at you." I stared at the domed ceiling. I concentrated on the rice-paper fixture.

"I promise I won't laugh. Here, I'll close my eyes."

"I wanted them to know . . ." I could not finish the sentence.

"That they can't shoot your dad?"

"No, not that." I was talking to the light fixture, wondering why the heat of the bulb never set the paper shade on fire. "That you can't, you can't fuck with the Blumenfelds. That there's someone you're going to have to answer to, and I know it's ridiculous that the someone is me."

Rachel did not laugh. "I think on some level your anger is because you *can* fuck with the Blumenfelds. That anyone who lives by the rules of civilization is vulnerable to people like that."

"So the price you pay for being civilized is being a victim?"

"It's being vulnerable to people who don't share those values. But I don't think the answer is to become like them. You guys were a quiet, middle-class, nerdy family from Long Island. You don't know how to fight. Part of the reason Rome was overrun by the Goths was they got all civilized and soft. Who would you rather be, a hyena or a gazelle?"

"A hyena. I don't know."

"I'd rather be a gazelle. They're noble, regal, intelligent and good."

"But what if you're attacked?" I said. "I'd rather be alive and bad than good and dead."

"Not always. Would you rather be good and hurt or bad and impermeable? How important is it for people to know 'you can't fuck with a Blumenfeld'?"

"Blumenf*eldssss*. Plural. Which I know is an extinct species, but—"

The phone interrupted. I jumped for it, eager to end a debate I knew I would lose.

"Is this my cute, crybaby wife who pokes and prods and pushes and pries?" Baruch sounded happy.

"I didn't cry all day," I joked, turning my back on Rachel.

"Wow, the whole day? Want to hear the headline from yesterday's *New York Post?* Finally some good news from the trial."

He read the article to me. I told him about the mastermind's house. "Shouldn't I come home? I'm starting to feel like this is kooky."

"No, it isn't. It's an adventure," he said. "It's not like you're going to shoot someone."

"But here I am, in the middle of my life, trying to get revenge for my father?"

"Or not getting revenge. You're exploring the idea of revenge. You're trying to figure out how to respond to an injustice."

I returned to my friend on the couch.

"Baruch and I do the same thing, but in different arenas," I said, feeling smart.

"Both ineffectually," Rachel said with a slung-back smile.

And we were even.

THAT EVENING, I went out to dinner with a journalist who was visiting from Washington. I took a taxi home.

"Yemin Moshe," I said to the driver. The neighborhood's windmill was a landmark that every taxi driver recognized. This driver missed the turn. At first I was irritated, then I saw his eyes illuminated by the green dash lights. I could see how disoriented he was.

His name was Suliman, a Bedouin Arab. He had lived all his life in the desert town of Rahat and had just come to Jerusalem two weeks before. When his grandfather broke a son-in-law's arm—payback over an unpaid loan—the injury started a blood feud. Suliman fled to escape the exchange of blows.

The story reminded me that there is another choice in the jungle, other than predator or prey. Every college student learns about it in freshman psychology. When confronted with danger, the choice is fight or flight. Fight back or turn and flee.

With the mastermind and his triggermen in jail, it made sense to leave. Pack my bags and join my husband in New York. That was what a reasonable person would do. I wished Suliman good luck, and walked through the lamplight to my door. Standing in the fragmented shadows of our apricot tree, I came the closest to defining my subject.

What is revenge?

Revenge is when you can walk away. But somehow, you cannot. Something pulls you back.

As my door opened, I heard the last ring of a missed call. I listened to the message:

"Happy Father's Day to me, happy Father's Day to me, happy Father's Day, dear father . . ."

The singing was interrupted by a cough. "Hiya, sweetypuss!"

I loved the bounce in my father's voice: "Where are you? What're you doing knocking around town at ten o'clock at night? Thanks for the Father's Day message; now my day is complete. I went to Rye Playland with Hal and the family. Anyway, sweetheart, thanks for remembering."

I wished that I could call him back and tell him how I had celebrated Father's Day. Instead, I wrote nonsense in a notebook:

> Options: 1. Get self arrested and follow them into jail.
> To get to them I have to become one of them.

Here was another problem with revenge. As Rachel put it, revenge means "stooping to their level." It is dangerous, not because of what it does to your enemy, but because of what it does to you. There is an imitative quality to revenge. In recent months, four Jews had been stabbed by Arabs in the Old City, as six Arabs were stabbed by Jews in the new city. Meanwhile, on the island of Crete, a land feud shrank the population of Patima from one hundred people to ten; those who had not been shot, fled. A symmetry develops between two people engaged in revenge, as they match blow for blow. The parties mimic each other's tactics—whether it is price-fixing in business or cheating in a marriage—which they might otherwise condemn.

Was there an alternative? I was trying to figure that out.

I contacted an agent from Israel's internal security service, the Shin Bet. He was a sinewy man in his forties, code-named "the Lion," who had spent twenty-seven years stalking terror suspects. I told him about Rachel and her belief that one should live life like a gazelle. The agent produced a thin-lipped smile.

"That's like walking around the streets of Manhattan naked," the agent said. "It's not socially appropriate here. Let her come here—she'll change. If not, she'll be erased little by little, until there's nothing left of her but ashes."

In Israel, talk of turning people into ashes was not a metaphor. The Holocaust still haunted many Israelis. When the country's chief rabbi, Israel Lau, granted me an audience to discuss religion and revenge, the sentence he uttered with the most conviction had nothing to do with God.

"The state of Israel is revenge for the Holocaust," the chief rabbi said.

Others had responded to this singular experience as prey with the hunger of a predator. For them, Israel was one big agency of revenge. Jews might still be killed, but not without consequences. In the decades following the Holocaust, the military had adopted a policy of retaliation to restore the equilibrium of self-respect. In 1953, a young officer named Ariel Sharon, who would one day become prime minister, led Squad 101, which specialized in reprisals. Sharon responded to the killing of three Israeli civilians by raiding the Jordanian village of Qibya. Sixty-nine people were killed. The reprisals did not improve Israel's security but they responded to the public's need to lash back.

Even today, the culture is marked by a revulsion of victimhood. One of the worst insults is to call someone a *freier,* slang for "sucker." The university offers a course analyzing this phenomenon, called Sucker Studies. After Rabin was assassinated, and after suicide bombers turned commuters into human confetti, Israelis elected the right-wing Benjamin Netanyahu. His worldview was summed up in a banner headline in the *Jerusalem Post* on the state's fiftieth anniversary. It quoted the prime minister: "WE ARE NOT 'FREIERS.' "

SO WHERE DID that leave me? Blundering around the Old City trying to figure out what to do, reconstructing the four shootings ordered by the mastermind. Meir Amit, the former chief of the Mossad and chief of military intelligence, had told me in an interview, "All my life I've taught military people—with retaliation, *you* choose the battlefield, *you* choose the timing, *you* choose the method."

Having not yet decided on any of the above, I wandered the alleys of the Arab market. As I walked the Via Dolorosa, the perfume and stench of the market soaked my hair and settled in my clothes. From one stand dangled bloodied sheep carcasses; from the next hung tote bags depicting the sheep from Christ's manger. I turned onto David Street, where one man sold fake Roman glass, another sold fake Persian rugs and another sold fake holy water.

And then I saw Tom, the shopkeeper. He was sitting outside his store on a stool, just as he had the night my father was shot. His dimpled chin was tipped toward the sun.

"How are you?" I said, not knowing what else to say. What do you do to someone who did nothing?

"Alive," Tom said, one eye closed, as if he were a dozing cat. "Trying to get a suntan."

"Oh, well." The reek of his cologne hit my nose. "You look good."

"You look good too." He straightened up. "Want to drink some tea?"

This was not an encouraging start, but I did want to check on Tom. I sat on the stool next to him.

"You married? I didn't notice your ring last time," he said, winking at a joke that I was not in on. He had a sleek-cat air, a twitch of the nostrils, sensing whether I was a mouse or just a pinecone.

Then a tour guide walked by. "Hi, Abed!" the guide called to another shopkeeper, ignoring Tom.

Tom shook a cigarette from its pack and began to mutter, "I hate tour guides." He reminded me of the kickbacks that they demanded, how his refusal to pay was ruining his business. "My mind isn't working. My stomach hurts. My head beats the drumsticks. It's all nerves." He made a fist, running his nails over the tendons in his wrist.

"I'm losing money. I owe the bank three hundred and fifty thousand dollars. I was thinking to leave the country, to Alabama."

He started to tell me how the stress was affecting his family. "I have problems with wife. Some people say it's better to get divorce, but I'm not getting divorce. Divorce is bad for the children."

"You have a nice shop," I offered weakly.

"I see it ugly. I see it black." He spit the words. "You see these colorful fabrics?" He pulled some Druze place mats off a pile. "All these colors look black. This is black. I am black. I don't come to a store anymore. I'm coming to jail."

Jail?

The word pricked my ears. Tom was free, tanning his dimpled chin on David Street, but he felt like he was in jail, and so he was.

If it was possible to be free, and to feel imprisoned, then it was possible to be in prison and to feel free. I was sure that this was the case with the shooter, if he was imprisoned. I was sure he did not regret it, that his conscience remained untouched. Jail had taught him nothing, except maybe pride. It did not make him sorry; it made him a hero. The state may have his body. I wanted to get to his spirit. Prison was beside the point, at least beside the point that I was trying to make. But how?

I would start by traveling to jail with the mastermind's family.

THE NEXT DAY was our wedding anniversary. One year of married life, half of it apart. Baruch was in the middle of closing arguments for his trial. He wired over an anniversary bouquet, long-distance flowers, tentacled and rust-colored. Rachel and her husband surprised me with dinner.

"Congratulations, you made it one year," Rachel said, raising her glass of wine. "Now you can keep your gifts."

The following morning, I called the mastermind's family and accepted their invitation to visit him in jail. They told me to meet them on Friday in east Jerusalem, outside the American Colony Hotel. A white Ford Transit would pick me up at 3:45 A.M. It would take an hour and a half to drive to the Shikma Prison in Ashkelon, a southern coastal city. I wondered how they would sneak me in. The only people allowed to visit prisoners were relatives. No problem, they said; they had a plan.

"Don't lie to government officials," Baruch said when I told him. "It's dangerous and stupid. The Israeli police beat people up, you know."

I knew, but there I was, standing in the hotel driveway on Friday at a quarter to four, my stomach jumpy. The streets were deserted. The traffic lights were dozing, flashing yellow until dawn. Far away, a rooster crowed. Closer, a recorded voice called the Islamic faithful to prayer, a voice so low it seemed to flow from an underwater cavern.

What am I doing here? Trying to get near him. No particular plan. Shocked how unplanned I am.

A half an hour passed, then forty-five minutes.

Low-grade panic. If they knew who I was, they might do something. They might be justified. Put that out of mind.

At 4:45, I was about to give up, when a white van turned into the circular drive.

"Sorry," said Mohammed, the mastermind's twenty-year-old nephew, sitting at the wheel. "We overslept."

I climbed into the second row of seats, over Noor, the statuesque niece who had shown me her wedding shoes. Beside her sat her cousin, whom I had not met before, an eight-year-old girl named Yasmin. An uncle and a cousin filled the front seats. In the back row sat two other women, traditional Muslims in long robes, relatives of a prisoner from the Islamic group Hamas.

The van was fragrant with morning, with the cardamom in their coffee and the strawberry in their soap. A box of tissues rested on the dashboard, reminding me of the tissues that I had swiped from their bathroom. Swinging from the rearview mirror was a *hamsa,* a turquoise amulet shaped like a hand, to ward off the evil eye.

That, I realized, was me.

Soon, the passengers fell asleep. I sat behind the driver, far from the door, next to the window. I could not get out, but at least I could look out. A vehicle pulled up beside us at the intersection, a white Ford Transit full of Hasidic teenagers, dozing on one another's shoulders. One boy was awake. We gaped at each other through the glass, making assumptions.

Our van turned, taking the back road out of Jerusalem, a route that wove us in and out of Palestinian territory. The landscape looked sleepy and innocent at this hour, puffs of olive trees and misty, terraced hills. Many days, I was charmed by the scenery. On this day, I resented it. In a few hours the sun would reveal its true harshness, the dry bushes and the rock-sown fields. The fight over the land, I thought, was like two men in a bar fighting over a woman, both too drunk to notice how ugly she was.

Up ahead, an Israeli soldier held up his hand, signaling us to pull over. The sudden halt woke Yasmin, who had been lying in her cousin's lap. She lifted her small, ringleted head. "Are we there yet?"

The soldier drummed his fingers on the base of his M-16. He spoke to Mohammed in Hebrew and nodded toward us. "Who are these people?"

"My friends," Mohammed replied in Arabic. He stuck his arm out the window, bending it sharply, as if the point of his elbow could hold back the soldier.

"What are you doing out so early in the morning?" the soldier said in Hebrew.

"Driving," Mohammed said in Arabic.

Mohammed knew Hebrew and the soldier knew some Arabic. Neither would speak the other's language.

Starting at the rear, the soldier walked the length of the van, his boots crunching gravel, his eyes landing on us one at a time. The women in the backseat had knotted their scarves in the Muslim fashion, under their chins. The mastermind's family had dark hair and dark skin, fitting the soldier's profile of an Arab. Then the soldier saw me, behind the driver. A sneer tweaked the corners of his mouth.

"Is she your sister?" he asked the driver.

"Sister-in-law," said Mohammed. If he was intimidated, he did not show it.

The soldier reached through Mohammed's window. He demanded my identity card. Every Israeli and Palestinian had one, which stated their ethnicity. The only identity card I had was my American passport. I passed it forward to the soldier, my stomach tensing.

In a matter of seconds he would find my name. My Eastern European Jewish last name: *What's a Jewish girl like you doing with these people?* the soldier might say. Or worse, he would blurt out my family name, cheerful and familiar, the same last name as my father, the name that had been framed in gold beneath a picture of the mastermind, sitting on the mastermind's coffee table for over ten years. *Hey, BLUMENFELD,* the soldier would say. *I go to a dentist BLUMENFELD in Tel Aviv.*

My stomach felt like a belt had been cinched around it. How would I explain myself to the soldier, or worse, to the family? They knew me only as Laura. They did not think I was Jewish. What would I say? I did not know. I never knew.

Then the passport dropped back through the window onto Mohammed's lap. The soldier did not open it. A truck was approaching, loaded with Palestinian laborers. The soldier waved us on.

So I was their sister-in-law, an American who had married the mastermind's brother. That was how they planned to sneak me past the prison guards. The mastermind did have a brother who had moved to Pompano Beach, Florida. He had opened a liquor store and was shot in the head by a robber. During my visit to their house, the mastermind's mother had told me that she saw a picture of her son's killer in a Florida newspaper. "He's black, he looks like a scary man, something says it between his eyes," she had said. "He's hard, not clean." Another brother tracked the killer down, she said, not the police. The suspect was tried and sentenced to twenty years. She said he deserved to die.

In keeping with Muslim tradition, the widow surrendered custody of their daughter to the mastermind's family. That was Yasmin, the girl asleep in the van beside me. I was supposed to be her mother.

I took all this in as we continued south, turning at the vineyards by the Latrun Trappist monastery. We traveled along a two-lane road, the white painted lines turning pink with the sunrise. Half an hour later, we reached the coastal highway. Soon we came to the exit for Ashkelon.

When I was a child, Ashkelon was a fabled place. It was the home of Samson, who uprooted mountains and rubbed them together as if they were pebbles. My father had told me about Samson when he tucked me in at night. He would sit on the edge of my bed and tell me Bible adventure stories, many of them about revenge: Joseph, the dreamer, who paid back his brothers while in disguise; Esther, the brave queen who hid her identity too. Now, hiding my identity as they did, I wondered how my own revenge story would end.

"We came late," Mohammed said as the walls of Shikma Prison rose in his windshield. Cars lined the curb along Israel Defense Forces Street. Passengers milled around drinking tea, picnicking on the sesame bread they had brought with them. The air was humid, a seaweed breeze wafting inland. Music blared, a Palestinian nationalist song: *"The one who has never seen the torture by the Jews is blind in the eyes of Zionism . . ."* It was 6:05 A.M. The rest of the industrial neighborhood was quiet. The palm trees were still.

"See how many people are ahead of us?" Mohammed lamented.

Another driver walked up to our van and greeted Mohammed: "Hey, you look terrible."

"I didn't have time to wash or change or even drink coffee."

We got out and approached a dusty courtyard where relatives of the other prisoners waited in line. Above us loomed an Israeli flag and a guard tower. Video cameras scoped us, our faces multiplied on a wall of screens inside a security booth. A handwritten sign in Arabic and English hung in the waiting area:

> In the name of Allah the merciful welcome our dear family and visitors,
>
> We hope you don't bring anything with you forbidden cause that will lead to search thorough and would upset us.
>
> Your sons,
> THE PRISONERS.
>
> - no cellphones allowed
> - no new clothes allowed unless take old ones
> - visiting days are Sunday, Wednesday and Friday, according to region
> - each prisoner is allowed 3 adults, or 2 adults and 2 kids

The mastermind's brother collected his family's identity cards for processing. I held on to my passport until the last minute, afraid he might recognize my last name. While the brother waited in line, the rest of us made small talk.

Mohammed told me that he wanted advice from his uncle, the mastermind. He wanted to sell his van and use the money to move to Florida. His grandmother had forbidden him. "Too many Cubans," she said. "Florida is a very dangerous place."

Noor was also looking for guidance from the mastermind.

"I'm thinking of breaking my engagement," she said. "But my father already paid for the wedding dress."

I asked her why she was having doubts.

"I don't think he's so nice. He has a big nose." She wrinkled her small nose. "I wish I could take English lessons and be a stewardess on Air France. I envy you; you can do what you want, and marry whoever you want." She said that she wanted to marry someone more like her uncle. "Someone strong and good-looking and good-hearted. He's understanding. He never forces you to do anything. And he likes small children."

Listening to Noor, I wondered if this was the same man who had planned the murders of so many people. Maybe he had become a different person; maybe he regretted it.

"He doesn't regret anything," Mohammed said. "If we could, everyone would do the same as my uncle. If the Israelis want to throw us out—I'll throw them out first."

Mohammed began to quote a popular Arabic saying. Noor joined in, singsonging the chant: "An eye for an eye, a tooth for a tooth, and he who starts it is to blame."

"I'll be wearing black," said Mohammed. "Holding a machine gun."

"If we can get our own arms," Noor said, "I'll have a machine gun. Knives are so old-fashioned."

Yasmin, who was hanging around the edges of our group, saw the excitement on her older cousins' faces and tried to jump in: "I think it must be a Jew who killed my father in America. Who else would kill him but a Jew?"

A relative of another prisoner, standing nearby, overhead our conversation. He saw me nodding and taking notes. He beckoned to Mohammed.

"Don't trust her," he said. "She works for the Israel Prison Authority; she's interrogating your family."

Mohammed brushed him off. "You're wrong."

A voice crackled over the loudspeaker. "Yoseph Zaid Ahmad . . ." A guard was announcing the names, the first shift of inmates to receive visitors. "Omar al-Khatib . . ."

That name sounded familiar. I scribbled it down as an afterthought. The mastermind's brother waved me over to join him in line. He counted out three cigarettes and dropped them into his breast pocket. He handed the rest of the pack to Mohammed, who had given up his spot on this visit to make room for me. Visitors were allowed to carry three cigarettes, but no lighters, no money, no letters.

The guard continued calling out names, like a maître d' announcing tables: "Hassan Abdel Aziz Al Atrash . . ."

Al Atrash's relatives rustled off their bench, leaving behind newspapers and sandwich wrap.

"Mohammed Ibrahim Hamadah . . ."

Hamadah's relatives surged through the revolving metal gate.

At 8:08 A.M., we heard the name we had been listening for: "Aladin Ahmad Bazian . . ."

This was it, my chance to meet the mastermind. And, I was convinced, my only chance. As a journalist I would never be allowed to enter the prison. I had checked that option through the prison press office and was told, no, never. Security prisoners were barred from talking to the press. The Israeli government did not want to reward violence with publicity.

The mastermind's brother and I—the two adult visitors—began walking toward the gate. The younger cousins trailed behind us, including my supposed child, Yasmin.

The twists in my identity were dizzying: I was the daughter of a man shot in the head, thanks to the mastermind, pretending to be his sister-in-law, widowed by a gunshot to the head. I was part of the mastermind's family, bringing him coffee and cigarettes. I was the widow from Pompano Beach.

In an instant, five guards wearing flak jackets surrounded me.

"You can't go in," a guard ordered in Hebrew.

"Visits are for family only," another guard said in Hebrew.

They did not ask me who I was or what I wanted. It was clear to them that I did not belong.

"I don't speak Hebrew," I said in English, pushing forward. I spoke Hebrew fluently, better than I spoke Arabic. I was afraid that my knowing Hebrew would make the family suspicious. In my desperation, I figured that if I kept walking, oblivious, the guards might let me through.

"Well, we don't speak English," the guard said. "Maybe you'll understand this." He planted his belly between me and the mastermind's brother, who was already half a turn through the revolving gate.

The Pompano Beach story was looking dim.

"Do you want me to tell him anything special?" the brother asked with a grin that begged me not to make a scene.

I backed away; he pushed forward. The metal gate turned. The clank rang inside and outside of my head, the sound of a slug rejected from a vending machine. "Tell him I hope to meet him one day."

And the family went inside.

THAT AFTERNOON back at their house, I was still reeling from the aborted visit. On the mastermind's dining room table, I looked for satisfaction in my father's initials, but the "*D.B.*" that I had written in the dust was gone, wiped away by a child's handprints.

Outside, the women had gathered in a courtyard embroidered with grapevines. They had been cooking since 7 A.M., preparing a feast for a visiting sister. Over the yard hung a vapor of steaming rice, cracked garlic and stripped ginger.

Squatting on a stool, in the middle of the bustle, was the mastermind's mother. A tub of zucchini sat at her feet. She wore a black head scarf and black reading glasses, keeping track of all the details that go into stuffed zucchini. One daughter-in-law was chopping parsley. Another poured the olive oil. A third woman sliced tomatoes, a plastic bag on her head that covered the streaks of bleach painting highlights in her hair. Children were dancing on clothespins that had fallen to the ground, and knocking into trays of chickpeas soaking in water.

Yasmin scampered up to her grandmother to tell her about the prison visit. "We got a whole hour with him. An extra fifteen minutes."

I had spent that hour waiting outside the gate, sunburned, defeated and grumpy. *Maybe I should go to the beach. What am I doing here?* At 9:45 A.M., the family had reappeared through the turnstile, carrying gifts from the mastermind. A box of cornflakes, a package of sesame crackers, a silver foil bag filled with chocolate wafers. "This is his present to you," the brother had said, handing me the bag of chocolate creme-filled wafers. He turned to Mohammed, who had also been waiting outside: "He doesn't want you to go to America. Something might happen to you. Your father would go crazy if that happened—the same as Uncle. He says, 'You can't go to Florida. Too many guns.' " Then the brother turned to me: "He says, 'Don't believe anything they say about me.' He wants to talk to you directly."

More than ever, that would be impossible. I would not have the chance to talk with him. Not with the mastermind, nor with any of his partners. Worst of all, not with the shooter. Security prisoners could not receive phone calls, could not send personal mail. The Israelis kept them isolated from political and military allies. How, then, would I reach him? I needed a new plan.

All this went through my mind as I sat, with a kind of exaggerated stillness, in the mastermind's courtyard. His mother was telling stories to the younger women, as she dragged a basin full of fish toward her stool.

"I was twelve when I got married. Your grandfather was fourteen. I never even had my period. I had no idea about sex. We never talked about those things. When I was thirteen, I was pregnant. The day came, and I didn't know I was having a baby. I thought I was taking a shit."

A boy ran into a table, knocking over a glass. It shattered on the concrete patio.

"A woman goes through a lot," said a petite woman, balancing on black, high-heeled sandals. "I used to get mad at him when he hit me."

This was Muna, a twenty-five-year-old mother of three with a delicately boned face. Her husband had recently punched it purplish-blue.

"He'll come home in the evening, he'll be upset, and I want to talk. And he won't want to talk, he just wants to watch TV. He steps on my stomach. I fainted a few times."

"Arab women respect their husbands, so they can't do anything back," the mastermind's mother explained to me. She picked up a silver fish from the tub and raised her knife. "We're different than foreigners." She began scraping the fish's scales. "We never get even with our men."

Another child dropped a glass. It crashed on the cement.

"One month after we married, he started hitting me," Muna said. She was talking as she walked in a tight circle around the women. "A black eye, a neck bruised with his fingerprints. I went to the intensive care unit, but I didn't press charges. A few sweet words, 'My darling, honey.' He hugs me and I forgive. It's stupid, I know."

The mastermind's mother sliced open her fish. She stuck her fingers inside and pulled out its ropy guts.

"His father abused his mother. That's the way it is," Muna said, still circling. "Once, I lay on the kitchen floor, and my lip was split, and I was thinking how to get back at him."

The mastermind's mother shook the fish by the tail, holding it upside down.

"Every night," Muna said, "I cook dinner for him. I make a salad for him and I squeeze a lemon on it. When I'm cutting up lemons, that's when I think about doing it."

The fish's jaw dropped open. The mastermind's mother lopped off its head.

"I think about cutting his dick off."

Muna stopped in front of me. "Do you know how to cook?"

"No."

"Good, you don't want to know. What's your husband's name?"

His birth certificate said Bernard. Everyone called him Baruch, Hebrew for "blessed."

"Bernard," I said.

"How's married life?"

"I don't know yet."

"Well, you're a gentle person. You'll have a good marriage."

Muna wavered for a moment, losing her balance on her high

heels. Then I noticed something moving beyond her shoulder. At the far end of the patio, a toddler around the same age as Hal's daughter had climbed onto the table and was inchworming across its surface. She was nearing the end of the table, unaware of the edge, about to plunge onto the cement. I opened my mouth, instinctively, to warn them. And then I paused: I had my next idea.

6

COLLECTIVE PUNISHMENT

JERUSALEM

"OUR CLAN AGAINST THEIR CLAN?" Hal said with a half-smile, refusing to engage in his little sister's fantasy. "Count me out. They'd decimate us in a second."

I was sharing a daydream that I had on a recent afternoon: our family versus the shooter's. A face-off in the valley on the road to Ramallah, the hillsides at our backs, the slabs of limestone volleying our sounds. It was only a daydream, an absurd one, but I wanted to know if, in principle, Hal was in. Were we members of a family that stood up for one another or not?

"Who's in our clan?" Doubt warped Hal's voice, curling the edges of his words. "All these hardened terrorists lined up against me and you and Eva and Michelle? We'd be hiding behind some rocks saying, 'How did we get ourselves into this?' At least Baruch and I know how to run fast—the other way."

My brother and I were sitting in a cafe across from the Old City walls. The restaurant was empty, the room quiet except for the background clink and jingle of the waiters setting up tables for dinner. Hal looked serious, his brown eyes attentive, his eyebrows pitched at a thoughtful slant. Faint shadows had settled beneath his eyes from all-night sessions writing scientific grant proposals. He was leaning forward on his elbows, a sign of affection, or maybe of fatigue.

Hal and his family were vacationing in Jerusalem. They had spent the morning at a petting zoo, feeding carrots to baby goats. While Eva napped, Hal and I went out for coffee. He knew, in the same vague way that my father knew, that I was looking for the shooter. I asked him how the attack had affected him.

First I had to remind him when it was: March 1986.

"It was a turbulent time for our family life," Hal said.

Our parents had separated. My father was in between homes. My mother had just bought a house with Bernie, a man fourteen years her senior whom she had met when she answered his personal ad in a magazine. He owned a company that made airplane and missile parts.

In big and little ways, our lives were changing. Our house was sold and our childhood bedrooms were boxed and stored in the basement of my mother and Bernie's new house. We were not always welcome at their house. Friends were restricted; Bernie liked his privacy. Bernie did not want pets in the house, so my thirteen-year-old cat was put outside and died. Our parents, meanwhile, took turns flipping a coin to divide twenty-five years of shared belongings. My mother said it was so amicable, she called it the "picnic divorce." My father said he would never set foot in my mother's driveway. When I went from her place to his, she left me in a shopping center parking lot; he picked me up on the curb by the grocery carts.

"We had nowhere to go on weekends, except Grandma's house," Hal said. "We were pretty much homeless."

I was floundering in college. Hal withdrew into his books in medical school.

"Then Daddy called from Israel to tell us we shouldn't worry in case we saw something in the newspaper the next day," Hal said. Initial reports said that he had been killed. "You wanted a lot of reassurance, like, 'He's OK, right? Is he OK?' To me it didn't seem real. Like one of those bizarre incidents: 'Strange but true! Rabbi shot in head and lives to tell story.' One centimeter, and it would have been in his skull. I've seen that in the operating room. Two centimeters, and the bullet would've tumbled inside, tearing his brain and his blood vessels. I remember thinking, What else could go wrong for Daddy? I wondered if he was feeling a little careless or suicidal, so he thought, 'Hell with it, I'll walk down David Street.' "

A ripple of memory crossed Hal's face that left him looking sad. "I think we hoped Mommy would feel sorry for him and take him back."

Hal took a last sip of iced coffee, the straw sucking against ice cubes. We had run out of things to say.

"What should I do?" I pressed him one last time as we stood up to leave.

"You can explore your feelings," he said.

"I don't want to explore my feelings. I want to hurt anyone who tries to hurt Daddy."

"Well . . ." Hal held up his hands as if to show me that they were clean. The padded fingertips, the broad span of his palms. They were hands that had reached out to me over the years. "Just don't involve me in any schemes."

TOO BAD, because my latest scheme involved Hal and the rest of my family. Revenge often is a group activity. Brothers and mothers and uncles and other kin. I was failing, I concluded, because I was on my own.

In its origins, revenge developed to preserve the integrity of a family, driven by feelings of esprit de corps. In the isolation of desert life or in grassland huts, where no one could defend himself alone, revenge ensured survival.

While nosing around the anthropology stacks at the university library, I had found a study on the Bedouin by the scholar Joseph Ginat. In his book called *Blood Revenge,* Ginat explains that revenge is the ultimate instrument of collective identity.

"A leader who is anxious to promote cohesiveness within the

group will encourage revenge," Ginat wrote. "By deliberately increasing tension, a leader can make his group aware of their collective responsibility."

In other words, by rousing the Blumenfelds, I was not only avenging my father but reasserting our unity. In seeking revenge I could confound the truth that our family had disappeared. We might have scattered—my father, mother and brother all married within three years of the divorce—but as long as we fought for each other, our family lived on. That, in itself, was a tantalizing goal. What was the definition of a family, anyway? In aboriginal Siberia, the word for kindred families is *cin-yirin,* meaning "collection of those who take part in blood revenge."

Hal was right when he said that I was trying to stir things up. I neither expected nor wanted a Sicilian-style vendetta. I was hoping my call for revenge would stir up something else. A familial call to arms.

THE TACTIC FAILED with Hal, though revenge has been bringing people together forever, in families, in nations and in the world of sports. Wanting revenge on Argentina helps define the English soccer fan in the same way that being a Boston Red Sox fan means dreaming of getting even with the New York Yankees.

Israeli sports have their own feuds. Danny Seaman, who worked in the Foreign Press Office, invited me to the soccer season's decisive game. Two rivals, Beitar Jerusalem and Hapoel Tel Aviv, were competing for the championship. "You'll see the meaning of 'playing for blood,' " Danny said.

That Saturday, as we climbed the stairs of Jerusalem's soccer stadium, he said, "This is our chance for revenge against Hapoel for taking our championship fourteen years ago. It was zero to zero until the seventy-third minute. Then Moshe Sinai scored two goals within three minutes, the son of a bitch. A triple humiliation."

As soon as we found our seats, Danny called his brother at another soccer stadium, where Hapoel, the nemesis, was playing its final game.

"How am I going to get through this without a heart attack?" Danny said.

Danny was tanned and handsome, a mix of hues and angles, blended by a Jewish Afghani mother and a Protestant American father. His dark eyes looked seared and imperious in their lids. He had a confident, even cocky face. On this day, though, he was nibbling the inside of his cheek.

All around us, Beitar fans dressed in black and yellow, cracked sunflower seeds, spitting the shells on the floor. They settled into rows, popping up, sitting down, popping up again, like nervous birds shrieking and eating seeds.

The announcer introduced the opposing team. Moshe Sinai, the player who had cost Beitar the championship fourteen years before, ran onto the field.

The crowd burst into song, "Moshe Sinai, you son of a bitch!" Thousands of fans were singing in one voice, bound together like one living organism.

This is a trait common to revenge groups. As the Irish saying goes, "You kick one of them, and the rest of them limp." In England, the Elizabethan gentleman and his family were called "one soul." In Arabia, the Bedouin tribe called itself "one bone." Among the ancient Israelites, the avenger was the "redeemer of blood." He recovered communal blood by taking that of the enemy.

Danny, the sports fan, might stand at the lighter end of the revenge spectrum, but the same solidarity defined him. Revenge helps answer the question, Who are you? You are what you avenge. Danny identified with Beitar, "the poor people's team," whose fans were Jews from Islamic lands. Hapoel represented the European Jews.

"Hypocrites and bigots," Danny said. "Their superior democracy is fine as long as you're not playing with their kids. Beating Hapoel Tel Aviv is a 'fuck you' to the elitists."

Like a true tribesman, Danny followed the principle of collective responsibility. While watching the games on television, he noticed that if he sat on the right side of his couch and ate nothing but potato chips, Beitar would win.

"We're not playing a sharp game; this is getting dangerous," Danny said. One of Beitar's stars was injured. Another one fouled out. It started to rain. The fans ducked and huddled, as if by pulling together, they could pool their might.

Danny's brother phoned in a report. Hapoel was winning 3–1. Danny jumped up, "Bastards!"

In the last seconds of the game, the ball flew toward the goal. A cry rose up. The howling, the fear, the wet, red faces of the fans were almost too intimate to watch. Danny stood on his chair, legs trembling.

The Beitar goalie caught the ball. Game over.

Fireworks exploded. Yellow and black balloons sprang toward the clouds.

The announcer taunted, "Moshe Sinai—"

The audience roared back, "Son of a bitch!"

Danny dialed his brother to check on Hapoel: "They were depressed? Great, so let them fuck themselves. They deserve it."

We squeezed through the crowd, past the ring of police guarding the Beitar locker room. I stepped into what felt like a steaming soup of happiness—hot spray spiced with fresh sweat and aftershave. The players were pelting each other with chunks of soap.

"It's revenge against everyone who isn't me," said the player Istvan Hamar. As he buttoned his shirt and zipped his jeans, we could hear the fans singing: "The whole league is sitting on my dick."

We waded out of the locker room. The rain had cleared.

"Oh, what great dicks we have!" the fans sang.

A smile erupted on Danny's face. "Now we're on top."

BUT WHO IS *we?* How far does a person's revenge territory extend?

I never gave much thought to the borders of revenge until I interviewed Israel's prime minister. Benjamin Netanyahu taught me, in a touchy exchange, that my assumptions about revenge borders were wrong.

On a July afternoon, I took a bus to the military cemetery on

Mount Herzl, where Netanyahu's older brother, Yoni, was buried. The cemetery climbed a hillside sprinkled with pine needles. The sun pierced the pine trees and dotted the white tombstones in a pincushion of light. Carved into Yoni's tombstone was the army's insignia, an olive branch and a sword. Visitors had left stones on the grave, a symbol of their heavy hearts.

On this afternoon, the anniversary of Yoni's death, his family would recite a memorial prayer. By 4:30, a small crowd had gathered: government officials; Netanyahu's mother, leaning on her cane; his father, with his white, blown-about hair; Netanyahu's younger brother, Iddo, in dark sunglasses. No one spoke much. They inhaled the perfume of old roses, wilting in bunches on top of the graves.

Netanyahu arrived late, his eyes straining as if he were trying to block something out or hold something in. He kissed his mother's powdered cheek. He shook hands with a veteran in a wheelchair who was crippled during the raid that killed Yoni.

In 1976, Yoni led a rescue mission at the Entebbe airport in Uganda, liberating 105 Jewish hostages seized by Arab hijackers. Israeli commandos stormed the airport. They killed the hijackers, but not before they lost their commander. As Yoni ran toward the terminal, a single slug hit him below the collarbone.

"It's hard to believe twenty-two years have passed," a former hostage said, his voice catching as he delivered his speech. "We can't forget the picture of a gun and hand grenade in front of our eyes. But the dream of our rescue—it's hard to believe it was real, hearing those words, 'We've come to take you home.' "

Netanyahu leaned over his brother's grave and laid a red rose on top of the grave. He stepped back, rubbing his fingertips as if they had been pricked.

"It's like losing a limb. You can't replace an arm or a leg that you lost," Netanyahu had told me in an earlier interview about Yoni. "There's permanent scar tissue on the soul."

From the day he could walk, Benjamin had waddled after Yoni, hunting for turtles in the fields near their home. When they were apart, Yoni wrote to him, "I didn't miss anyone at home as much as I missed you . . . you're the only true friend I ever had."

Benjamin Netanyahu grew up to be a politician who believed that the only peace possible was one of chilly deterrence. Still, I wondered if his attitude toward Arabs was influenced by something more personal than politics, if he was reluctant to shake Yasir Arafat's hand because he believed it was stained with his brother's blood.

"I'm interested in talking about brothers," I had said to Netanyahu at the beginning of our interview.

"Brothers?"

"Brothers. Going back to Isaac and Ishmael, and all the way up until today."

Isaac and Ishmael were the sons of the patriarch Abraham, contenders for the birthright. The Koran and the Bible relate how Isaac became the father of the Jews, and Ishmael the father of the Arabs. Four thousand years later, their descendants were still fighting. Both claimed Abraham's inheritance.

"You're especially interesting for this subject because of your own family," I said. "And I know that it's not something that you talk about easily."

I circled the subject until I worked up the nerve to ask about Yoni. "Has Arafat ever expressed his condolences to you?"

He lifted his eyes from the revolving gears of my tape recorder. "No."

"Have any Palestinians you met with ever said, 'I'm sorry'?"

"I don't remember. In any case, I try to think more than feel."

The prime minister and I were sitting side by side. His security agents hung back, lining the walls. He had just finished a session with reporters and editors, and was enjoying the afterglow when I pulled up a chair.

Usually, Netanyahu glided through interviews with scripted answers to policy questions. At forty-eight, he still had the face that made him popular on talk shows and faithless to three wives. It was a roguishly asymmetric face, with one brown eye open and inviting, the other one leering.

"Have you ever thought about finding out where some of the hijackers came from?" I asked.

Accounts of Entebbe called the terrorists "Arabs and Germans." I assumed Netanyahu had traced their identities. The Mossad, the General Security Services and army intelligence all worked for him. Given Netanyahu's reputation for vindictiveness, I figured that he had settled the score with their families.

"Did you ever try to find out who they were, or find them?"

"No, no, I haven't."

"There was no curiosity?"

"We-ell," he stumbled. "It's not going to bring my brother back."

He was caught off guard by my questions, and I by his answers. *He never wondered about the man who killed his brother?*

I understood that the context of the death was combat, that Yoni was a soldier, and that soldiers were in the business of blood. But these were not battalions massed against battalions. This was not an all-out war, where collective bloodletting erased the individual. This was one row of an Air France jet booked with hijackers. It was possible to hold someone accountable for Yoni's death.

Unsure of what to say, I rambled, "People say it's bad to hold grievances and I always think, well, what about 'an eye for an eye'? And that's the kind of thing you talk about, the dreams of peace 'crashing against the rocks of the Middle East reality.' "

I paused, hoping the quote from Netanyahu's book would encourage him to speak. "There was never a sense, like, where was the revenge?"

"The terrorists were killed," he said precisely.

That was Netanyahu's way: reciprocity. He offered concessions if they were mutual and when attacked, he countered. Reciprocity is the engine of cooperation, but it also drives revenge.

"So that's it?" I said.

"I've never thought of it in terms of personal revenge."

He looked like he meant it.

"When I was in Hebron, near the Tomb of the Patriarchs," I

said, "I came across the brothers of one of the people who hijacked the plane, the head hijacker, a guy named Fayez Jabar. Does that name mean anything to you?"

Netanyahu shook his head no.

I motored on: "If you were in Hebron and you met these brothers, is there anything you'd say to them? I mean, not as, you know, prime minister of Israel, but as a brother?"

His chin pulled back, as if the inch could make the difference. "I don't know. I haven't tried to track down the identity of the hijackers."

He cast around for his spokesman. He gestured toward the door. "Is it time to go?"

"Is this OK? Are you all right?" I said. A disturbing sensation began to wash over me: Was I hurting him? Or was the death of his brother so impersonal that knowing who did it meant nothing?

"No, no, I'm good," he said, swiveling to reach for a Danish.

"These brothers, the ones in Hebron, they didn't know I was coming. I went to their house and asked them about the hijacking, and one of the guys reached into his pocket and pulled out a picture, which he gave to me. He said this was the leader of the cell."

Later, I would regret what I did next, too hard-hearted, I thought, even to a hardened man: I placed the photograph before him. A three-by-two-inch snapshot. A man with a thin smile and a bootblack mustache.

Fayez Jabar, head hijacker. A face for Netanyahu's faceless Arab.

"You don't recognize him?"

"No."

He glanced away and muttered that maybe it was not the hijacker. He tried to make a joke with an obscure historical punch line. He slapped the table and said, "Gotta go."

After he left, I sat for a moment, ashamed. I thought I might have crossed the line of what was fair. But another thing bothered me about the encounter: Netanyahu had seemed indifferent to his brother's killer. It was hard for me to accept that murder could be so impersonal.

Killing a person is personal, no?

"No," replied Iddo, Netanyahu's younger brother over the phone. I had asked him if he wanted to find the hijacker's family. "It's not a personal issue, it's national."

For the Netanyahus, personal identity and collective identity were one. Their nation was their family. Unlike America, which celebrates the individual, the Middle East cultivates a collective existence. The Netanyahu brothers knew that the hijacker was an Arab. That was enough. All aspects of life were part of a larger, existential war. And a man killed at war, as far back as the Hebrew Bible, does not demand blood revenge.

The Netanyahus taught me that each individual stands at the center of his own revenge map. Concentric circles radiate outward, as far as he is willing to avenge. The circle might contain only the person himself—avenging the slights suffered directly by him. Or it might include the circumference of his entire race—harm any Asian and he takes it personally.

The Netanyahus' revenge borders stretched far beyond mine. They would defend and avenge their entire population. I would redeem my family, but no one beyond that, because Blumenfeld, more than anything, was me.

OR AT LEAST it had been. One morning in July, I got an e-mail from Weiss@Justice.gov—*Thanks for being with me. I need you. YOUR HUSBAND*—and I knew that the jury would reach their verdict that day. If Baruch, who turned inward during hard times, was reaching out, he must have been anticipating the worst. Two years of legal maneuvering, four months of trial, three days of jury deliberations, and in the end—one gavel-clap of justice.

After midnight, Baruch called and said that King had been acquitted. "This is a major defeat," he said, his words slurred with exhaustion.

"No, it isn't, not for you." Although I knew it was. "No one could have done a better job." And that was true. No lawyer was more loyal to the law than Baruch.

"But I believe in the core of my soul that Don King was guilty," he said. "And he is not being punished for any crime."

"That's why my simple justice is better," I said.

He tried to laugh, but it came out like a groan.

The next day, a column ran in the *New York Times* sports section under the headline A LESSON IN FUTILITY. My father saw the article and wrote to me: "Well, it's all over. Yesterday's news. Like the breath vapor on a window—it's quickly vanishing. Unfortunately, Baruch will be replaying the trial in his mind for some time to come—so be real supportive. Tell him he's your hero!!! A man's essence, more than anything, is his job."

To celebrate his acquittal, Don King flew the jurors to the Bahamas, an all-expense-paid thank-you. He feted the jury and cavorted with his legal team on the beach, toasting them with tropical drinks. Baruch flew to Israel, to me.

The day of his arrival, I scribbled down baby names. I prepared the one dish I knew how to make, pasta with garlic. When his taxi pulled up, I opened the door, saw his smile, and was overcome with shyness. I had been dreaming of Baruch for so long, the reality scared me. Baruch, my childhood crush, lived largely in my imagination. As with the shooter, I never had expected I would actually have him. I had conjured up two men, one to love and one to hate, and now in this peculiar honeymoon year with the shooter, I would discover who they were.

A FEW DAYS LATER I set out again for Ramallah, looking for the shooter. I waited until Friday, when Hal, Michelle and Eva went to the beach, so I would not have to answer questions about where I was going.

"Have fun," I called after Hal as he lugged the baby car seat down our walkway.

"That's not even an option," he cracked.

An hour later, the bus driver dropped me halfway between Jerusalem and Ramallah. I wandered along the road, navigating a narrow, gravelly shoulder. Trucks jouncing vegetables drove by, blowing my hair into my eyes. A white glare bounced off the cars' windshields. The summer was the hottest in forty years. Everything along the road was cooking in the sun: oil cans wafting greasy fumes, sneakers smelling of burned rubber, squashed tomatoes oozing the odor of rancid tomato soup. Even my leather purse was stinking like an exercised cow.

Folded inside it was the list of suspects, gleaned from newspaper articles and the DA's letter. I had starred the names that appeared in both, and noted where they lived.

Issam Ali Jendal—?? shot British tourist
*Ali Mislamani—Aram
*Omar Khatib—Kalandia
Mohammed Khatib—Aram

Although I had worked in the West Bank for the *Washington Post,* I did not know these places. There were no street names, sidewalks or pedestrians. I picked my way up and down the curving road, going nowhere.

A van pulled onto the shoulder. The driver reached his arm out the window. "Hi, what are you doing?"

It was Mohammed, the mastermind's nephew, who had driven me to the Ashkelon prison. He was working as an unlicensed cabdriver.

"Come on in," he said, slapping the van door.

I climbed in without thinking, relieved to be somewhere cool. "How's business?"

"Not good. Too many police."

I explained that I was trying to get to an interview but could not find the home. I read the four men's names to him. He recognized them all, activists arrested with his uncle.

"You're closest to Omar Khatib's house. It's down there, to the right."

We turned onto an unmarked road. Strung up on the wires overhead was a tattered, black shirt. Later, the black flag would become my navigational star. We bumped over potholes, past a torched car, a burning Dumpster, flattened soda cans. Birds hopped on black banana peels. Red and green nationalist graffiti streamed by. Mohammed stopped at an empty lot and called out to a boy, "Where's the Khatib house?"

"I live there." The boy picked up his soccer ball. "Turn left, turn right." He gave the ball a hug. "By the quarry. The one with the red gate."

Our van squeezed down a steep alley, its concrete walls pressing in on our windows. At the bottom, the walls gave way to a view over a limestone ravine. Trash spilled over the precipice. Dust clouds whorled below, and gray, humpbacked boulders ran all the way to the horizon. There were no trees, no birds. The air was powdery, full of something that was once whole and had crumbled.

"Here," Mohammed said, braking at the edge of the ravine. He pointed to the red gate. It was the last house, at the end of the road, at the far end of town. He said good-bye and chugged back up the hill.

I looked at the house, a pile of small houses, really, that together became something big. They were cement improvisations with raw concrete steps and half-stacked cinder blocks. They jutted from the hillside like a row of broken teeth. A chained dog barked and jumped.

I knocked on the first of many doors. A woman appeared wearing a pink embroidered robe.

"Hi, my name is Laura." I tried to smile. "I'm looking for Omar Khatib."

"Come in," she said. "Would you like some orange soda?" She waved me out of the sun and through her front door. I entered a dimly lit living room full of children.

Omar was not home. Omar was in jail.

"That's him," the woman said, pointing to his photograph.

I looked at his face and sank into the couch.

"He tried to kill someone," she said.

"Who?" I asked.

"Some Jew." The boy on my right smiled, a pleasant look of commiseration.

"He was a person from the outside, the head of a municipality in New York," said Saed, Omar's brother, shifting into the room in his army fatigues. He came closer. "It happened inside the Old City, near the Western Wall. He shot the man one time in the head."

My heart hesitated, then resumed with a thump. I had found the right home.

AT SUNDOWN, as I walked away from their house, the facts that I had gathered sizzled and popped inside of me: The shooter was a black belt in karate, a militant who had bragged and smirked at his trial. He lived, literally, at the edge of civilization. The only injustice, his family believed, was that he had been jailed at all. When they recounted my father's shooting, they laughed.

I turned and looked back. The shooter's family was gathered on the front steps, waving. Standing together, they looked strong. The shooter was the youngest of eight children, all married with kids. There was Imad, his brother, his orange head higher than the others. "It wasn't a personal vendetta," Imad had said when I asked if he thought the victim's family would seek revenge. "It was public relations. It was like telling the media to pay attention to us."

For four hours, I had sat in their living room, nodding. A journalist on a story. Taking notes was the one thing I could do to stay calm. It kept my mind off the reality of where I was, who I was and who they were. My forehead kept furrowing, though. I lifted my hand, trying to wipe away the lines.

"Your face, I know it from somewhere," the brother Saed said, with the angling smile of a secret revealed.

As I listened to him, to all of them, outwardly sympathetic, I felt a rising anger that made me scrutinize them for the ugliest details. The father's split toenails. The ceiling's cauliflower-shaped stains. The flies raving in circles. The feces floating in their toilet. I noted the mother's breasts lumped beneath her pink robe, and hated them for suckling him.

By the time my bus arrived back in Jerusalem, I was so repulsed—by them for dehumanizing my father, by me for accepting their sugared tea—that I wanted to break something, or someone. During my visit, the idea of collective punishment of the shooter's family had taken hold of me, but by now I was so diffusely angry that I hated pretty much everyone. I glowered at two tough guys sitting on a rail. *I'm not afraid of you.*

The vendors outside Damascus Gate were closing their stalls. As I hurried past the stone-block walls, the scene outside the shooter's house replayed in my mind: walking away, turning back to wave. It was an odd mirror image of the scene at Kennedy Airport six months earlier, when I walked with Baruch toward our airplane and turned to wave to my father. Moving forward, while looking back.

I was grinding through these scenes, when I heard a whizzing sound. Something struck the back of my head and skidded across my scalp. A tremendous weight slammed into my legs, knocking me onto my back. I lay on the sidewalk, dazed.

Did I fly? My purse lay five feet away. *Did my purse fly?* I touched my head. I touched my elbows. Elbows bleeding, not head. Good. Pedestrians stared. Then two Palestinian men came running toward me. One had a broken tooth. The other wore a green shirt.

"Are you OK? I'm very sorry," the broken-toothed one said.

His Saint Bernard had been chasing a corncob that he had pitched. The cob grazed my scalp as it soared overhead. The dog ran into me from behind, knocking the wind out of me. It was comical, slapstick, really, but my legs were shaking. I stood up, my white pants streaked with dirt.

"Your dog hit me. Very hard."

"It's no problem?" he said.

"Well, he hit me."

I huffed away, tears stinging. Forgiveness was not an option. I would never forgive the shooter. I continued, unsteadily, along Paratroopers Street, corncobs and bullets mixed up in my addled mind. *I was cobbed,* I tried to joke. Was that all that had happened to my father, a conk on the head, albeit a homicidal conk? There had to be more, something more hurtful, but in my wet-eyed confusion, I could not say what.

As I continued tracking the walls, I passed the Notre Dame center, where a statue of the Virgin Mary and Jesus watched over the courtyard. In the failing light a big white cross glowed like a reprimand.

Maybe I should have told them it was OK.

As I turned the corner, coming up to the arches of Jaffa Gate, two Arabic-speaking men approached from behind. One of them wore a green shirt, graying in the dusk. The corncob men. They had trailed me all the way from Damascus Gate.

"Are you OK?" the green-shirted one said in English. "My friend is very sorry."

"Oh, it's OK," I said in Arabic, in a voice that came out in a squeak. "No problem."

I descended into the valley, elbows burning. Feeling better that I forgave them. Hating their big, brown dog. They walked away, smiling and nudging each other.

WHEN I GOT HOME, the lights were out. Hal, Michelle and Eva had walked to the Old City, to the Western Wall for Friday-night prayers. Relieved to be alone, I called New York.

"Thank you for calling Sound Shore Medical Center of Westchester."

"I'm calling for David Blumenfeld, room four seventy-four."

"I don't think he has phone service where he is," the operator said.

"This—is—his—daughter. I'm calling from Israel."

There were some clicking sounds and then ringing.

"Hell*ooo!*"

A smile bloomed. "Hi, Papa, how you doing?"

"Dynamite on wheels. I have my own clothes on, and Fran is coming soon, sneaking me a Swiss-cheese sandwich."

"Are you comfortable?"

"Yeah, I was just reading." The weekly Bible portion, read on the Sabbath. "It talks about God commanding the Israelites to get revenge against the Midianites. It's at the end of the forty years in the desert. It's kind of brutal. I never noticed before that God says 'Thou shall *surely* take revenge,' not just 'take revenge.' "

I looked out the window at the Old City. The night was lightless, no moon, no flicker of stars. "How are your tests going?" I asked.

"So far, the medicine hasn't done anything. They woke me up in the middle of the night. I was dreaming I was in Jerusalem walking past these shops and something was shaking me—a nurse was waking me up to take my blood pressure."

I tried to blot out the image of my father in a hospital bed. That was what had hurt about the shooting so many years before, confronting the reality that my father was vulnerable. As a child, he was the only one stronger than the monster in my closet. At night, he sat on the side of my bed, tucking me in, all around the edges. His voice carried me safely through the dark as I drifted. I would close my eyes and listen to his Bible stories. My favorite was Queen Esther, who hid her identity from her husband, the Persian king. When the king signed a decree to kill the Jews, she told him she was a Jew. Suddenly the king saw Jews as human beings. The political became personal. His love for her saved the day. I always wondered—could that story be true?

Now my father was the one lying in a bed. A hospital bed. What could I say to comfort him?

"My father had heart trouble," he said. "Grandma too. She used to call it 'pumpitations.' I have a little arrhythmia. Like when you see a boyfriend, and your heart skips a beat, only it skips and loses control."

Palpitations. The shooter's house came back into my mind. "Dad, what did the Midianites do that was so bad?"

Just then, I could hear a man and a child singing outside my apartment. I said good-bye to my father and opened the front door. It was Hal, holding Michelle's hand and carrying Eva on his shoulders.

Hal had taken Eva to the spot at the Western Wall where my father liked to pray, close to the stones, alongside the Vishnitzer

Hasids with their fur-brimmed hats. Eva was gabbling about the men she saw wearing porcupines on their heads.

Friday evening at the Western Wall with the victim's grandchild—Hal had scorned the shooter more than any of my scheming had. He had done it without trying.

HAL WENT HOME to New Haven. My father, out of the hospital, soon arrived with Fran. One morning, he joined me and Baruch at the kitchen table while Fran was taking a shower.

"You see," he said, pointing to an article on the front page of the newspaper: A Palestinian had stabbed an Israeli settler to death. Settlers called for revenge. "They say they'll settle up with the Palestinians, but not on an individual basis."

My father knew that I was interested in stories about collective revenge. He did not know why; I had not told him that I had found the shooter's family.

Baruch mentioned a settler who was brain-damaged by Palestinian stone throwers. "His friends said when a war breaks out, they're going to kill the guys who did it. They know where they live."

"Yeah," my father said, getting up from the table to get dressed. "But then they'll go inside the house and meet the family. It's not so easy. They'll see the little children and won't be able to get revenge." He walked down the hall, his words trailing behind him. "It's very easy to say you're going to kill people until you meet them."

He opened the bathroom door a crack. "Fran, what should I wear?"

"Whatever you want."

"But don't you want to be twinsies?"

I sent a smile across the table to Baruch, who was smiling too. I whispered, "Do you think they really targeted him?" Both the mastermind's and the shooter's families had said they had. "How could a terrorist group target my dumb old dad?"

"To you he's just your dad, but to Palestinians, he's a big Jew from America."

"You've got the Australia T-shirt laid out," my father was saying to Fran. "I'm wearing Nantucket. So we won't be twinsies. Should I change?"

Just then our doorbell rang. A hand reached through the bars of our front window, into the living room. From the kitchen, we could see the hand, cupped and tendony. A beggar. A regular, known among the neighbors for her weepy tales. One week her daughter was sick; the next, her daughter was dead; the following week, the same daughter was sick again.

"No," Baruch said, pushing back his chair, uncomfortable.

"Sorry," I said. "Sorry, sorry, sorry," until the hand withdrew.

My father, walking back into the kitchen in his Australia shirt, looked at us, surprised.

"I usually give money to the first beggar I see in Jerusalem. I have a dollar." He took out his wallet. "It's from Mommy." He had seen my mother at a birthday party for a mutual friend. She gave him a dollar for charity, turning his trip into a good deed, helping to safeguard him.

My father went out the door, holding his wallet. I followed him. The beggar was moaning to a neighbor, "My daughter is sick." She was a large woman, with full-lidded, enveloping eyes. She was speaking Hebrew, but wore the long, embroidered dress of a Palestinian.

"Is she Israeli or Arab?" my father asked, walking toward her.

"Arab."

He hesitated, ten feet from her. "Should I give it to her? She's an Arab."

An Arab. Did he blame them all? Were Arabs a moral collective?

"It's up to you," I said.

He took out a dollar and looked at her, crinkling his eyes at the corners. Our neighbor was telling the beggar to go away.

"Well, I always give to the first beggar I see," my father said. He stepped forward, "Excuse me."

The woman turned around in a heavy sweep, spotting his dollar. She burst into tears. "My daughter, she is sick." She plucked the bill from his hand.

As we walked back to the house, my father shuffled a bit, embarrassed. "Tell Mommy," he said.

Back in our kitchen, Fran was chatting with Baruch. She was pretty in a way that was startlingly like my mother. Wavy brown hair, elegant nose, optimistic eyes. They had the same way of launching themselves into the day. People often mistook them for sisters. In fact, they had met in the dorm at Barnard College. When my father's best friend, also a rabbinical student, was looking for a date, my mother had introduced him to Fran. He died twenty-five years later, leaving Fran a widow the same month my mother left my father. It was natural that my father would gravitate toward her. He once described their union as "two souls in the dark, finding each other."

My mother liked to joke, "I got Fran both her husbands."

Fran was a chemistry teacher who brought common sense to the Blumenfelds. Neither dreamy, shallow, repressed, or scattered, she did not deny the injustices of life, but she did not dwell on them, either.

A few days into their stay with us, my father and Fran rented a car and drove to Caesarea, a beach town with an ancient Roman amphitheater. I came with them so that I could interview a member of a kibbutz that was on the way. As my father drove north I asked Fran about his injury.

"Oh, yes, you can feel the scar with your finger," she said, touching her own scalp. "There's a little ridge there."

Then I asked about wanting revenge.

"Inherently, life is unfair," she said, puncturing my mission with a single phrase. "If you accept that, then you don't have vengeful feelings. My first husband died a terrible, painful death. Was that fair? No. My father always told me, the good subsidize the bad in life."

I knew that she was right; revenge was immature. Only children were animated by an absolute sense of justice. Only a child would say with simple conviction, "But it's not *fair.*"

"Dad," I said, leaning through the break between their seats. "Look for Kibbutz Ein Horesh. It's coming up on the right."

The kibbutz member I wanted to interview was a seventy-eight-year-old woman. Decades before, she had participated in an act of collective revenge.

"I'm trying to figure out if it's ever considered OK to get collective revenge," I said to my father and Fran.

I told them a story about a man from the Qashqui tribe in Iran. The man wanted to avenge his brother, who was shot by a peasant. The man got revenge by shooting another peasant, the first one who wandered by. Asked why, the man shrugged: "Well, they were both peasants."

My father seemed to be only half listening. He was driving past strip malls, reminiscing about how they used to be orange groves.

"So what I'm saying is," I continued, "does revenge have to be against the exact person who hurt you? Can you ever punish someone else?"

Fran said, "The Palestinian who shot your father must've felt that someone had done something horrible to him. So he shot someone else. That doesn't make sense." She kept her eyes on the road, watching for the sign. "If we followed that logic, everyone would be running around with guns, shooting people."

Soon Fran found the turnoff. The road to the kibbutz wound past cows and bales of hay. We parked and walked among the trees, breathing air grained with fresh mud and chicken feed. Israelis had founded kibbutzes as utopian societies. This one in particular was known for its pacifism. There were no roads, just sidewalks for strollers and bicycles. The only sounds were the sputtering of water sprinklers outside the members' dining hall. A single bird called from a branch.

"Here I am!" A woman stepped from between the trees. She was small and solid and pumped our hands. Her gait was strong, her posture erect. She wore glasses and a long dress blooming with white flowers. This was Vitka Kovner, raised in the Polish town of Kalisch.

Vitka now worked as a child psychologist. During World War II, she lived in the forests of Lithuania, blowing up railroad tracks. At the end of the war, she helped organize a revenge plot against the Germans that, had it been successful, would have made her one of the biggest murderers of all time.

"I'll make some coffee," Vitka said as we crossed her porch. "Americans like coffee, yes?"

"Cold water would be wonderful, thanks," Fran said.

It was hard to swallow the water without thinking about Vitka's revenge. She and fifty other Jews called the Avengers had conspired in 1945 to poison Germany's water. Nuremberg. Hamburg. Weimar. Munich. Berlin. The goal was to slaughter six million Germans, one for every Jew slaughtered in the Holocaust.

"After all these years," my father asked, "do you still feel it was a good thing?"

Vitka squared her shoulders as if testifying, not for a judge, but for posterity. "It was a cruel and cataclysmic plan. But at the time, I thought it was right. It answered the need to return blow for blow."

We were sitting in Vitka's living room, paintings and poetry books crowding the walls. In the middle of the room hung a literary award honoring her husband, the poet Abba Kovner. Abba, who died in 1987, had been the leader of the Avengers. He had described Jewish victimhood as "lambs to the slaughter." He also had proposed a response, the water plot, known as "Plan A." Abba procured the poison. Vitka had delivered messages, money, and supplies, coordinating Avengers in Italy, Israel, Austria and Germany.

"As a psychologist," Vitka said, "I think it's good to get revenge. It's not good to be helpless and oppressed."

The last time Vitka saw her family was the day Germans corralled the three thousand Jews of her town into a church. Vitka, a teenager then, pushed open a window and escaped. The other Jews, for the most part, were shot, burned, gassed, clubbed or starved to death. Her mother died in the Treblinka death camp. One brother was killed in the Majdanek camp; another was killed by a Polish partisan.

"When we met camp survivors in striped uniforms, I felt a terrible rage. I felt if we don't get revenge, the world will do it again. We didn't want to kill individual Germans. I had no impulse to get revenge on any specific person."

"Even the German who killed your mother?" I said.

"Because he killed my mother, I should kill him?" She looked at our faces, waiting for one of us to nod. "No. He probably killed a hundred other people too."

The Holocaust, the Avengers reasoned, was a collective evil. An entire population had collaborated to make it happen, and so the revenge should be collective, as indivisible as drops of poisoned water.

Another Avenger named Joseph Harmatz had led the team that infiltrated the Nuremberg waterworks. He had told me in an interview, "I would ride the train and look at the Germans and think, 'For now you live, but the day will come, and you'll be dead.' And the German children? We thought only about our dead children."

Before the Avengers could carry out Plan A, Abba Kovner was detained while transporting the poison. He sent a message to Vitka, "Arrested. Proceed with Plan B."

Plan B was a plot to poison the bread fed to Nazi SS officers awaiting trial, held in American barracks. An Avenger named Leibke Distal worked undercover in a bakery that served the prison camp in Nuremberg. On April 13, 1946, with help from other agents, he painted a gray mix of arsenic and glue onto the bottom of loaves of black bread.

"After we completed a thousand loaves, we kissed each other and continued," Leibke told me. "I didn't think about anything. Not about my murdered parents. I just thought how more SS officers should die—and I kept on brushing."

In her letters to other agents, Vitka referred to the poison as "medication." For the Avengers, half-starved orphans and refugees, revenge had a healing effect.

"The day of Plan B was a happy day, strange to say," said Vitka, offering us a plate of poppy seed cakes. "I felt we accomplished something. To kill the way they killed us."

The Avengers claimed to have tainted three thousand loaves

of bread, which, divided into four pieces, would have poisoned twelve thousand Germans. It was never clear how many, if any, died. Historical records contradict one another. The Associated Press reported that American medics had pumped the stomachs of 2,238 Nazi prisoners of war who suffered from arsenic poisoning.

"However many SS were killed, it wasn't enough," Vitka said.

As she spoke, there were breaks in the conversation while my father translated the Hebrew for Fran. During one of them, I brought up the subject of guidelines. It was obscene to compare any aspect of Vitka's experience with mine, but I was interested to hear what she had learned about collective revenge. "I'm writing about people who make their own justice," I said.

For the first time, Vitka looked as though she had tasted something sour.

"But that's criminal. Only criminals do that." Her fingers bent at the knuckle, driving poppy seeds into the cake plate. "We're not criminals, we're people of ideas."

She got up to look for napkins. My father whispered to Fran, "That's going overboard with an idea."

"What about the Arabs?" my father called to Vitka.

"It's a different issue," she said as she returned to her seat, tucking her flowered dress neatly under her legs.

"But when terrorists kill Jews, shouldn't Jews strike back?" he asked.

"How would it help us to kill Arabs? With Germans, it was the fact that they dehumanized us. They turned Jews from people—not even into cats but into ants, who had to be sprayed. The dehumanization was what made me want revenge."

Vitka would have a lot to say about the right conditions for collective punishment, I thought. I brought my pen close to the page. "So when should you take collective revenge?"

"Never."

Surprise crossed my face.

"You should never take collective revenge," she said. "The

Holocaust was a unique event that demanded a unique response. Collective punishment is primitive."

She made the sour face again. "It's backward. Biblical."

THE ATTORNEY GENERAL of Israel rose from his dining room table and reached for a Bible. We were dinner guests of Eliyakim Rubenstein, a classmate of Baruch's from Harvard Law School. He had asked about my research. I told him that I was learning about collective punishment.

He set down his spoon beside his bowl of chicken soup and opened the Book of Ezekiel.

" 'The fathers have eaten sour grapes, and the children's teeth are set on edge,' " Rubenstein read from chapter eighteen, his voice booming like an old-time prophet's. " 'As I live, saith the Lord God, ye shall not have occasion any more to use this proverb in Israel.' "

In this passage, Ezekiel, one of the later Hebrew prophets, introduced a new standard of justice: Every person would be held accountable for his own behavior. The position of the Bible, and of many ancient cultures, had been that moral responsibility was collective. God punished all the Israelites with exile. Moses smote all of the Egyptians with the plagues. Abraham convinced God to spare Sodom and Gomorrah if ten innocent men could be found—"Will you sweep away the innocent along with the guilty?"—but he stopped at ten because even Abraham had a sense of collective guilt.

Reading from Ezekiel as his guests blew on their soup, Rubenstein tutored us on a pivotal moment in the evolution of punishment. Individuals would be judged for their own deeds. Democracies thrive on this principle of individual rights and responsibilities. They discourage collective revenge because a person's position reflects what he alone has done. Modern Israel stands among those democracies, although it makes exceptions.

"What about when the government blows up houses the terrorists live in?" I asked.

"Go ask Ezekiel," Rubenstein joked.

Baruch laughed respectfully, then shot me a look. *Objection. Indelicate line of questioning.*

"Seriously," Rubenstein said, "the terrorists live in those houses, and the family often knows what they're doing."

When Israeli soldiers had arrested the shooter, his family had told me, the soldiers sealed the house. Twenty-four relatives moved into tents until they found another house to rent. Eight years later, the Palestinian Authority blowtorched open the doors.

In an odd coincidence, I wrote about the reopening of homes in 1994 for the *Post,* during the first days of Palestinian self-rule. I visited so many sealed houses in the Ramallah area, they blended together in my mind. The shooter's brother Saed said he remembered my face. He said he saw me taking notes as they tore off their welded doors. Maybe I had. I checked my article. It described another family:

> Neighborhood men bring chisels and picks. Women pass around Turkish delight and trays of lemon soda. The matriarch is hugging everyone, planting wet kisses on their eyes. . . . The moment is too full of promise to keep them back. The girls hold hands and run up the stairs. The doors are open now.

Collective revenge was an extreme option, especially for me. The year after the shooting, when I graduated from college, I had volunteered for a program called Interns for Peace. I lived in a Palestinian village for a year and helped organize get-togethers between Arab children and their Jewish neighbors in Israeli towns. I hoped that if the children played together, they would stop seeing each other as the enemy. The Arabs and Jews would get to know each other as individuals and become friends.

I never had been enthusiastic about collective identity. And what I really needed now was not a collective, but the shooter. "So, are you thinking of pardoning any more prisoners?"

"No, that was last month's trend," Rubenstein said dryly.

Recently, the attorney general had granted amnesty to some Israeli prisoners. If he pardoned the shooter too, he would be free, for me.

If not, I would have to find a way inside. "I want to interview a security prisoner. Do you think I could?"

"Very unlikely," Rubenstein said, his diction turning crisp. "We don't want to give them publicity. What did they do to deserve an interview?"

"Only bad can come of it," said Rubenstein's wife, with a smile that signaled the end of the conversation.

"So, who decides?" I pushed. I could not help myself. As attorney general, Rubenstein could visit any prisoner. And here he was, sharing a pot of soup with me. Looking back, it is hard to believe that I asked the state's top legal official for help. But by then, I already had compromised myself with Israel's military chief of staff and the prime minister. Ethics? Professionalism? I was nearly too far gone to care.

"You can try the prime minister's office," Rubenstein said vaguely. "But I would leave it alone."

Baruch nudged me under the table.

"Eat your soup," he said. "It's getting cold."

"TONIGHT FRAN LEAVES and we can get down to business," I wrote in my notebook. My father would stay for a few more days.

That evening, Baruch went to a friend's house for dinner. Finally, I would have some time alone with my father.

"I have some stuff to show you," I said. I approached him, lightheaded with uncertainty. He might approve. More likely, he would not.

I told him that I had found the mastermind and the shooter. They were in prison in Ashkelon.

"Ashkelon?" my father said. His associations were of sand dunes and of Samson. "I was going to go look at the archaeological ruins down there. I didn't know there was a prison."

He was not as surprised as I had been. Nor was he disappointed—as I had been—that the gunmen were in jail. I handed him the picture of the mastermind.

"This guy with the sunglasses looks like a tough cat," he said. "Like a truck driver or a—uh—terrorist."

"And here's the shooter when he got arrested." A photographer had snapped the shooter outside the police station. "Look how young he is."

"He's young, but he has wild eyes." My father felt for the top of his head. "He looks like an intelligent person. Like a university student who has powerful ideological motives."

"Exactly right," I said, impressed. The shooter was in college, his mother had told me. "He had finals that day. He took an exam in the morning and tried to kill you in the afternoon."

My father laid the picture on the coffee table and put his feet up next to it. "I'm just wondering how this guy got involved with those other guys." He yawned and checked his watch: 10:30 P.M. Time for his situation comedy.

While my father watched his show, laughing out loud at the jokes, I went into the kitchen. In the back of a cupboard, I had hidden the bag of wafers from the mastermind.

My father came in during a commercial break.

"Would you like some chocolate wafers?" I said. The bag crinkled in my hands.

"Nah, I'm trying to watch my weight," he said.

The phone rang.

"Hi, sweety-pie dolly darling!"

My mother.

I took the phone into my room to talk. My mother and I spoke nearly every day, though I never told her that I was pursuing the shooter. In a few weeks I would see her. Bernie had rented a beach house in North Carolina to celebrate my mother's sixtieth birthday. She asked Bernie to fly me in as her birthday present.

I could hear Bernie in the background: "I'm jealous. You talk to Laura more than you talk to me."

"My sweet little boy is walking away with his head hanging down," my mother said. "I have to give him a kiss."

After we said good-bye, I found my father in the kitchen poking around the cupboard. A cup of coffee he had just made sat steaming on the counter.

"Got any cake?" he said, with a sweet, caught smile.

"No. Well." I avoided his eyes. I picked up the silver bag. "I have these yummy chocolate wafers."

The wafers were a gift from the mastermind. He had given them to his family to give to me when I visited the prison. I had saved the wafers because I wanted to use them, in my own unhinged way, to undermine his intentions. He wanted to kill my father? I would sweeten my father's evening with his chocolate cream–filled wafers.

Ha! I thought as my father bit the wafer. *It's true, revenge is sweet.*

My father opened his mouth to speak, still chewing. He looked sheepish: "Did Mommy complain that I'm staying at your house for too long?"

"What? No." This was his moment of triumph. Why was he talking about *her?*

"I still don't understand why we broke up," he said.

He was leaning against the counter, swallowing the bite. "I was brought up with loyalty. When you're playing ball, you do whatever you have to for the team. I was raised during World War Two, when you'd risk your life for the country. You didn't abandon someone. That's the problem with divorce. If you have rough times in a marriage, you work it out, you don't abandon it. I know she was unhappy with me for being bossy. But go down the list of our neighbors—a gambler, a womanizer, an alcoholic. Our problems didn't compare to their problems. They didn't abandon their marriages. We had a beautiful family for twenty-five years. We were always there for each other. Then I get shot and she doesn't care. How do you understand that?"

My heart was sinking. I had to get him to stop.

"I hope this isn't stressful for you to talk about the shooting," I said, moving us into the living room. I put the bowl of wafers on the coffee table.

"It's not stressful, it's interesting," he said, taking another bite. "Now I have faces to see. They're people now."

"Did you talk to someone about it, someone professional?" I said.

"Yeah, I did, but I can't remember who." Munch, munch. "Oh, wait, it was the guy me and Mommy were seeing. The marriage counselor. He said I was fine."

"Do you ever touch the scar?"

"I think if I touch it, it hurts. So I don't." Munch, munch. "That might be psychological, though."

I counted the number of cookies left in the bowl. He had eaten two and a half so far. I felt ashamed and foolish.

"Aren't they good?" I said.

"Um, yeah." He sounded doubtful.

A few minutes later, Baruch walked through the door carrying a plate from his friend's house: chocolate fudge pie, caramel cheesecake, peach cream torte. My father appraised them with the eye of a man who had bought high and sold low.

I leapt up and hugged Baruch.

"I thought you were sick and couldn't come." Baruch wriggled free. "How can you be jumping around?"

Then he saw the bowl of wafers.

Later, as we undressed for bed, Baruch closed the door and lowered his voice. "What are you tricking your dad for? He's the victim."

"It's not a trick." I took off my shoes and pitched them into a corner.

"Maybe your dad didn't want to eat the wafers."

"He had to, it's his revenge. He just didn't know about it."

"A *chocolate cookie* is revenge?" He took off his shorts and folded them. "Next time you're mad at me, eat a cookie and we'll call it even."

"It's symbolic revenge. The mastermind loves control and this was totally out of his control." I knew that I was wrong, that I was going to lose. I clamped my hands on my hips, defiant. "In church a wafer can represent God, so why can't a wafer represent revenge?"

"That's not revenge, that's contrived, silly girl."

"But it's something. I did something." I tapped my collarbone in congratulations. Yes, it was contrived. Revenge *is* contrived. It is enjoying the illusion of control, playing God. Many rituals were contrived, I said. "Tossing rice at a bride isn't contrived? You have to think symbolically. You have to have imagination."

I followed him to the bathroom.

"Silly. Period. Silly. I have nothing more to say about this," he said, and closed the door.

I stomped back to the bedroom, resenting him for being right, angry at myself for being so self-dramatizing, so much of the time. I stubbed my toe on something hard under the bed. I reached down. A black, plastic cylinder. I had bought it from a vendor outside Damascus Gate the afternoon that I came back from the Ashkelon prison. A toy machine gun.

I got into bed and pulled a pillow over my head.

The next morning, I woke up with guilt in my stomach, a feeling that congealed like grease as I came to. "Daddy?" I said, wandering into the kitchen. He was an early riser. "Dad?" The house was quiet.

What if those things I fed him were poisoned? Guilt, more than fear, drummed the thought around my temples. I walked through the living room to the window. I pushed open the blue metal shutters.

"Hey!" The voice came from outside. "You almost knocked my eye out." I opened the door and there was my dad, smiling in his Nantucket T-shirt. He was carrying a bag of sesame rolls from the market.

We went into the kitchen and got out a jar of apricot jam. He handed me a roll. "Are you ready to continue our talk?" I said.

"Shoot away," he said, pulling up to the table. "Let 'er rip, kid."

Then I told my father everything, everything, that is, except for the part about the chocolate wafers. I told him about the mastermind's militant relatives. Riding with them to the prison. Driving up to the shooter's house on the edge of an abyss. Finding out that the shooter knew English, that I could try to sneak a letter to him.

I spoke for half an hour, flushed from the reliving that comes from retelling. I picked at the crust of my roll, making a flurry of crumbs.

"Whoa. Isn't that incredible," my father said, rubbing his cheeks. "You put yourself in dangerous situations."

I expected that reaction. What followed, though, surprised me.

"But you know, there's a little bit of *g'neyvat daat*"—"stealing knowledge"—"in what you did. You're not allowed to do that." His tone was instructive, not scolding. "It says 'Don't steal' in the Ten Commandments and it says 'Don't steal' in another place in the Torah. So why does it say it twice? Because you're not supposed to steal objects, and you're not supposed to steal a person's mind—like deceiving them. *G'neyvat daat* is when you try to benefit from the information people give you, and you're not telling them the truth. It's when you sucker someone. Even to the point of going into a store and asking a price when you have no intention of buying."

Baruch joined us at the table, noting my crumbs with a flicker of disapproval.

"At some point you have to be honest," my father said. "There's a point when you have to have a sense of decency."

My neck felt warm, a rising pang of guilt. I knew that I was being manipulative with the families—the shooter's and my own. That knowledge hummed like a stinging insect in the back of my mind.

"It's OK what you did so far," my father said, softening. "But to write letters to the guy, that's *g'neyvat daat.*"

For the first time, Baruch spoke up. "Don't you think it's OK to deceive a terrorist who tried to kill you?"

"He's serving time for the crime. That's the punishment," my father said. "Actually, I feel worse for the family. They gave her all this information. Imagine how they'll feel when they learn the truth. It's *g'neyvat daat*—even with an enemy."

"I think there's a difference between the family and the shooter," Baruch said. "In law enforcement we often deceive criminals."

"You do?" I reached over and touched his hand. This was Baruch's way of making up, I hoped.

"Sure, we send in undercover cops."

"Maybe you're right," my father said. He tipped his head from side to side like a scale balancing weights. "OK, it doesn't matter if you deceive a criminal. He's a killer, and you're the daughter." He nodded, growing more certain. "You have a right."

I told my father that the shooter's family visited him every other week. Political prisoners were not allowed to send or receive letters. They used them, prison authorities said, to direct terrorist attacks on the outside. Even so, the family offered to try to smuggle my letter.

"Do you want me to ask him anything?" I said.

"Yeah, ask him why he didn't shoot me a second time." He closed one eye, focusing his thoughts. "And I'm curious why he wanted to kill me. A man wants to kill me for being a Jew? What is it about being a Jew that you're sentenced to death?" He glanced around the table like he was about to give away a secret. "I hate to go into the New Testament and the Christians, but there's collective guilt against the Jews."

This was where my father and I disagreed. I did not assume that he was targeted for being a Jew. Two of the other people shot by the gang—the German tourist and the British pilgrim—were Christians. But he had grown up during the Holocaust. For him, the attack was part of the general, collective punishment of Jews.

"I once had a knife put up against my stomach in high school," he said. "I was in New York, at One Hundred Eighty-fifth Street and Amsterdam. We saw five guys heading in our direction and we were three guys. They were drunk, staggering around. We didn't wear yarmulkes in public back then; we used to put them in our pockets. But they could smell a Jew. One guy pushed me against the wall. He held me with one arm and put a knife to my stomach. I could feel the blade push against my skin. I remember thinking, It's not cutting me yet, maybe it's a dull knife. He breathed in my face: 'You son of a bitch. You killed Jesus! I'm going to kill you.' Two thousand years ago, and the guy acts like he heard about it this morning. I looked across the street. Herb Gross was getting punched around. The third guy got away and ran to Yeshiva University. He burst into the study hall, where they were studying Talmud, and yelled, 'We're being attacked!' A guy named Green led the pack. He was a short, skinny guy with his yarmulke flapping on his forehead. He was carrying a board, part of a desk he wrenched free from the study hall. Ten yeshiva boys were charging down the street. And the drunk guys ran."

Once again, a memory had animated him—he was twisting his mouth like a drunk, throwing air punches, thrusting a finger to lead the charge—more than the shooting ever did.

"The point is," my father said, "these guys are ready to kill a person walking on One Hundred Eighty-fifth Street in Manhattan. They're not even mugging me. What money? What wallet? I'm condemned to death because I'm a Jew. Why? Because I killed Jesus. Why is there a death sentence on David Blumenfeld's head, some guy from Newark, New Jersey, who killed Jesus?"

This talk of collective revenge on the Jews struck me as irrelevant. In my mind, the shooter did not shoot "a Jew." He shot my father.

My father must have read the impatience in my fingers as I rolled bits of bread into dough balls.

"Look, I don't want revenge," he said. He let his statement hang over the table, between us. "My revenge is that I'm alive and I keep coming back here."

He looked out the window to our flowering vines. He addressed a face visible to him alone: "You think you're going to have a victory, killing a Jew? In your face, I'm coming back." Then he looked at us, his voice upbeat again. "You have one shot at life. It's great to be alive. It's not all about the Holocaust and suffering and 'The world is evil.' You have to believe the world is good."

"How can you believe it's good if you were almost killed twice?"

"Their way to mend the world is terror. They solve problems by blowing up people. I don't condemn him for the fact that he wants Palestine. But killing doesn't work. What does? Strengthen yourself and your culture. I think it's marvelous that people are studying Jewish books. I don't look for any other revenge."

"Even though he's not sorry?"

"Look, I don't want to shoot this guy. If they gave me a gun and said, 'Here, take a shot,' I wouldn't want to shoot him."

"You wouldn't even want to graze his head?"

"No, no, no!" His voice was rising.

"Why?"

By now, we were yelling and waving our arms. Neither of us was angry—that was our style—cloudbursts that cleared.

"What good would it do?" my father said. "He's an ideologue, the most dangerous kind of killer. I don't think he would stop being an ideologue because I grazed his head. I would give the gun back. I'm not a person with a gun. I was a chaplain in the army. I used to give character guidance lectures. I wouldn't even say 'I could kill you,' because I couldn't kill anybody—unless someone killed *you,* God forbid."

The sun was tilting against the window, heating up the room. The light burned the back of my neck. I needed a break. Here I was, trying to avenge my father, to be our family redeemer, and no one would play along.

"I feel bad for his family," my father said. "His mother may hang up his picture and say she's proud. But in her heart, she would rather have him home, married with children. When you reach my age, all that ideology goes out the window. Where is her son? In prison. She sees her other sons running around with kids. Ideology isn't worth it. A family is."

Baruch sat there quietly, a hand under his T-shirt, cleaning out his belly-button lint, thinking, He's noodging us already to have a kid.

MY FATHER WENT BACK to Fran, to America. I went back to the shooter's house. I was returning articles about the shooting that I had borrowed to photocopy. I asked my taxi driver to wait while I ran inside. Imad, the beautician brother, led me upstairs. We sat in the shooter's room, on a couch where the shooter had slept.

"His head was here, his feet were here," his mother said, brushing the upholstery with her fingers.

"He used to study here too," said his father.

The mother sat beside me, her feet falling out of her slippers. The shooter's black attaché case was on her lap. Years ago, she had given away his clothes, but she kept his papers in the case. "It's all karate, karate. We're sick of karate," she said as she clicked it open.

A karate poster rolled out. A karate manual. A picture of the shooter, in karate costume, kicking. A black belt certificate from 1979. (He wore his black belt to his trial.) The mother began digging through the rest of the pile: a Koran, a book called *The State and Revolution* by Lenin, Shakespeare's *Measure for Measure.*

"He was at the University of Bethlehem, studying English," Imad said.

"And business too," said his mother. "He got a ninety-five in public relations."

There were report cards, his birth certificate from the Mount of Olives, and a high school certificate: "The school administration certifies that Mr. Omar Kamel Said Al Khatib was a student in 1980–81. His conduct was very good."

Imad clucked his tongue, pleased. "Omar is the educated one of the family," he said.

I dipped my hand into the pile of papers and came out with a British Council library card. It had expired the month before the shooting.

"He's civilized, not a thug," he went on. "Murderers are people who are ignorant. People who struggle for their country are enlightened."

A child began to cry in the other room. Dogs were barking outside. Imad's manner was as mysterious as ever, his face unreadable. Unsure of what to say, I coughed. I looked out the window into the cracked, parched ravine. The sky held the sun straight down the middle. For weeks, I had been thinking about collective revenge, but now that I was finally inside the shooter's home, resting on the couch that had cradled the shooter's head, all I wanted to do was run.

"I have to go," I croaked. "Thank you. I'm sorry. My taxi won't wait."

I hurried down the raw cement stairs. My driver, a Palestinian, was yelling at a German shepherd. We drove off, along the ravine, up the alley. The dog ran howling after our car.

"Wait!" a boy cried, chasing us too. "Wait! We want a ride to Jerusalem."

"No, let's go," the driver said. He pressed the accelerator.

A little girl scrambled after the boy, waving at us to stop.

"Just a minute," I said.

The driver grumbled and backed down the alley. As we rolled backward, dust clouds blocked the rear window. Our bumper scraped against a cement wall. An older man, his head wrapped in a red-checkered kaffiyeh, walked slowly toward us. I opened the back door, and the little boy and girl jumped in next to me. The man eased in next to them. I looked over the children's dark bangs at the man. It was only then that I recognized him, the small, tapered nose, the bony face, the tattoo on his thumb. The shooter's father.

We rumbled up the hill. *The shooter shot my father.*

"So where do you know English from?" I said, my spine rigid.

"From school."

"In Jerusalem?" *Am I supposed to shoot him now?*

"No, I'm from the West Bank, Khalkilyah. My wife is from Jaffa," he said. "We're visiting Omar in prison tomorrow. He told me he wants to see you."

"Yes?" The small talk was excruciating. Every light along the way turned red. "And how is Omar?"

"Good," said the little girl. She was going to visit him too.

"Do you know English?"

She shook her head no.

"In English, *salaam* is 'hello,' " I said in Arabic.

Finally, we reached my stop at the Hebrew University. I paid the taxi fare. The father wanted to go to Damascus Gate, ten minutes farther down the road, but the taxi driver refused without extra pay. He asked the old man and the grandchildren to get out.

I handed another ten shekels to the driver.

"You want to tell Omar anything?" the father said.

"Oh, well, *salaam.*"

The Arab taxi snaked down the road, the red kaffiyeh in the back window fading to black, taking with it the idea of collective revenge. I was not going to do it. I never even came up with a plan.

Collective revenge misses the whole point of revenge. At its cathartic best, revenge focuses diffuse rage on a specific, guilty party. Taking revenge on any other person turns its moral purpose upside down. Stripped down, it is a fancy word for terror. Terrorists believe that there are no innocent bystanders, that all people of a kind are guilty, even civilians. That is how they justify killing children.

During my father's visit, we had watched news footage of rescuers dragging bodies from the American embassies in Kenya and Tanzania. A Saudi dissident named Osama bin Laden wanted to attack America, and his followers had blown up the embassies killing 224 Americans and Africans, and wounding thousands of others. Innocent lives shredded, collective punishment.

My intentions were not violent, but they were not kind. I would aim them only at the shooter. I walked into the university, through the security checkpoint, where a guard searched my bag—everyone's bag—for bombs.

AMERICA RETALIATED for the embassy bombings. Missiles targeted a factory in Sudan and terrorists camps in Afghanistan. Newspapers referred to it as a "reprisal." Headlines announced the expected response from the other side: "Bin Laden Promises to Avenge Bombings: Alert in the United States," "Wave of Revenge Attacks Threatened Over Bombings," "Bin Laden: Muslims to Take Revenge."

Baruch and I soon left Jerusalem for the Outer Banks of North Carolina, where we biked and windsurfed and built sand castles, doing the things that people do when they are living in the moment, when they forget about revenge.

"Isn't this fun? Are we having fun?" my mother said repeatedly.

In a lonely moment, I called my father. He said, "I hear children. Who else is there?"

Everyone but you.

One muggy afternoon, my mother and I sat outside on a wooden deck overlooking the Atlantic. The waves were nudging a flock of sandpipers up and down the shore. I took out my notebook and asked her about the shooting. She nestled into her lounge chair as if it were naptime.

"What do you remember?"

"I was in a hotel room in Hawaii," she began, "and you kids called and said that Daddy had been shot and that it creased his skull. I realized that you kids must have been really shaken up if you called me all the way in Hawaii. I remember thinking that you guys were overreacting."

We looked at each other, waiting for the other to speak. Whatever I might have wanted to say, I held back. I was a journalist, an observer.

"That's all I remember. That's it." She laughed drowsily. "I was glad that he was fine. Bernie and I were having fun. Around then we decided to make a commitment to get married. It was a very happy time."

"Did you call Daddy?" My voice sounded sour following hers.

"You know . . ." She leaned her head back and stared at the clouds. For a moment her eyelids fluttered. "I don't even remember. I have so little to say about it, I'm falling asleep."

There was a knock behind me, knuckles on the glass door, coming from inside the house. My mother perked up and blew a kiss over my shoulder.

"Who's that?" I did not turn around.

"Bernie." She said his name as if he were her six-week-old kitten. "You know, I haven't a clue why you're writing about this. I would never think of revenge as part of your gestalt. You're such a darling, thoughtful person."

She patted the wooden arms of her chair. "If you were actually going to find the guys who did it, I'd be extremely concerned about you. I'd call Daddy and we would talk you out of it."

I was about to close my notebook, when she added with a sideways smile, "Want to hear my revenge story?"

I frowned, skeptical. She was too happy for revenge.

"I'm going to go to Jake Shain's funeral," she said.

"What?"

Jake Shain was alive and well. He had been the head of the cemetery committee in my father's old congregation and had led a faction of congregants in a synagogue power struggle. My father, the rabbi, had tried to make peace, and ended up enraging him. I was too young to understand the politics. All I knew was that Jake Shain, a fat man with hair plastered to his skull, did not like my father. In my child's imagination, he became the monster in my closet. He had a jack-o'-lantern mouth and eyes that sank like wormholes when he grinned. I slept with my closet door open because of him.

"Why would you do that?" I said, amazed.

"Because he threw Daddy out of his job. And he threw our family out of our home. The worst part about it was how hurt Daddy was. And it hurt all of us. Our whole family. So I vowed I would go to his funeral one day."

"And what'll you do?"

"I wouldn't laugh out loud, because he had a nice wife and children, but I would sit in the back and have the quiet pleasure of being there."

Bernie stuck his head outside. "Norm, where's the bread?"

"In the fridge." Her voice lifted for him. Then it fell back, dull and angry. "I think Daddy was much more hurt by Jake Shain than by the jerk who took a potshot at him in the Arab market. It was a much more terrible injury. Because it was an attack on him personally, and on his work, an attack on his essence as a rabbi. The shooting was an anonymous shot that missed. What Jake Shain did to Daddy was a direct hit."

"Isn't it strange that both of our revenge fantasies are about Daddy?" I said.

There was something unsettling about her story. A problem. A clue. Some secret meaning tucked inside the narrative, and all I could see was its tail.

"Jake Shain did more than hurt Daddy," she said. "We had to move out of our home. He hurt you. He hurt Hal. He hurt our whole family. Maybe that's the key about revenge."

The key?

Her words came quickly and unfiltered in a rush of discovery: "Maybe someone who attacks your family merits revenge. Someone who hurts your family, that's really a bad person. Someone who throws you out of your home—that's a person who deserves revenge."

The tail again, I could see it. And now it was twitching. A person who hurts your family, she had said, deserves revenge. I was startled by what she was implying, though she seemed unaware of it.

"That's very interesting," I said.

"What's very interesting? I'm falling asleep." She smiled lightly, closed her eyes and drifted away.

7

DIVINE VENGEANCE

ATHENS, GREECE

OUR CONVERSATION in North Carolina was troubling in ways that I was not willing to confront, at least not directly. My father's pain, I still believed, had not been addressed. But it was more complicated than I realized. I had vowed to get back at the person who hurt my dad; I was not sure, anymore, that I could.

What if I left revenge to divine forces? Even if it was a false exit, an artificial deus ex machina escape from insubordinate characters and an unruly plot, anyone's God seemed like the way out.

Now, Baruch and I were lost in Athens traffic, trying to find the road to the Temple of Vengeance. We had a half-day layover before our flight back to Israel. I wanted to visit Rhamnous to see the ruins of a sanctuary from the fifth century B.C., where ancient Greeks had worshiped Nemesis, the goddess of revenge. Nemesis was a daughter of Night, depicted with the face of a beautiful girl, feathered wings and the claws of a lion. Mentioned in Homer and Hesiod, she embodied retribution for evil deeds.

There were advantages to divine vengeance, and I was eager to consider them. Gods get the job done. They do not agonize or make mistakes. People judge actions. God does too, but He also can see into the heart of a man. In the Hebrew Bible, in Deuteronomy, and in the New Testament, in Romans, God said, "Vengeance is mine, I will repay." Revenge is not evil, God seemed to be saying, rather, revenge is too delicate for humans to do right. From the time of Cain, the first murderer, God tried to limit human revenge. God put a mark on Cain, threatening sevenfold vengeance on any person who avenged Abel's death. In Islam, one of Allah's ninety-nine names is al-Muntakim al-Jabar, the "Greatest Avenger." A Muslim who relies on Allah instead of taking revenge himself is rewarded.

The directions in our guidebook to the Temple of Vengeance looked easy: take the Neo Makri-Marathona road, turning right toward Kato Souli. A quick, thirty-three-mile ride northeast of Athens.

We had not counted on the signs being in Greek.

Baruch shouted a request for directions to the driver next to us, who replied in a flood of merry Greek. We kept looping around helplessly onto the same wrong road. When we rented our car, a gust of wind had shattered the windows of the agency, sending tourists from Waterloo, Iowa, to the emergency room. Then a forest fire closed the main road out of town. We never would make it to Rhamnous and back in time for our flight. I did not care, but Baruch looked at his watch and said, "I'm turning around."

As he steered into a U-turn, I slunk down in my seat. "I wanted to pray at the Temple of Vengeance."

"Yeah, right, and you have a golden calf in the trunk of the car."

"No, really."

"What? I assume you're joking. That's heretical. That's idol worship."

"Oh, what's the big deal?"

"Believing in a goddess? You're a polytheist?" His fingers tightened around the wheel. "Do you know how many Jews died so they wouldn't have to pray to a goddess in a Greek temple? All it takes is one bow to an idol."

"It isn't an idol, it's a god." And not my first choice either. Nemesis just happened to have a Doric temple. The avenging spirits that really intrigued me were the Furies, or the Erinyes, the guardians of parents' spilled blood. They so terrified the ancient Greeks, Heraclitus wrote, "even the sun will not transgress its course," for fear of them. It was the Furies who hounded the Greek hero Orestes with whips and burning eyes. Orestes was caught in a revenge dilemma: he wanted to avenge his father, but his mother was the guilty party. Honoring one parent meant hurting the other.

Baruch looked uninterested in the details of Greek tragedy.

"Sorry, but this is outside the realm of 'I'm OK, you're OK,' " he said, changing lanes so abruptly that we were honked at on three sides.

"Well, whatever works."

"We already know—idol worship doesn't work. It's the first commandment: 'God is our Lord.' That was the whole reason Judaism came into being. The one thing we've persuaded the world is that multiple gods is ridiculous. My wife's going to worship idols? She's violating the Ten Commandments? Why don't you commit adultery too?" His thigh muscles tensed beneath his shorts. "Why don't you break all Ten Commandments while you're at it?"

In all our disagreements, I never had seen Baruch react like this. Baruch took religious law more seriously than I did. He observed the Sabbath laws; I did not. "Why are you so upset? I didn't say I'd do it. I was just thinking about it." It was just a fantasy.

"But the first commandment is the only purely thought commandment."

Better not tell him what else I was thinking.

I had been reading about revenge in Polynesia. When a Polynesian sorcerer wanted to get back at a man, he stole something connected with him—nail clippings, a lock of hair, some earth dampened with his spit—and cast a spell over it. On one of the islands, the sorcerers used scraps of household paper. I had this idea, one of my more clownish schemes, to take the tissues that I had swiped from the mastermind's house and bring them as a kind of sacrifice.

Baruch saw a smile skim across my lips.

"I don't think this is funny," he said. He pulled the car to the side of the road and drew me into focus. "I have very fixed ideas of what's right and wrong. There are certain fundamental beliefs. I would hope that my wife—"

"Your *wife*?" Now it was my turn to huff. "It doesn't bother you that your wife is obsessed with revenge, that I refuse to forgive? That doesn't bother you as long as I'm not breaking your commandments?"

"They're your commandments too."

And he looked so sorry, I was sorry too.

WE LEFT ATHENS for Jerusalem, and I began looking for my own God, for the things that made Him hurl lightning bolts. We arrived in Israel on the eve of the Jewish New Year, Rosh Hashanah, also known as the Day of Judgment.

"Man is judged on the New Year," says the Talmud, "and his fate is sealed on the Day of Atonement," or Yom Kippur, which falls ten days later. During this period, God presides over a heavenly courtroom. He considers every person's behavior over the previous twelve months. Then He decides who gets hit by a car.

In the month leading up to the holiday, life in Jerusalem is infused with self-consciousness. People stop themselves from gossiping. They blow rams horns every morning like an alarm clock for repentance. Bus drivers remind squabbling passengers that Judgment Day is near. On talk shows, political enemies who have sniped at each other all year ask for pardons; God only forgives those who forgive each other.

On the eve of the holiday, as the sun turned the Old City walls deepening shades of pink, my father called to wish us a happy New Year.

"Also, I wanted to ask for your forgiveness," my father said, suddenly formal. "If I did anything wrong to you this year, or if I said anything to hurt you, I'm sorry."

This is an annual ritual, prescribed by the rabbis, that always made me squirm.

"You didn't do anything wrong, but, yes, I forgive you." Then I was supposed to reciprocate. "And do you forgive me for anything I did to you?"

A neon chocolate wafer blinked before my eyes.

"Of course," my father said.

It was the time of year to petition the Divine Avenger. One evening I asked Baruch, as we crossed the street, "Do you really believe God decides your fate for the whole year?"

"I don't know," he said cautiously. An oncoming car beeped at our shadows. "But it's helpful to act like He does. It forces you to think about being a better person."

We were walking through Mea Shearim, a tightly packed neighborhood of alleyways and mossy walls and God-fearing Hasids. Women wore black scarves knotted over shaved heads. Men rushed about in long black coats, as if they were forever late for prayers.

We had come here to watch a medieval ritual called *kapparot,* performed during the Ten Days of Penitence. *Kapparot,* as a form of repentance, is one of the ways, along with charity and prayer, that a person can avert God's evil decree. Divine vengeance is punishment for disobedience, or sin. *Kapparot* cancels sin.

Rounding a corner, we came upon hundreds of Hasids, their faces pale against a darkening sky, murmuring and swinging chickens over their heads. Children were chasing the chickens that had escaped. Workers in plastic aprons were pulling the animals from their crates. Customers spread the chickens' legs and thrust them into the workers' faces, asking, "Is it a male or a female?"

Women were swinging hens; men were swinging cocks. A husband circled two birds over his pregnant wife's belly, one of each sex, covering all options. A British couple, the only other foreigners, wrinkled their noses and held up their chickens with a handkerchief. In England, they said, the ritual fowl wore diapers.

As each person hoisted a chicken by its crusty legs, he repeated a chant three times, announcing the transfer of his sins: "This is my substitute, my vicarious offering, my atonement. This cock shall meet death, but I shall find a long and pleasant life of peace." Any divine vengeance intended for him would be reassigned to the chicken. Then its throat would be slit and it would be given to the poor.

Kapparot is a kind of Jewish voodoo, a scapegoating ritual. Scapegoating is the twin brother of revenge: the person who deserves punishment is replaced by someone else. The Aztecs of Mexico used human scapegoats to appease Xipetotec, their god of pain, with human sacrifice. Jews offer chickens as stand-ins because in Hebrew the word *gever* means both "cock" and "man." (My father, like many modern Jews, substitutes eighteen dollars for the chicken and gives it to charity. Eighteen, in Jewish numerology, symbolizes "life.")

"I'm afraid I'll get pecked," Baruch said as a worker held out two screaming birds. Neither of us had performed this ritual before. Taking pity on us, the worker found two plastic baskets to hold the chickens. A Hasid handed us the prayer.

We retreated to a corner, away from the trampling feet and the screeching of damned souls. I looked at my hen through the square openings of the basket, a white, skinny bird with a beak like dried corn. She was quiet and quivering. The lights from the slaughterhouse shone in her eyes.

"It's going to die for my sins?" I said.

"Uh-huh," Baruch said, lifting the basket over my head. He began circling it three times.

"Like Jesus?" I said to needle him.

"Will you let me concentrate? Otherwise I'll get henpecked."

I mumbled the prayer, feeling less like someone cleansed of sin than someone committing a new one. A feather dropped from the basket onto my head.

THEN CAME THE Day of Atonement, or Yom Kippur, the most somber day of the year. From sunset to sunset Jews would fast, wear no makeup, jewelry or leather, abstain from bathing and from having sex. No planes flew, seaports were closed, land border crossings were sealed. An apocalyptic, eerie air overtook the city.

On the holiday eve, the radio was dominated by news of a Hamas bomber who accidentally blew himself up as he was fitting his car with explosives. Then at 2 P.M., Prime Minister Netanyahu delivered a radio address, signing off in a sad voice: "I know very well, I know *very* well, the pain of losing a loved one. We are still a country surrounded by hostile nations, struggling to survive." Then there was silence. The radio and television would not broadcast until after the holiday.

That evening, we walked to the Great Synagogue, where Israel's chief rabbi preached. Baruch gave me a gift, a prayer book inscribed: "To my beloved wife, So that we may pray together for a year of forgiveness and understanding." I apologized to him for being impossible. He joked that God had paired him with me as divine retribution for mistreating past girlfriends. We entered the crowded sanctuary, and he was swept up into the service. Restless, I went out for some air.

The synagogue sat on the city's busiest street. Every store and office building was shuttered. The only things moving in the pale pink lights were children from nonreligious families, bicycling down the middle of King George Street, their voices resonant in the silence. I turned into a pedestrian mall, deserted except for a street sweeper leaning on her broom.

Another form approached. A Hasid floated up the hill in a white holiday robe, worn to invoke the purity of angels and the gravity of a funeral shroud. He talked to the street sweeper and then moved on. As he came closer I could see he was a plump man in his twenties, with big feet and little teeth, and a rambling, light brown beard. He wore a round fur hat, a prayer shawl, and was holding a prayer book.

I wondered what he was doing out of synagogue.

"Excuse me," I said. "Who are you?"

"I'm a messenger."

I was surprised that he answered. Hasids do not talk to women in public. But this man—Mattityahu was his name—was sent from the Sanz Hasids as a messenger to wandering souls.

"Can I ask you a question?"

"Of course," he said.

We began to walk uphill, past the empty cafes. A light breeze brushed back his earlocks.

"I wanted to know, does God take revenge on his people?" Odd as it sounded, the question was not unusual for Jerusalem.

"Ah, it's called 'revenge,' but it's not really revenge." God's revenge is more like a parent punishing a child, he said.

I looked up at a pharmacy and recalled a recent terrorist bombing. Rescue workers had found a scalp blown on top of the pharmacy's red and white sign.

"Do you remember the suicide bombing here last year?" I said.

"Yes, I was standing nearby, at the bank machine."

During the first week of school, a group of fourteen-year-old girls were walking here, shopping for textbooks. Three suicide bombers erupted in a fireball. The blast killed five people, including two of the girls, and wounded 190 others.

"Did God do that to punish people for their sins?"

"Oy," he said. "It's complicated." He started to tell me about a vagrant and a rich man, a folktale that explained why the good go unrewarded and the bad unpunished, a mystery as old as the suffering of Job.

"OK," I said, cutting it short, "but if someone did something wrong, don't I have to pay them back?"

"No, you should forget it."

"But what if it wasn't me who was hurt? Someone hurt my father."

"God is up there right now deciding who will be punished. You can't get between God and your enemy. Let them fight it out."

"But how can I be sure God will punish him?"

"Because it's the truth."

"How do you know?"

He exhaled, *pssssh,* the sound of air from a punctured tire.

"Well," I said. "Am I allowed to at least pray that God take revenge?"

Omar Khatib, the shooter, a member of the Abu Musa gang, on the day of his arrest, 1986.

Omar Khatib, 1997.

Ala-din Bazian, the mastermind of the Abu Musa gang, 1997.

Omar Khatib's brother, Imad, center, with his parents and daughter in their home in Kalandia, the West Bank.

Suraya Khatib, Omar's sister-in-law and family with me during one of my visits to their home.

Tom, the shopkeeper, in his souvenir store in Jerusalem's Old City.

(*Left to right*) Brigit, Isolde and Hermann Raith at their home in Munich, Germany. Isolde was wounded by a member of the Abu Musa gang on the Via Dolorosa, 1986.

Isaac Ben Ovadiah pointing to a picture of his wife, Zehava, who was murdered in her office by the Abu Musa gang.

Paul Appleby, the British tourist who was killed by a member of the Abu Musa gang as he sat outside the Garden Tomb.

(*Left to right*) Sam, Liz and Julian Marsh, Paul Appleby's adopted family in Portishead, England.

My father, David Blumenfeld, visiting me in college shortly before he was wounded by Omar Khatib in the Old City.

My family in 1966. (*Left to right*) me; my mother, Norma; my brother, Hal; and my father, David.

My mother in fall 1998, when she accompanied me on a reporting trip to the Sinai Desert.

My friend Rachel with her newborn baby boy in the hospital.

Baruch Weiss and I shortly before our wedding, in 1997.

Grand Ayatollah Abdul Karim Musavi Ardebily, formerly Iran's chief of the judiciary. He now runs a seminary in Qom.

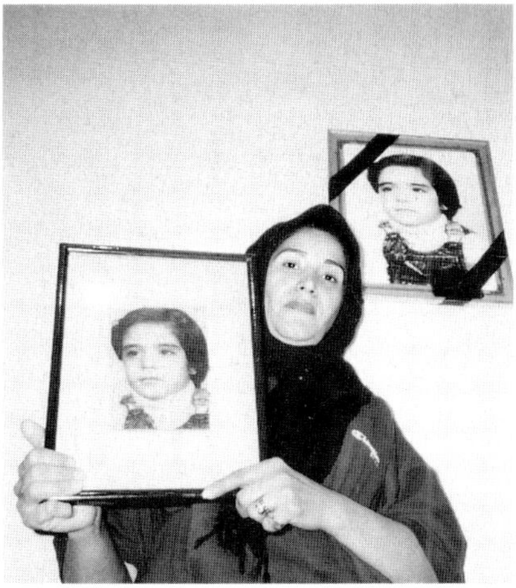

Nahid Najibpoor, in Tehran, Iran, holding a picture of her murdered daughter Arian. According to Iranian law, Nahid can get revenge by executing the killer if she can pay his blood money.

Me on the street in Qom, Iran.

Mark Pashko Malotaj, one of six members of the provincial Blood Feud Committee, in Baldre, Albania. The committee advises the 12,000 inhabitants of the region on issues related to revenge.

Moaz Jabari, a Palestinian from Hebron, the West Bank, who saw his father killed by a Jew and was haunted by dreams of vengeance.

Maytal Khatib, a Druze teenager from Ein Al Assadd, Israel, who was strangled by her brother to avenge their family honor.

Vitka Kovner outside her home on an Israeli kibbutz. In 1945, to exact revenge for the Holocaust, Vitka took part in a plot to poison the German water system.

Rafi Eitan, one of the Mossad agents who, in 1960, kidnapped Adolf Eichmann, architect of the Nazi's Final Solution.

Anez abu Salim of the Arayada clan, and the Tarabin Hasablah tribe. Hashish smuggler and ringleader of hundreds of Bedouin smugglers in Sinai, Egypt, he got revenge on his unfaithful wives.

"You can't ask God to hurt someone. Maybe he'll repent."

"No, he definitely doesn't regret what he did."

"Not last year. But maybe next year. You can't ask God to destroy your father's enemy." His eyebrows rose like a scholar divining a new reading of an old text. "He may turn out to be someone your father cares about."

WHEN THE HOLIDAY was over, when God's judgment was done, I did what I often did that year when I felt lost. I went to the Old City alleyways and lost myself. The labyrinth led to David Street and Tom's souvenir shop.

I found Tom outside his store, his gold chains glinting, his black curls shining like patent leather. He sat hunched over an eggplant crate, playing cards with another shopkeeper. It was easy to imagine him there, witnessing my father's shooting.

"How are you?" I said.

"Existing." He extended a foot and dragged over a stool. "Sit down."

Tom scowled into his cards. He licked the corners of his mouth. I sat quietly, the purpose of my visit hanging unbalanced between us. Maybe he thought I was lonely or weird, or fascinated with him. Looking back, in a sense, all three were true.

I tried to sound clever.

"Kill any tour guides lately?" I said.

"Not yet."

He folded his hand of cards. The other shopkeeper emitted a dull, victorious snort and retreated to his store. I took out my notebook to resume our interview, which, over the months, had evolved into the life of Tom.

"I tried for ten years to make the marriage work," Tom said. "We had a daughter and I started coming home late, playing cards. After another year and a half, I have another baby. I make it with her like animal work, not love."

He tapped my knee to be sure I understood.

"She is always shouting, always blaming. The same shit. I sleep on the couch, sleeping in her bed is sleeping with snakes. No divorce. How will it be for the children with divorce? Even if she is stupid, even if she is dead, just a body lying in the house, at least she is the mother and not divorced."

"And you're OK?" I said.

"It's not like I'm hungry and the only thing I can eat is cheese." He tapped my knee. "I have a girlfriend from Alabama. She's Christian."

I had noticed that Tom's English was improving. His American girlfriend worked in a Jerusalem body-waxing salon.

"Are you a Jew or a Christian?" he said.

"I'm learning about all three religions. Islam too."

"I'm born Muslim. I learned Christianity from my girlfriend. In Islam everything is from God—good and bad. In Christian, I learned a better thing. God gives us good. The devil gives us bad. There's no punishment from God, according to Christians. I like this."

Finally, an opening. "Do you think God punishes you?"

"Maybe."

I thought I saw him wink. It was hard to tell in the market's filtered sunlight.

"So your religion says . . . ?" I asked.

"My religion is not to hurt people. I'm well known in the market for helping people." He raised his right hand as if taking an oath. "I was sitting in front of my shop, eating watermelon seeds, and one stuck in my throat. I couldn't breathe. My friends didn't know how to help. I said, 'Now I'm dying. My children will be sad and will bury me.' Then I fell over."

He paused, waiting for my face to arrange itself in awe.

"When I woke up I said, 'What happened?' My friends said a tourist did the Heimlich maneuver and disappeared. My girlfriend said maybe it was an angel. But I want to see this person. He saved my life."

"How do you imagine him?"

"He'll be my height and educated. He won't mind that I'm an Arab. Maybe he's a Jew. He'll be the same as my personality, he'll just help someone in trouble . . . how do you call it in English?"

"A Good Samaritan?"

"Yes. I owe him. Maybe God will pay him back."

Maybe God paid Tom back?

"In my people," his voice dropped so low I had to move my stool closer, "if someone is hurt, if it's a Jew, they won't help."

I kept writing. Now he was going to admit to witnessing my father's shooting.

"Once I was driving out of the gas station," he said, instead. "I was upset about the wife. A car came zooming and I have accident. The side of the car was crushed. I have my shoulder gone out of its place and cracked two spines. My face pressed against the steering wheel."

He pointed to the scar that ridged his forehead.

"I couldn't move or talk, but I could hear." His voice thickened. "I heard people say, 'Leave him, he's Jewish.' "

"Why did they think you were Jewish?"

"The car was a white Ford Fiat, new Jerusalem plates." Israelis drive Fiats. "My brother accidentally passed and rescued me. The people said, 'Leave him, he's a Jew.' He said, 'Get lost. He's my brother.' I understand if someone doesn't want to be friends with a Jew, but to see someone in an accident? It's very sad and very bad." As he spoke, he leaned closer.

"Do you remember a man shot here, in the market?" I said.

"Did I tell you I remembered?" He pulled back.

"We talked about it. There was a man shot."

"An Arab?"

"A foreigner."

"I remember a stabbing, a Jewish man on a bicycle."

I started to insist, "a shooting," but he was too absorbed in his own story: "Maybe it was for my good. It's the opposite of when I choked. When I choked, the man who saved me knew I was Arabic. He didn't think if I am Christian, Muslim. Like when you have feelings . . . what do you call it? Human manners. The people who left me to die have no manners."

"What would you do to those people if you saw them?"

"I would spit in their face and say shame on you."

"Why not just walk away?"

"If me shut up, and you shut up, and he shut up, how we change? I won't change the world alone. But if everybody say something about a wrong, we can change."

"What if they say they're sorry?"

"I will not accept it." His lips shivered around his cigarette. "They just sorry they're caught. They're just sorry I'm an Arab."

He looked at me long enough to see something off in my expression. I was thinking about the symmetry between his story and my father's. Two men who needed help, abandoned. It reminded me of God who meted out retribution measure for measure. Tom saw my father hurt and did not help; the same thing had happened to Tom. If you believed in divine vengeance, Tom had been punished.

He puzzled over my face, his nostrils flaring with concern. "Are you on the board?"

I did not understand. "What's 'on the board'?"

"Sorry, I mean—are you on edge?"

FOR MONTHS I had avoided ministers and church, and all things Christian. The Christian message, from the little I knew, was one of forgiveness; I thought it might compromise my resolve. But I could not omit the Christian God from my divine search. So I packed my New Testament and walked through the Old City, out St. Stephen's Gate. I crossed a valley to the Church of All Nations at the foot of the Mount of Olives.

The church stood inside the Garden of Gethsemane, where Jesus spent his last night in agony.

"People come here and realize it's not a fairy story," said Father Edward Dillon. We sat inside a dark, domed room. Over the door hung a figure of Jesus nailed to a cross. "There was a girl, an Italian stewardess, she came here and finally decided to make her confession. I let her tell her story. She wept and wept."

The friar crossed his legs beneath his habit, and rotated his sandaled foot. "We sat right here, in fact." He folded his hands over his Bible. "So, what brings you here?"

To confess—to cry? I pictured the Italian stewardess, sitting on the couch where I now sat, her mascara leaving wet, grainy trails down her cheeks. The urge to confess was both frightening and seductive, a giving up and going numbly under. Father Edward impressed me as a kind man, tall and rangy, with a sculpted, ageless face. He was from Long Island, the grandson of Irish immigrants. There was something appealing about confessing to him, to leave revenge behind inside this dusky room. Secrecy and deceit had separated me from the people I loved and from the part of me that was lovable.

All along, while I considered different plans, I struggled with two competing impulses. The first was an expression of anger—shake the shooter and scream. But what kind of revenge was that? And my second plan was even less realistic. I wavered for a moment, going over my second plan. It was an impudent girl's dream, borrowed from my father's bedtime story of Queen Esther. But I could not let the Esther idea go. Not then, and maybe never.

"I'm interested in revenge," I said finally, all doubt scrubbed from my voice.

"Giving forgiveness is godly. Getting revenge is ungodly." He adjusted the collar on his habit. "It's a sin."

"A deadly sin?"

"Well, let me see." He counted on his fingers. "Pride, covetousness, lust—that's, you know, erotic stuff—anger, gluttony, envy and sloth."

"So it's not deadly?"

"Sometimes it is. It's deadly for a marriage. When I do weddings I say to the couple, 'I'll tell you what marriage is all about—it's a whole series of forgiveness.' "

"But what if, say, someone did something bad to your sister?"

"My first reaction would be anger. But I wouldn't attempt to get even. It wouldn't make me even. It would make me guilty."

I thought of a group most deserving of revenge. The Nazis. I told him about Vitka Kovner and the Holocaust Avengers.

"Oh, what a naughty thing to do," he said. "Oh, my. I understand how they felt, but I don't approve. God would have taken care of the Nazis."

"How do you know?"

He patted the Bible on his lap. "It's in Revelations."

The Book of Revelations talks about the hour of God's judgment, when the wicked will be punished in a lake of fire.

"I'm afraid I have bad news for you," he said. "The human race is not getting better, it's getting worse. Man has thrown aside all restraints. Even war used to have a certain dignity, World War One had its class. On Christmas Day, all the guns stopped."

He turned the Bible facedown on his knees, then turned it over again.

"I felt it when I first came here," he said. "It grabbed me from inside, a sense of evil hovering over the land. It's a dark sort of feeling that the Evil One is trying to discredit God and prevent Jerusalem, the city of peace, from having any peace. It's Satan's way to show Him up by fanning the flames of hatred and revenge."

Behind the friar's head shined a table lamp, the only light in the room. It gave his quiet words a backlit intensity. "Eventually, God is going to say, Enough. And he'll come and end it all."

"And then?" I said.

"The end of the world. The Last Judgment."

In the New Testament, the "day of vengeance" was God's final reckoning. Jesus spoke of it farther up the slopes of the Mount of Olives, not far from where the friar and I now sat. The Book of Matthew describes the "son of man" or a king sitting on a throne, judging the nations, separating souls like a shepherd divides sheep from goats. The righteous people will go to the right, to eternal life. The wicked ones to the left, to everlasting fire.

Many religions promise a future divine judgment, one that will finally set things right. They offer a theological exit from the puzzle: Why do good people go unrewarded and bad people die unpunished?

Because God will get them later. The Vikings believed evil people went to an icy hell where a goddess, with green rotting flesh from the waist down, made them vomit. For many Buddhists, Hindus and other believers in reincarnation, a wayward soul is condemned to an endless cycle of rebirth. The Gallinomero tribe of native Americans believed bad people returned as coyotes.

Divine vengeance evolves with the needs of its dreamers. When I asked Sheik Ikrama Sabri, the chief Islamic cleric of Jerusalem, about Allah's revenge, he said, "The land we lost to the Israelis, God will give to us in heaven." In his weekly sermon at the Al-Aksa mosque, he promises disheartened Palestinians, "The revenge of Allah is near."

Medieval Christians were perhaps among the most creative in their rendering of hell. Those who had indulged in the seven deadly sins would be elaborately tortured: For pride, you were tied to a wheel and grilled over a fire. For envy, you were dunked in ice water. For lust, you were singed with hellfire and brimstone. For anger, you were dismembered. For gluttony, demons forced toads, snakes and rats down your throat. For ambition, you were boiled in oil. For sloth, you were tossed into a snake pit; every time you escaped, the demons flung you back.

I was not sure why medieval scholars drew such vivid pictures of hell. I wondered if it was because forgiveness was their only choice as good Christians. They channeled vengeful feelings into dreams of the afterlife. Other religions condemn revenge too, but then riddle it with loopholes. In Islam and Judaism, restraints on revenge apply largely between believers. On nonbelievers, revenge often is tolerated, if not encouraged. Christianity set itself up as the religion of mercy, separating itself from Judaism, the religion of justice.

"You have to forgive, because Jesus forgave," Father Edward told me. "Even on the cross, Jesus said, 'Forgive them, Lord, they know not what they do.' "

All this he said reflexively, like a prerecorded message. Then he leaned forward and spoke in an urgent whisper, as if the words were escaping from a crack inside.

"I used to say when I was a kid"—he raised his fist—" 'they did *so,* Jesus.' It was always inside of me, They did *so* know what they were doing! They hated you, they knew they wanted to kill the Lord."

For a moment he was young and angry and stinging to do something about it. Then he let out his breath and slumped back. The lamplight shadowed his eye sockets, making him look older than his seventy-one years.

"But Jesus forgave them anyway. It's in line with my faith," he said. *Forgive them, Father.* "But it goes against my grain as a human being."

IF DIVINE REVENGE was going to be my exit, I needed to find it quick. This year was perhaps my last chance before I disappeared—like my mother, father and brother had—into the forgetfulness of another family.

One way to speed up the process was through a human intermediary. In the Holy Land, there were catalysts for divine revenge, people who could bring down hell.

I visited a mystic, Yossi Dayan, a snake-eyed Cabalist, with peppery breath and bristly gray hair who had put a death curse on Yitzhak Rabin. Three years earlier, he had stood outside the prime minister's home and recited an obscure Jewish prayer called a *pulsa denura,* or a "scourge of fire." "God killed Rabin—divine vengeance," he said. "I was just the messenger."

Yossi was a settler who believed that Yitzhak Rabin was making too many concessions to the Palestinians. The curse he cast on Rabin called for his death within thirty days. That month, a fanatical Jew shot the prime minister.

"I expected Rabin would die, but not by a Jew," said Yossi. "I would've preferred that he go to synagogue on the Day of Atonement and have a heart attack."

Yossi was sitting at his dining room table in Psagot, a Jewish settlement of 230 families overlooking Ramallah. Like other Jewish enclaves in the West Bank, Psagot evoked a surreal mix of armed conflict and serenity. A ten-foot electric fence, a concrete bunker and Israeli soldiers guarded the town. But once inside children wandered by themselves among flower beds, dropping their bicycles on the sidewalks unlocked.

Yossi lived in a small apartment with his Tunisian wife and six children. He was born in Mexico City, worked as a Hebrew-Spanish translator of holy texts. The books filled the room with the sweet smell of decaying paper. He was surrounded by religious objects, a Hanukkah candelabra, Sabbath candlesticks, all coated in dust that blew across his balcony from Ramallah.

"I want to learn about divine vengeance, but I can't interview God," I said, getting right to the point.

"You can interview God through his emissaries," Yossi said, his dark eyes fluttering with modesty.

"After Rabin died, I went to the dentist for a filling. He was afraid to treat me. The dental hygienist told him I have the power to curse."

"Can you tell me the basics?"

His shirtsleeves rolled up, he began his lesson, flicking and tapping his pen as if it were a magic wand. "When you curse, be specific. Not just 'Have a bad life.' Mix in famous curses from the Bible. Killing someone is just one option. You might prefer to limit it to sickness or poverty. And don't forget, there are dangers to cursing. If God doesn't like the curse, it'll come back and hurt the curser. If you curse someone to grow old fast, maybe your wife's hair will turn white. If you curse someone's business and he doesn't deserve it, your business may fail and God may make him win the lottery."

"If someone shot my father and I wanted to get revenge, could I curse him?"

"Yes, if you pray, something should happen to the gunman. But then you have to do something. You can't rely on miracles."

"But how does an ordinary person curse?"

"All you have to do is feel it. If you really want something bad to happen, you don't need a manual." He said with the patient enthusiasm of a fourth-grade teacher, "Let's try an exercise. Make the request you want most."

"To have a child."

I gulped. Why did I say that? I was supposed to be a he-man avenger, and instead I had wished for a baby. Lately, Baruch and I had been talking about having children. I wanted a family now; he wanted to wait. In his reasonable, measured way he listed five problems he wanted to work through. In my impatient, roiling way, I stamped around the kitchen and slammed the refrigerator and said that if we waited for things to be perfect, we would waste the rest of our lives.

The mystic, meanwhile, smiled at my answer.

"A child?" he said. "I promise it will come true. But why didn't you ask for a good child? You might have a child, but he's not healthy. Or he's healthy, but a troublemaker. Don't just wish for any family. You want a good family."

That prompted my next question. "What about putting a curse on a parent?"

"You can't curse your parents."

"Are there any excep—?"

He cut me off with a wave.

"Never. No matter what. Honoring your parents is a commandment above all else."

Yossi reached for his pack of Marlboro Lights. "Let's go outside. My wife doesn't let me smoke in the house."

We walked out to his mangy backyard and peered through his barbed-wire fence. Ramallah stretched out below us, the rooftops wrapping the horizon. "See that antenna?" he said. "That's Arafat's headquarters." I knew that the shooter's brother Saed worked there.

"Until we kick out all the Arabs, this nation won't be safe," Yossi said.

I looked at the mystic looking down at Ramallah and decided that I did not like him. Not that he was rude or overbearing. In fact, when I sneezed he said, "God bless you," three times, which from him might amount to something. But curses, hexes, sorcery, black magic—if you believed in them—struck me as a coward's way out.

They demand no showdown with the enemy, no risks. Which is probably why they are so popular.

In almost any culture, you will find revenge voodoo. On one of my scavenger afternoons at the library, I opened a dictionary of Chinese mythology and turned to "Revenge": "The god of revenge is a straw man. A straw image of the enemy or the thief is made, and daily worshipped; needles are stuck in the eyes, blood is made to issue from the nose and ears, and the arms and body are pierced and it is confidently believed that this process will send pains, sickness and probably death on the object of hatred. The practice is universal in China."

Similar practices are common worldwide, especially in desperate places like the Gaza Strip. Crowded and poor, Gaza breeds superstition. People believe in spirits called jinn, or genies, who possess them, often as agents of revenge.

Shortly after visiting the Jewish mystic, I traveled south to Shajaeia, in the Gaza Strip, and spent time with Sheik Ziad Tatar, a genie exorcist. The sheik, a thirty-eight-year-old Muslim and the father of seven, ran "The Koranic Clinic to Treat Maladies by Koran." Inside a three-room shack with a green tin roof and plaid blankets for doors, Ziad treated people who believed they had been cursed.

"There are three ways to make curses," he said, standing in his open-air waiting room. "They can be drunk, poured on the steps of a house or cast over the hair or handkerchief of a person. Curses can be made of anything impure—cat's urine, dog's urine, rat bones ground up and mixed with water. One woman I know was jealous of her husband's second wife. She wanted him to love her more. She took her menstrual blood and cooked it into his rice. The magic worked, but there were side effects, and he got cancer and died. Sometimes the magic turns against the person because he is inexperienced."

Ziad had seven years of experience, dismantling curses using the anti-Satanic forces of Islam. He had a 60-percent success rate, he said.

"The genie inside a human body is like a mouse in a hole. When you pour water in the hole, the mouse escapes. The same thing happens when a genie hears Koran. There are antimagic verses, antienvy verses, antirevenge verses," he said, scanning the list in his appointment book. "Revenge genies usually separate a husband from a wife, make a person go crazy or have epileptic fits."

On the morning I arrived, several families sat in his waiting room. A pretty woman named Najat with a heart-shaped face was next. She was twenty-two years old, wore peach lipstick and black eyeliner.

"Why are you here?" the sheik said, ushering her into his treatment room.

"I have a problem," Najat said, squeezing her sister's fingers.

"In your stomach?"

"In my head."

Ziad placed his calloused hands on her head and examined her pupils. "A genie can live in the stomach, womb, chest, head," he explained to me. "Genies can fill up a space as big as a mountain but when they enter a body, they get compact."

Ziad had no more than a high school education, though his glasses, the pen in his breast pocket and the white shirt and pants all lent him a medical air. He asked Najat to lie on the mattress on the floor. A poster of Mecca hung over her, and a spray of ostrich feathers. Ziad propped open a Koran, like a tent, over her chest. He covered her face with a scarf and clamped headphones over her ears.

Sometimes, Ziad recited passages from the Koran over cups of olive oil and massaged the oil into a patient's neck and shoulders. If the patient had drunk a liquid that had been cursed, he had the patient swallow holy water and throw it up. The Koranic blessing would bind with the curse inside the patient's stomach, and the genie would be vomited out.

In Najat's case, he played Koranic verses to help establish a diagnosis. After a few seconds, Najat sat up.

"I feel a stone on my chest," she said. "When you touched my head, my throat tightened. When I heard Koran, I couldn't breathe. I feel the power of the curse in me."

"What kind of curse?"

Najat looked at her sister as she spoke: "We are becoming old. All our friends are married. And some have children too."

She breathed back tears. "Men come to our house to get engaged but they run away. A fortune-teller said someone cursed me. Someone cursed a jug of water and poured it on our front steps."

"Who did it?"

"Our cousins, when my brothers refused to marry their sisters. My cousins put a curse on me in revenge."

Najat's sister said, "We know we're young, we know we're beautiful, but we're cursed."

I listened to Najat and to the other patients. They described the kind of slights people everywhere might wish they could avenge: a woman who was dumped cursed her ex-boyfriend with impotence on his honeymoon; a woman whose son-in-law insulted her stew cursed him with insomnia; high school students who failed an exam cursed their teacher with diarrhea.

The sheik wrote out a prescription for Najat: "Make ten photocopies of ten verses from the Koran. Boil the paper. Wash the body and hair with the boiled water. Pour the used water outside the house. Repeat ten days."

"I tried that one, it didn't work." She crushed the strip of paper in her hand. "The revenge curse is very strong."

I HAD ONE QUESTION LEFT before I gave up on the spiritual world: What kind of people relied on divine vengeance?

Many interviews followed, in hotel lobbies, in rest rooms, on a pier while a reggae band played. I even attended an adult education class on forgiveness, trolling for people with grudges.

I came across three types of people: 1. the pious; 2. the devastated; 3. the weak.

The first type were a lot like Stefan Bialoguski, a thirty-three-year-old writer. Stefan had just moved into a new apartment in Sydney, Australia, when the music in the apartment downstairs began "vibrating the walls like a violin." He asked the neighbor to lower the volume. The neighbor blasted the music.

Stefan stamped on the floor and wrote to the tenants' association. The neighbor responded by turning off his fuses. "It was a primitive struggle, two guys marking territory. The only thing we didn't do was pee against each other's door."

Meanwhile, Stefan was becoming more religious. He knew revenge was wrong, but he could not stop thinking about it. He fantasized about dumping a can of schmaltz herring soaked in oil with strips of onion through his neighbor's ground-floor window.

Finally, Stefan moved out with help from a police escort; his neighbor sat on the curb drinking a beer while he loaded the moving van. Then Stefan noticed something else on the curb. The carpet that he had been dreaming of ruining was blackened and burned. The night before, the neighbor had fallen asleep while smoking and had set it on fire.

"At the risk of sounding like a pious git, I really do thank God," Stefan said. "When the whole thing came to a climax, I couldn't help but be struck by the similarity of what happened to my neighbor and my fantasies. My budding faith was vindicated."

The second type of person who relies on God for revenge is not necessarily pious. They were people who had been devastated, like Lilah Shamshashvili. The saddest moment I ever witnessed was the night Lilah said good-bye to her husband. Gabriel's body lay in the middle of their living room under a red velvet blanket. Lilah smoothed the red velvet one way and then the other, talking to him quietly in Georgian.

"Don't go, please," she said, stroking his arm. "I want to spend one last night with you."

Lilah and her husband, Gabriel, and their teenage son and daughter had emigrated from the Republic of Georgia three years before. One Sunday morning, Gabriel, a forty-three-year-old baker, boarded bus number 18 on his way to work. A suicide bomber blew up the bus, killing nineteen people, including Gabriel.

When I knocked on Lilah's door again, more than two years had passed. I waited, listening to the muffled sounds, to the slow, shuffling feet of an old woman.

Lilah opened the door wearing a black housecoat that made her pale skin look paler. Her eyes were puffy and half open, floating and aimless in the flat plane of her face.

"I'm thirty-seven. My heart is eighty-seven years old," she said, huddling near an electric heater, despite the mild afternoon.

A portrait of Gabriel smiled over the couch, a vibrant man with a Slavic face and dark, burned coffee eyes. A picture of their nineteen-year-old son sat on the coffee table. Lilah picked it up. "Every morning when he wakes up, his pillow is wet. He still cries."

I asked her if her sadness ever expressed itself as a desire for revenge.

"No," she said. "God will avenge my husband." There was doubt in her expression. She was not a religious woman. "God will punish them," she said, "if He can."

Sometimes, when an offense is so great, it is not possible, nor is it conceivable, to take personal revenge. Most often, people who suffer the worst crimes do not attempt revenge.

A question that came back to me many times that year: If my father had been killed, would I be contemplating revenge? The answer was probably no. I was not capable of avenging a murder. The crime was overwhelming. The criminal terrifying. That was one important lesson I learned about revenge. People often seek revenge for the smaller slights because they think it's possible to achieve.

It was the inconsequence of my father's injury that allowed me to entertain thoughts of revenge. It was a blow that I thought I could return. If my father had been murdered, I would have been too broken to do anything except, perhaps, believe that God would take care of his killer. And so the second type of person who believed in divine vengeance, the devastated soul, did not resonate with me. I was lucky—my father had lived.

The third kind of person who relied on divine vengeance surfaced in the most surprising place: The diamond district near Tel Aviv. Businessmen dominated the streets during the day, but women took over after hours, in a squat, windowless building, inside a lavender, perfumed haze.

Sixteen women greeted customers at the Paradise Club. They arranged themselves like confections on a pastry cart. The men could have their pick: a short blonde wearing platform shoes. A chubby young one in orange spandex. A redhead with feline eyes.

The first customer of the evening, a clean-cut young man in a blazer, chose Lucy. They retreated to a room with a narrow bed and a clock with a second hand. A two-hundred-watt bulb would flash above the door when he had used up his half hour.

After six minutes, Lucy walked out.

"That man has to learn not everything is permitted," Lucy fumed. "I don't give kisses above the neck. We don't make love here, we just have—you know. I told him a few times. He still tried to kiss me. I slapped him. That was the end."

In her native Russia, Lucy said, she had worked as an accountant. She knew the importance of balancing the plus and minus columns. Now she slapped her customers when they crossed her. And when they overpowered her, she settled accounts another way. In between her breasts swung an amulet. A rabbi blessed it and told her that as long as she wore it, God would hurt anyone who hurt her.

Lubia, a Christian woman from Kiev, heard Lucy talking about God.

"When I was seventeen, I was a virgin," Lubia said. "A friend's friend locked the door and raped me. He was very strong. I looked out the window and asked God to make justice. For three days, I was hysterical, asking God to punish him. Then he called and said he was sorry. I said, 'I won't forgive you. I'm right and God will judge us in the end.' Two years later, a policeman called and asked if I knew this guy. He said his address book had five numbers in it and one of them was mine. They pulled him out of the river that day. A current dragged him under. I thought God punished him. I felt guilty, but he deserved it."

I had not expected to find divinity in the Paradise Club. Later, though, Lucy and Lubia's faith began to make sense. God's role in the economy of revenge is to guarantee satisfaction to disempowered people. God is the last tribunal of a failed revenge. He is the One people turn to when they have no choice.

In my jumbled state, I had considered divine revenge. Let the All-Knowing One sort it out. Yet after months of trying, I could not believe.

I began to look for another way. One evening, I had dinner at the home of an English professor, a friend of Rachel's named Ellen Spolsky. Ellen had moved from New Mexico to the Old City.

"Simplify," she said at the end of the evening, standing above me on the stoop. "That's the secret to revenge."

I looked up at her. "Huh?"

"You can't think or analyze too much, or it messes up the straight line of fanatical thought. Look at what happened to Hamlet. He wasn't an avenger, he was a philosophy student." She gave me a hug. "Hamlet should have kept it simple."

As I walked out of the Old City, on a path fringed with rosemary, I experienced what felt like a revelation:

If I could simplify, block out glimpses of alternate villains, then I might be able to complete my task. Why complicate the plot? Hamlet failed at revenge because he complicated matters. He wanted to avenge his father but that meant turning on his mother. He talked about it for five acts, and his mother was killed in a mix-up and then he died. I had always found Hamlet a little irritating.

I would focus on the shooter and no one else. Reduce a complicated truth to simple justice.

8

SIMPLE JUSTICE

SINAI DESERT, EGYPT

FOR SIMPLICITY, there is no place like the desert. The landscape is reductive. Tan sand, blue sky, two blocks of color stacked on top of each other, one solidly below you, and one above.

I decided that I needed to simplify, to block out nuance. For inspiration, I traveled south to hear a simple story from a Bedouin. I had heard about him from a neighbor, who had heard about him while traveling in Sinai, where his revenge story was told as if it were a legend. A trip to see the Bedouin was the perfect expedition, stripped down and uncomplicated.

Then my mother came along and things got complicated.

"Put your seat belt on," she said as our jeep jostled off the road, turning into a windy canyon. "I don't want to lose you."

My mother was touring Israel with Bernie and a group of New York suburban friends. While the rest of the group went on a glass-bottom-boat ride in Eilat, an Israeli resort, my mother insisted on joining me at dawn as I crossed the Egyptian border.

"It's dangerous. You could get lost, or worse," she said. "You could get kidnapped by wild people." She would protect me, she said.

Now we were rumbling through a dry riverbed, volcanic mountains rising on either side. Our legs jiggled, our teeth chattered. There was no road, and even if there had been, the wind and sand would have erased it. We were looking for Ayn Umm Ahmad, an oasis in the southeastern reaches of the Sinai peninsula, where the Bedouin had an encampment. A young man from his tribe escorted us as a translator and guide; the route was unmarked to discourage outsiders. In two hours we passed few landmarks: a sluggish donkey, a widow sitting in thin shadows wearing a red mask, a camel skeleton reclining in the sand. An acacia tree sprang up here and there, the dust and sun silverplating its leaves. We picked up a Bedouin boy who was wandering on foot. My mother gave him a hard-boiled egg from her hotel box lunch.

"Wow, this is Sunday-school land," she said, gripping the brim on her sun hat. "All those years learning about Moses in the wilderness and here I am."

In the distance we could see a camel hoofing the ground.

"Look," my mother said. "The camel is dancing."

The camel's owner had chained its ankles. It struggled in a kind of tortured jitterbug, trying to break free. We got out and walked up to it to get a better look.

"Look at its teeth," my mother said, extending her hand toward its mouth. "The camel needs braces."

"Please be careful, Moron," our guide said. He had trouble pronouncing "Norma," reversing the letters. He took my mother's camera and told her to pose with the camel.

"Smile, Moron!" he said.

We climbed back into the jeep and lurched up and down the gullies, past a tinted cliff—a thin wash of red color over the stone. In our final approach to the oasis, we crossed a riverbed, the white mud cracked and dried in circles, like clay plates set on the ground. All at once, two hundred date palm trees poked their shaggy heads over the horizon.

It was Ayn Umm Ahmad, or "the Spring of Ahmad's Mother," a withered stream reflecting brackish green. Six hours after we had crossed the border into Egypt, thirsty and covered with powdered rock, we had arrived.

Girls wearing orange floral dresses and veils emerged from the palms to greet us. Forty people lived at the encampment, though the men were often roving the desert. The girls gave conflicting accounts of the Bedouin's whereabouts. He was at the Santa Katrina monastery at the foot of Mount Sinai. He was on the other side of the peninsula, watching camel races. He was at a friend's funeral and would be gone for three days. After all, he was a nomad. He roamed and if you were persistent and lucky, you found him. I would have to return another day. We got into the jeep and left.

"Here," my mother said, handing me a fudge and halvah sandwich she had prepared at her hotel breakfast buffet. "I put lotsa good stuff in there."

"You sound like my father. He says 'lotsa good stuff.' "

"You can say 'Daddy.' "

"You call him 'Dave Blumenfeld' when Bernie is around."

Her voice began to climb the four-note flight of steps that leads from relaxed to defensive. "Dave Blumenfeld and I have a wonderful relationship ever since the divorce. I really enjoy him now that he doesn't control my life."

We had not talked much on the drive to the oasis. We were caught up in the adventure and the wonder of the desert. On the return trip, grimy and tired, we talked to pass the time, staring at a landscape that had grown monotonous.

"Daddy called yesterday," I said. "I felt guilty when I hung up. I always get the feeling he's hurt when I'm with you."

"Why?" she said, chewing on a bite of chocolate sandwich.

"Maybe he's sad about me being with you."

Since my parents had separated, I spent more time with my mother than with my father. Sometimes my father complained that I neglected him. Unlike so many of my friends who were irked by their mothers, I actually liked mine. "Maybe he's just sad about the divorce," I said.

She dabbed her mouth with a napkin. "Oh, I think you're just imagining that. He's very happy with Fran. He's a much happier person, and I am too. He deserves to be loved, and Fran really loves him."

"Maybe, but I still think he would've preferred that it didn't happen."

"Me too."

I looked at her, surprised.

"I never wanted a divorce," she said. "When I visited Jerusalem last week, I thought Daddy and I were so happy back then. Maybe if we had stayed in Jerusalem, life would've turned out differently."

This was the closest my mother ever had come to voicing regret. I listened hungrily.

"I married Daddy because he was so idealistic. He believed in religion and helping people. Anyone could be a lawyer, but Daddy believed in something."

Drops of moisture appeared on her forehead. "Then there was the reality of being a rabbi's wife. The congregation was not idealistic. They were backbiting and horrible to Daddy, and they destroyed our family. Daddy was willing to sacrifice everything for the job, including me. He would say, 'Go to the Sisterhood board meetings and don't open your mouth.' "

"Oh, Mom, why didn't you stand up to him?"

"I was too immature. He was too stubborn. He thought my life was an appendage to his. I don't want to say bad things about your father. He's a good father"—she wiped her forehead with the back of her hand—"but he was very old-fashioned. He's changed a lot since then."

"Why don't you remarry him?"

She answered me with silence. I found hope in it, even though I knew better. Maybe she did wonder what it would be like to be married to him now. I looked out the window, at the ground rushing past, and imagined that I could see tiny things beneath our wheels. The beetle tracks. The yellow scorpion footprints. The slither lines from lizard tails. Then I grew impatient.

"Why don't you marry him now that he's changed?" I said.

It was not as simple as that, even for me. I could step back and say that I was happy she was happy. There were moments when I was proud, even, that she had made a good life for herself. But she was my mother, and I wanted her to love my father.

"It's too late. It was lost. I don't love him anymore," she said.

Our jeep rolled past the camel skeleton. Its vertebrae curved in a graceful arc. Its ribs were bleached so white it was hard to believe they ever held a beating heart.

"So we made a mistake," she said.

"How do I know Baruch and I aren't making the same mistake?"

My mother smiled. "I asked Hal, 'Should I worry about Laura and Baruch because of all of their fights?' Hal said, 'No one worried about you and Dad, and look what happened. No one worried about your marriage, Mom, because you didn't tell anyone.' "

"But you did tell." An old pang sliced down my middle. "You told *me.* Don't you remember?"

"No."

I turned away from her so I could say the words: "I was in high school, we were on the subway. I was telling you about my friends and all their parents' terrible marriages. And I said, 'You guys have a great marriage, right?' And you stiffened and said it was 'adequate.' And you'd tell me your problems with Daddy. I was your confidante, Mom."

I was dousing her with guilt, too much of a kid to stop. The adult in me wondered how she was taking it. "I felt so guilty knowing—like we were conspiring against him. I knew you were going to leave him, and I didn't know how to stop it. How can you not remember?"

I kept my head turned away. She was quiet. I thought that she must be remembering. She had to remember. After a minute, I looked at her. Her head was resting against the seat. Her breathing was slow, eyes gently closed. She had that light smile on her lips as if she were somewhere pleasant, as if the rumble of the desert had rocked her away to a lovelier place.

• • •

THE NEXT DAY, my mother relaxed with Bernie in Eilat at her hotel pool. She splashed down the water slide again and again, blissful as a five-year-old. With Bernie, she felt for the first time in her life "free to be myself, to say anything, to do anything, to be anything I want."

I returned to the desert alone. *Simple justice,* I told myself.

As my jeep approached the oasis, rounding a bend, the wheels knocked loose stones over the edge of the goat path. A moment later the Bedouin appeared and climbed into the jeep next to me. Anez abu Salim of the Arayda clan, of the Tarabin Hasablah tribe, hashish smuggler and ringleader of hundreds of Bedouin smugglers, was a tattered, regal sight to behold. He wore a long black robe, the hems dusty and frayed, his head wrapped in a white kaffiyeh. His beard was white and spiny. His raisin eyes were buried in layers of wrinkles. His toenails were thick as bone. His brown feet were so calloused they looked petrified. The dirt under his fingernails was permanent.

"Where's your mother?" he said, glancing around, disappointed. A messenger had told him she had come the day before. "I'm looking for a good wife. How much does she weigh?"

"Fifty-five kilos," I said, slimming her a bit.

"I want someone one hundred and twenty kilos." That was 264 pounds. "I've had many wives. Six died from hunger." He smiled at his little joke. "Where's your mother from?"

"America."

"Is America bigger or smaller than Sinai?"

The one thing Anez knew about America was that our president had a twenty-year-old girlfriend. This prompted him to rethink marrying my mother. "She's too old. I want a young wife. Will you marry me?"

He grinned. There were gold teeth, broken teeth, silver teeth, brown teeth, no bottom teeth at all. He was seventy-eight years old.

"No."

"If your father agrees, you have no choice. Your father has camels?"

"No, but he likes camels."

"Then he will agree."

The jeep stopped and we got out in a thicket of palms that Anez had cultivated. He told me to pick some dates from a pile where they lay beneath a swarm of bees. As I bent over, I could hear him a few feet away, his stream of urine hissing as it hit the sand.

We walked past the dark stain to a clearing near his well. Anez threw down a brown goatskin for himself, a white sheepskin for me. The oasis had been his family's home, he said, for eight hundred years.

Off in the distance near the roosters and the goats, the girls worked in a mud-brick hut. They were peeling vegetables and flattening balls of dough. The young men joined our circle, facing a red, rutted mountain.

They gathered twigs, built a fire and served me tea in a tin can. Anez gave me one of his warm, honey-colored dates. I bit into it and noticed white, threadlike things wriggling.

"I'm very happy to be here," I said haltingly, uncertain of the customs of when to speak and what to say. "I'm sorry I missed you yesterday."

"Meeting once is more romantic." Anez pulled out a small package wrapped in purple cloth.

"I have a present for you," he said to his son Maish, a man with a black beard and a white turban.

"A new pistol," Anez said, stroking the black metal. "German." He loaded it and aimed at the red mountain. "Let's try it out."

When his finger hooked the trigger, I got nervous. When I got nervous, I interviewed. I tried to distract Anez with questions about smuggling. Soon he announced that he was taking a nap. He stretched out on his goatskin, pulled his headdress over his face, hugging his gun like it was a teddy bear. A loose bullet rolled to his knee.

He poked an eye through the folds of his headdress. "What do you say when someone dies in your culture?"

The first thing that came to mind was the Jewish custom: "Blessed be God, the True Judge."

"And if the person who died was a bad guy?"

"You still say something nice because he's dead."

"And when he dies, his wife marries again?"

"Yes."

He adjusted his pistol so that the tip touched his chin. "Nothing wounds a man like a wife who leaves him. Even if he's already dead."

He curled up and rolled onto his side.

Maish sat with me in the shade of a nearby acacia tree while his father slept. His father had been a well-respected, prosperous smuggler. Then the Egyptian police arrested him, tortured him and convicted him of smuggling. A court sentenced him to fifteen years at the Egyptian Military Prison in Abbasa. One by one, his wives betrayed him. Maish's mother, Subhiya, ran off with a fellow tribesman.

"Always in life, there's love between man and woman," Maish said, clicking through his red and black worry beads. "In the beginning, they have love; in the beginning, they have hopes."

Frail, long-legged birds tiptoed past us through the sand. "Then they disagree and leave each other," he said. "This is also true in America, yes?"

"Yes," I said, letting the sand run through my fingers. "Do you ever wish it could be different with your parents?"

"I used to dream my parents would get married again, but the dreams didn't help."

"Do you want revenge on your mother?"

"No," he said. "I believe she still loved my father."

After an hour or so, Anez woke up. He sat up suddenly, pushing his headdress from his face, and said to me, "I dreamed I married your mother."

Anez joked about being a bachelor, but there was a poignant bite to his humor. For lunch, we shared a tray piled with zucchini, lamb and lebne while the camels stood nearby eating buckets of straw. Then Anez reclined and told the story of his revenge on his wives.

He was in solitary confinement when news of his wives' disloyalty reached him. A faithful wife was the measure of a Bedouin's honor. As the Bedouin proverb says, "The wife is a tent's main pole."

Anez said, "The shame I felt was worse than dying."

He began thinking about ways to get even. "If I was outside prison I would've taken a different kind of revenge."

"Like what?" I said.

"Like kill her, or shoot her brother."

That would have been one of the oldest acts of revenge—the cuckolded husband killing his wife. It sprang from a place so instinctive, many societies sanctioned it. In England under King Alfred, the law allowed for it, and until recently in Jordan the law looked the other way. In the United States, many states treat it as a lesser form of homicide.

Anez, instead, planned a more sophisticated revenge. He set out to replicate the crime—being shamed—with the roles reversed. He wanted to get back at his wives, but more than payback, he wanted them to feel his pain. This kind of revenge is very calculated, an imaginative, psychological art. It has to be staged and manipulated. It is why revenge can take a lifetime. To stab an unfaithful wife in a spasm of rage offers no lesson. To bring the women around to Anez's own psychological state, to shame them—that was satisfaction.

How could he do it, handcuffed in an Egyptian prison? Anez was illiterate, but he was a skilled oral poet. He devised a form of poetic justice for his wives.

"I wanted to get the sadness out of me," he said, opening a pack of Cleopatra cigarettes. "Like when you need a cigarette, and you light the end and inhale."

He composed poems reproaching his wives, poems of ridicule. He dictated them to a literate prisonmate, who passed them along to a visitor, who passed them along to a merchant friend. The merchant traveled among all the Bedouin of the region, reading the poems out loud. In time, eleven different tribes knew Anez's poems by heart. It was as if Anez had posted news of his shameful wives on the Bedouin Internet.

Anez quoted from the poem he composed to his wife Khadra:

Rush her these words ere I hear more of her,
Quick: as though the whir of bright bullets were heard.
They tell me it seems that she's losing her mind,
That she's having trysts of a secretive kind . . .

As he recited the poem in Arabic he closed his eyes. Then he opened them and said, "If you are shamed, it's bad. But when other people know the shameful thing, it's even worse. This was my revenge. It was like spitting in her face."

Next, Anez turned his anger on the man who seduced Khadra, an unworthy suitor who owned only one camel, who was too cowardly to be a smuggler. He was a first cousin, a member of his own blood-revenge group, heightening the insult.

The one thing Anez could do was publicly humiliate him. He quoted from the poem he had sent to his cousin:

He who shames with a slut, his disgrace is the same,
Though for some men disgrace isn't really a shame.
And taking no note of what strangers might say,
They'll appear in our camps with a wife gone astray.
So, the little blind worm's now sprung teeth and can bite,
And what once was a cur's now a wolf out at night.

To save face, Anez divorced all three wives. He announced the divorce with a poem, which he summarized: "And, lest every Zed and Abed laugh at me, I've set my three nonbearing she-camels free."

There was one more embarrassing episode. Subhiya, the mother of Maish, married her lover. Anez heard the news while he was being tortured.

"Two guards held me, and one beat me, three times a day, like meals. And then they'd feed me a piece of bread. Now if someone hits me, I feel hungry."

Still, he would not be defeated. "The words of my poems were like bullets that I fired on all the people who hurt me."

At first, it was hard for me to understand how a poem could

be so powerful. But among the Bedouin, reputation determined everything, from social status, to financial security, to physical safety.

He recited from his poem following Subhiya's remarriage:

But you, fancy dresser! By your news I'm dismayed:
But you surpass all in behaving with shame.
You let down your hair tassels loose on your back
While they hung me and beat me on rack after rack.

Anez walked me to my jeep and offered one last thought.

"Revenge with words is better," he said. "When I kill someone, he dies, so he won't feel my punishment. But when I write a poem about him, he must live with it and suffer for all of his life."

Just as Anez did.

ON MY MOTHER'S last day in Israel, I suggested we go for a walk to see my parents' apartment from their newlywed year. The visit had filled my father with nostalgia. Maybe it would awaken something similar in her.

My other witless scheme already had failed. I had given her one of the mastermind's chocolate wafers, the same ones I fed to my father. It was a corruption of the custom of sharing the first piece of wedding cake: when my father was shot, my mother was golfing in Hawaii with Bernie. Now, if she shared the sweet wafers with my father, then, symbolically at least, she shared his experience; my father would not be alone.

Before I could stop her, she had turned to Bernie. "Here, Bern, have one."

"Ucch." She pinched her face when she bit into her wafer. "It's stale."

The wafers had been sitting in our refrigerator for months absorbing odors—cheese, gazpacho, salmon with chives.

"This tastes terrible," Bernie said, spitting it out.

"I want to get rid of this," my mother said. She dropped it into a garbage pail.

Now, as the two of us strolled under a canopy of trees, my mother gave me a long look.

"What?" I said.

"I love you." She patted my back. "I'm so glad to be with you."

My father had led the way to their old home. My mother did not remember the way. Eventually, we found Salant Street.

"Yes, there are the flowers," she said, quickening her pace just as my father had. "It was the first time I ever saw bougainvillea."

We stood outside number 7, looking up at the second-floor balcony. Like my father had, she began to reminisce. "We had to heat water in a kerosene stove; the woman next door gave me a recipe for chocolate cake; I used to sit up on the balcony and watch the Hasids pee against the wall."

Then her expression dimmed.

"I didn't remember it being that dumpy."

"It's not dumpy," I said. It was dumpy.

She put her hand on the rusted gate. "I wonder if we could go in. I'd love to see inside."

"Want to try?"

She tipped her head sideways. "Nah," she said. "You can't go back after forty years."

We walked slowly back to the King David Hotel. I was sorry she was leaving.

"This has been the most incredible visit," she said. "I feel like I've been breathing laughing gas for two weeks." She inhaled. "I love the smell of cedar everywhere."

As I hugged her good-bye in the lobby, she stepped back. "Do you know what day tomorrow is?"

"Sunday."

"Yeah, and?" she challenged. There was a trace of hostility in her eyes.

I always remembered dates, which explains my affinity for revenge. I reminded Baruch of piddly events, like the third anniversary of our first rollerskate through Central Park.

"I have no idea," I said, worried by her tone. I could not imagine what I had done wrong.

"Me and Bernie's wedding anniversary."

"I didn't realize."

"Yes." She hit the consonants hard. "Our wedding anniversary. Twelve years."

I swallowed. There was the taste of an old anger. "Happy anniversary."

SETTLING ACCOUNTS, I realized then, was not a neat procedure. The thought came to me while walking past the windmill, after I had said good-bye to my mother.

You could not always separate grudges and sort them in tins labeled "Rice," "Flour," "Salt." They were stored inside of you, sifted together. Getting even, for me, anyway, was like picking out flecks of pepper once they were blended into a gray pile with salt.

I had decided to pursue simple justice. A man shot my father, shot to kill. I had to pick the gunman out of the pile.

Anez the Bedouin had reminded me of the power of words. Words, as he had shown me, could penetrate anything, even prison walls. I would write a letter to the shooter.

I went inside, turned on my computer:

> *Dear Omar,*
>
> *I'm writing to you as one wretch to the next.*

I erased that, and called my friend Rachel for help.

"How are you?"

"I have no belly button," Rachel said. She was seven months pregnant.

"Oh. Well." I told her I was writing a letter to the shooter. "What I really want to know is, why did he shoot my dad?"

"Well, you know how you fantasize your parents will die during finals just so you can fly away and be excused from your test?"

"Yeah."

"Maybe he shot your dad as a technique to get out of an exam. He was in the middle of finals, so he told his professor, 'I was at the frontier of the struggle between my people and the Jews.' "

"I'm going to ask him if he was getting revenge."

"It was probably for the Jews stomping his people," she said.

I refused to believe that. He was mad about something else. It was an act of "displaced vengeance"—when you take revenge on someone other than the one you are angry with because you cannot, or dare not. You "displace" revenge on a convenient target.

Who was the shooter angry at? Not my father. Not even Israel. He was angry at his parents, I suspected. There were hints of it in a poem he wrote in English some time before the shooting. The poem was called "I May But I Can't." His mother showed it to me along with his other papers. I had photocopied it and read it many times, trying to decode it. I had to get the shooter to open up about these things.

I asked Rachel, "How do I get him to respond thoughtfully?"

"This is what I do when I make up essay questions for my students: try to word questions in a way to bypass three pages of essay drivel. Like, 'In addition to the proud, beautiful reason of the independence, courage and fortitude and glory of your nation, is there any other reason you fired that gun?' You want him to admit to doubtful thoughts, not the platitudes he'd say at a press conference—" She interrupted herself. The baby was kicking. "I'm in baby panic, I have to go buy a stroller."

I went back to my computer.

Dear Omar,

Hopefully, one day we can meet and talk in person. In the meantime, I was hoping we could write each other letters.

I reread the letter. It looked a little cold. I added a first sentence:

I hope this letter finds you happy and in good health.

" 'I hope this letter finds you *happy*'?" Baruch had walked in and was reading over my shoulder. "How about 'I hope you're miserable'?"

I changed "happy" to "in good spirits."

I followed Baruch into the living room to watch the news. Two Palestinian suicide bombers had blown themselves up in the vegetable market. Despite the violence, peace talks were progressing. In a few days, the Israelis would hand over West Bank land to the Palestinians. The Israeli prime minister announced that he would free "a batch" of Palestinian prisoners. (Israelis called them security prisoners. Palestinians called them political prisoners.) At first he said "not ones with blood on their hands." When the Israelis could not find enough Palestinians to fill the quota, they modified the conditions to include prisoners with "a little blood on their hands."

That sounded like the shooter. He had a little blood on his hands.

After the news, I went back to the letter. Baruch suggested that I sound chatty and informal. He did that when he interviewed witnesses in criminal cases; it helped them to relax.

Lucky for me, you speak English. I am an American journalist writing a book about the region. Through conversations with your family, I learned a little bit about what has happened to you, but I would like to hear your story directly from you.

First, I was wondering about your life before prison—what you liked in university, your interest in karate, the family and career you were planning, the things that made you happy and the things that made you angry.

Your mother showed me an interesting poem you wrote in English titled "I May but I Can't." It seemed to be about your role in your family but I wasn't certain of the message.

Next, I was wondering about your life in prison: your inter-

> *ests, how you spend your days, what your plans are for the future. And finally, I would like to hear about the events that led to your arrest. What happened? When you think back on it, what were your feelings then? How do you feel about it today?*

The phone rang. A familiar, upbeat voice.

"Hi, Papa. Did you hear, on Friday they're releasing two hundred and fifty prisoners?"

"You don't think it'll be those guys, do you?" my father said.

"I don't know. Do you think they should let the shooter go?"

"No," he said. "It isn't that I want retribution. I think he's dangerous. They should lock him up for at least twenty-five years, until he isn't a threat anymore. When you're fifty years old—even if you're a black belt—you don't run around killing people. You don't have the stamina. So," he took a breath that signaled a change of subject, "what's happening on the baby front?"

"Baruch's not ready."

"Tell him he has three obligations to a wife according to Jewish law: to clothe her, to have sex with her and . . . I forgot the third one."

"Sex isn't having babies."

"Sex is supposed to be for having kids," he said. Hal's wife was pregnant again. "What's the matter with Baruch? Tell him I'm waiting for a grandchild. Tell him life doesn't stop at a certain point. It can't stop."

I got off the phone and finished my letter.

> *I know these are a lot of questions, so sorry if I've overwhelmed you. Feel free to write about anything that is important to you. I look forward to hearing from you.*
>
> *In the meantime, take care—*
>
> *Laura*

I printed out the letter and trimmed the margins with a pair of scissors. His family would be sneaking it past prison guards. I figured small was good.

The next day, I delivered the letter to the shooter's brother Imad. My fingers were icy as I passed it to him.

"Do you think your brother will be freed tonight?" I asked.

Imad sidestepped the question. "Part of our country will be liberated tonight. I wish it were Jaffa and Tel Aviv and Haifa too."

He invited me to stay for dinner. I declined—my father's ethics speech about "stealing knowledge" playing in my head.

The next day I woke up early, wondering whether the shooter had been released with the other prisoners in the middle of the night. I heard on the news that they would be bused from prisons all over the country to an Israeli army post in the West Bank. From there, they would ride to Ramallah for a welcome rally.

I set out for the army post. If the shooter were free, I wanted to be the first to see him.

About fifty Palestinians and I stood by the roadside in a scrubby patch of West Bank. The crowd was young men mostly, brothers and cousins, in tight black leather jackets.

Aside from the tents of the Israeli army post, the land was desolate all the way to the horizon, where a minaret poked up from an Arab village. The Palestinian Authority cars parked to the left of the narrow road; the Israeli military vehicles parked on the right. The wind blew circles of yellow dust around us. The dust that they were fighting over. If you stuck out your tongue, you could catch it and own part of the land.

I searched the crowd for the shooter's family. Most relatives were waiting at the rally in Ramallah. If the shooter showed up, I thought slyly, I would be his welcome committee. Would I recognize him? What would I say?

An Israeli officer's walkie-talkie chirruped with the signal.

"They're here!" the officer announced. He shook hands with the Palestinian commander. A minute later, a convoy of four Israeli buses crested the hill, their headlights on. They curved down toward us. A cheer went up around me.

What's my plan? I had no plan. When the moment came I would know what to do.

The prisoners were hanging out the windows all the way up to their hipbones, whistling and chanting: "With blood and spirit we redeem Palestine!" Some flapped pictures of Yasir Arafat, some waved kaffiyehs, others were holding models they had made of the Dome of the Rock. Police cars were honking. A few mothers started to dance in a circle, clicking their tongues against their palates as if it were a wedding.

"Ahmed! Hey, Ahmed!" A man blew kisses to his brother on a bus. "Mommy is waiting at home."

The four buses drove through the gate into the army post, where the freed prisoners would be transferred to Arab buses. The relatives scrabbled up a thistle-covered hill overlooking the parking lot. I picked my way up to the barbed wire with them.

"Boys, are you from Ashkelon?" an older woman called out. "Is my son with you?"

"What prison are you from?" called Akhtam Falana, a man standing next to me. Akhtam was looking for his cousin. "Where's the Ashkelon bus?"

A good deal of yelling back and forth followed. Akhtam found his cousin Bassam on the third bus to the right. Bassam had served seven years.

"Bassam, are you handcuffed?"

"No," Bassam shouted with a smile.

Akhtam and I had been stumbling around the thorns together. I asked him if he minded shouting out a name for me. I was looking for someone from the Ashkelon prison. I was too shy to yell.

Akhtam cupped his hands around his mouth and called to the parking lot, "Is Khatib on the bus?"

"Which Khatib?" a voice volleyed back.

"Omar," I cued Akhtam. My voice sounded strange. My heart beat faster. I could not help being lifted into the excitement of family reunions.

"Is Omar Khatib with you?" Akhtam yelled. Bassam stuck his index finger out the window and wagged it no.

More than half of the prisoners released were petty criminals, car thieves, not political activists.

Akhtam shook his head and said to me, "Better luck next time."

Disappointment drained down my legs. It took a minute to remember why. For a moment on that thistle-covered hill, hopping and waving with the others, I had forgotten everything, including that I hated him.

IT WOULD TAKE two weeks for the shooter to reply, if he replied at all. Typically, his relatives visited him every other Friday. His family would smuggle out his letter during their next visit.

Two weeks passed with no visitation. Then four, then five. The Palestinian prisoners had staged a hunger strike, demanding their release. From inside the prisons, they orchestrated demonstrations in the West Bank that turned violent. The prisoners wrote their instructions to outside activists, sealed them in plastic capsules and slipped the capsules to visiting relatives, who swallowed them. That was how Hamas prisoners sent instructions to detonate five car bombs.

Israeli prison authorities struck back, suspending family visits. There was nothing for me to do but wait. I filled the weeks with interviews, looking for the simplest revenge stories. No ambivalent protagonists, no hazy crimes. I collected stories about simple justice: a businessman who felt "burned" by his lawyer brought a can of kerosene to the lawyer's office and set him on fire; an academic with a grudge against her grandfather evened the score by delivering a bruising eulogy; a farmer who caught a tractor thief stripped the thief and painted him green; a diplomat's wife who was mad at her neighbors beheaded their chrysanthemums at night; a saleswoman in a butcher shop whose boss was merciless waited until he left for the weekend—and unplugged the meat freezers.

All of these stories shared a simple logic, one that I was trying to distill. I realized what they had in common over dinner one night while listening to Baruch. We were waiting for our pizza at a restaurant where the service was slow. Baruch and I had been together long enough to have told each other all of our best stories. He glanced at the dessert listings and said, "At summer camp, whenever kids would go to the mall, they'd go to the parking lot, to all the German cars, and piss on the driver's door."

"And you didn't do it?"

"I'm not the sort who pisses on car door handles."

American Jews played out their revenge fantasies on Nazis in quirky ways. Some Jews refused to buy German cars. Bernie owned a Mercedes sedan, but he would only play Yiddish music while driving.

"Did you ever get revenge on the Nazis?" I said to Baruch.

I expected him to ignore my question. When Baruch's mother and father were teenagers, they were deported to the Auschwitz death camp. On the train platform, they were selected for labor by Josef Mengele; he pushed them to the left with the crack of a whip. Almost all of their relatives—grandparents, uncles, aunts, cousins, their fathers, a mother, an older sister, a baby brother—were sent in the other direction, to the gas chambers. Baruch hardly ever talked about it. I did not expect him to now. I had been edgy lately, and he had been remote.

"I've always had dreams of Nazis deporting me to Auschwitz," he said with a vulnerable look around his eyes I had never seen. "I'm always a child in the dreams. I'm in a school bus and the bus stops, and Nazis get on. They take over the bus and ship us off to Auschwitz. And I'm terrified and absolutely powerless."

There was nothing Baruch could do to stop the nightmares. When he was awake, though, he balanced them with dreams of getting even.

"I've always had daydreams. One I still have—I show up secretly during the Warsaw Ghetto uprising. I knock on the door of resistance headquarters. I say, 'I'm a Jew from America,' and I supply the resistance with food and vitamins and infrared binoculars so they could shoot at night."

"Do you help them fight?"

"It doesn't go that far. More recently, I have another daydream—I'm in one of the death camps, and I grab the kids of the commandant and hold them hostage unless he stops the crematoriums."

"What happens?"

"It never gets that far. One more"—his voice was hurried, the dreams leaking out for the first time—"the Allies are in the air over Europe, about to go on a bombing raid, and I'm a member of a secret unit that goes back in time with all the most modern equipment. We have big Jewish stars on our planes and we join the Allies. We broadcast, 'Don't shoot, we're friendly.' And the Allies say, 'Who are you? Identify yourself.' And we say, 'We're Americans and we're Jews out to get the Nazis.' And they don't know whether to shoot us until they see us start bombing the hell out of the Nazis. They radio back to headquarters, 'We don't know who these guys are, but they're good.' "

The glow in Baruch's face was boyish and strong, like that of a teenage comic book hero scaling a building.

"It makes me feel better for a moment, but then I realize it's a fantasy." The color in his face began to fade. "Everyone died. And I feel powerless."

Powerless—power. That was it, the common thread. In all the simple justice stories the avengers reversed the balance of power. The weak became strong, the strong became weak. That was what made their revenge a success. Baruch's fantasies worked so well because they transformed him from a powerless child on a bus to Auschwitz to a powerful pilot dropping bombs.

Faisal Husseini, Jerusalem's most important Palestinian politician, told me that he too had revenge fantasies about being a fighter pilot. His father, Abdel Kader al-Husseini, a commander in the 1948 war, was killed by Israelis. As a boy, Faisal would dream that he was flying over the Israeli soldiers, gunning them down in revenge, changing places with the men who had killed his father.

Every simple revenge story pivots on this reversal of power. Societies with honor codes demand it. Revenge can be taken only on equals or superiors. There is no point to taking revenge on a slave, a woman, a sleeping man or a man from a lower class, because they are weak. Their defeat brings no honor.

The most spectacular story about a reversal of power was told to me by Rafi Eitan. Short, rotund, with thick brown glasses and a bad ear, he might easily be mistaken for a benign old man. But his deafness had come from dismantling explosives. He worked for Israel's General Security Services and the Mossad. Among other operations, he was responsible for Jonathan Pollard, the American intelligence agent who spied for Israel.

"An eye for an eye gives you nothing," he advised. "You have to go after the head."

Rafi followed his own advice, literally. In 1960, he joined a team of Mossad agents to kidnap Adolf Eichmann, architect of the Nazis' Final Solution. The agents tracked him to Argentina and ambushed him outside his house.

"Three of us carried him back to our car. One carried his legs, one his middle. I wanted to hold his head."

Inside the car, Rafi lifted Eichmann's shirt and looked for the number SS officers had tattoed on their arms. A scar with blue dots puckered the skin where Eichmann had had it removed.

"He tried to shout," Rafi recalled. "Our driver, who knew German, told him to be quiet. He breathed heavily. I kept his head on my lap. This man was a Caesar and all the Jews would quake to hear his name. I felt I should touch his head, to show him, 'You tried to destroy us—we're still alive. And your head is in my hands.' "

Of course, most revenge and most power reversals are not nearly that dramatic. Most involve the slights and jabs of our daily lives. After my interview with Rafi at his Tel Aviv home, I hailed a taxi. The driver, a twenty-nine-year-old Druze named Jamal, saw my notebook and asked what subject I was reporting.

"Revenge?" he said. "Talk to my wife. I wanted to sleep with her last night and she said she was tired. Now *that's* revenge. I don't love her and she feels it. Now she's getting back at me. And she knows where to get me—in the balls."

Jamal's wife might feel powerless to win his affection, but when her husband begged for sex, she was omnipotent. Here was the important difference between power-reversal revenge and the predator-prey vengeance I had explored earlier. People who live in the anarchy of predator and prey, characters like Smitt the burglar, or Shahak the Israeli military chief of staff, retaliate because they think they have to. For them, revenge serves as a deterrent. There is little, if any, spite involved. Reprisals are part of a perceived Darwinian struggle.

The more recent interviews, those people who went from feeling powerlessness to powerful, had a choice. They could let the offense pass and move on. If they got revenge it was partly for their own psychic pleasure. Baruch's fantasy about bombing the Nazis was not about deterrence, but the satisfaction of giving back.

Baruch's dreams about payback surprised me. I thought of him as someone defined by logic, not fantasy. Meanwhile he was walking around screening action movies in his head that starred himself. Knowing that made me feel tender toward him. Maybe that was why he encouraged my exploits. He was enjoying the catharsis of vicarious revenge.

As we waited for our pizza, I wondered, What else don't I know about my new husband?

"Did you ever get revenge on the Nazis?" I asked again.

"The closest I ever came was working as an intern at the Nazi-hunting office at the Justice Department. The school bus nightmares stopped because for the first time in my life I didn't feel helpless. My work gave me a sense of empowerment."

After that summer at Justice, Baruch decided to become a prosecutor. "Becoming a government official was a way for me to be part of a legal system that's fair. We catch people who've killed, cheated and defrauded and—unlike the Nazis, who rewarded criminals—we send them to jail. I don't think you understand how satisfying that feels. My parents would describe the Nazi officials as emissaries of tremendous fear. For me, working for a government that's fair is turning the Nazi idea on its head. That's empowering."

This was something else I did not know about Baruch. I had always wondered if working for the government reflected a lack of imagination. Meanwhile, he was feeding his need to get even, doing something my father called "constructive revenge."

• • •

From time to time, my father would phone me and say, "Don't forget about constructive revenge. You should say that's the best revenge."

In deference to him, I looked for these constructive avengers. They change the power equation by building themselves up rather than putting others down. They come from the "just you wait" school of vengeance. The ones who, when spat at, lying in the dirt, vow, "one day, you'll see."

There was Zevadia Vidge, a twenty-five-year-old Ethiopian, born on a farm near Addis Ababa. When his family moved to Haifa, Israel, the basketball players snubbed him. "I don't choose little guys," the captain sneered.

"I asked myself, 'Do they hate me? Why was I made so small?' " He remembered how he used to run two miles to the river in Ethiopia carrying jugs of water, and five miles to the forest to gather wood. He felt the ping of an idea. He could run, fast and far. He started training, and today, at five foot four and 118 pounds, Zevadia is Israel's champion marathon runner.

"I proved it to them," he told me. Recently, after he won a race, he got a call from a man whose husky voice sounded familiar: "Remember me from the basketball game?" It was the captain who had tormented him. "You're a big media star and I'm a night security guard at a construction site."

When Zevadia finished his story, he stood up and stretched. "I'm little, but my victories are big."

Sefi Visiger was another constructive avenger, a slight twenty-six-year-old with the scruffy hair and the baggy clothes of a skateboard kid. Sefi grew up a misfit in his own home. While his father was a soccer player and his mother was an artist, he was lousy at sports and a clod at art.

"I thought I was adopted," Sefi told me. "I'd sit in my room with my computers all day."

He overslept so often, arriving late for school in Herzliyah, that in eleventh grade he was expelled. "The vice principal, a very mean lady, made a speech: 'You'll fail in life.' " He tried to find a job, but his erratic habits got him fired.

One day, he and two friends locked themselves in together and agreed not to leave until they developed an idea for an Internet business. Three weeks later, they emerged with an e-mail messaging system called ICQ. Eventually, America Online bought their startup company for $287 million dollars in cash.

Now he wakes up at 1 P.M. if he likes. When I met Sefi at his Tel Aviv office at 3 P.M., he was eating a breakfast of french fries and Coke. He is president of a company with seventy employees. He bought a house on the beach that has a projection booth to play movies. He installed sensors that light a path to the refrigerator in case he wakes up hungry in the night.

"I ran into the vice principal who kicked me out. She was like, 'Hey, Sefi, remember me?' I was, like, 'No.' "

The marathon champion and the computer multimillionaire achieved the kind of revenge that people applaud. There is nothing threatening about constructive revenge. No one gets hurt.

When I asked my brother if he ever got revenge, he recalled his supervising physician on the epilepsy ward who made his life miserable. "I went to the library and looked up his scientific publications. I realized, 'Ha! I have more publications than he has.' " Hal yawned. "Is that revenge?"

"You're pathetic," I said. "What a goody-goody."

Hal, Baruch and the others followed the Sunday-school proverb: Success is the best revenge. Which was why my father often phoned me with the advice, "Get constructive revenge, OK?"

"OK, Dad," I would say, with no intention of doing so.

ANOTHER FRIDAY scrolled around—visiting day in prison. I dreaded calling the shooter's family. It was awkward, I felt guilty, they were so nice, they hated Jews so. I forced myself to dial.

A girl answered who seemed to recognize my voice. There was a lot of rustling, as if the phone were being passed around the room. Eventually one of the shooter's nephews came on the line. My conversations with the family, especially on the phone, were hopelessly mangled. They barely spoke English, I barely spoke Arabic. They knew Hebrew, but they did not know that I knew Hebrew too. Somehow, from the stream of Arabic rushing past my ears, I was able to fish out the phrase: "We have a letter for you."

I struggled to keep my voice steady. *He wrote back!* I said I would pick up the letter the next day.

Baruch was in the other room working on a law review article called "The Mental State of the Federal Accomplice." He had rings around his eyes, as if someone had cupped them with shot glasses and pressed hard. I walked past him and said hello politely.

The night before, as we got into bed, I had suggested that I start taking prenatal vitamins. It turned into a three-hour discussion. Baruch told me that for the past three months he had been keeping a record of our relationship in his checkbook. He marked every day that he went to sleep feeling like our marriage was "intolerable and insufferable." The average: one out of every four days.

No prenatal vitamins.

"And this is supposed to be our carefree honeymoon year," he said.

"But that's not true," I said. "It may be our honeymoon year, but for me it's not carefree. I've been agonizing about revenge."

"If you have moral problems with it, then forget it."

"Of course I have moral problems. So I have a reason, OK—but what if my plan doesn't work? Rachel's about to have a baby. Hal's finding the cure for epilepsy. And I'm running after some guy in jail?"

Baruch turned off the light. He lay his head on his pillow.

"You remind me of music class in college," he said.

"Of what?"

"I got A's in all my other classes. But I didn't 'get' music. Even though music was the most important class to me. I tried the hardest and cared the most. No matter how hard I tried, there was something about music I just couldn't understand."

He rolled over and went to sleep. I stayed up, lolling in my own thoughts of failure. I was back at summer camp, an eleven-year-old taking my swimming test with Baruch my counselor on the dock. He was flunking me again.

Serves me right for marrying a lifeguard I had a crush on. What an asinine idea—to make a fantasy real.

The next day, when I got the news about the shooter's letter, I was still too mopey to tell Baruch. I went to bed early. I dreamed that the shooter wrote to me in Arabic, in coiling, snaky ink. I dreamed his mother took off her pink robe and showed me her eight-children breasts. She reached between the blankets in her bed and said, "Here's the letter from my son, and here's the money." What money, blood money? I refused it. She asked, "How old are you?" A year younger than the shooter. "Too old to be my son's wife," she said. I dreamed his letter was all pictures and words and symbols cut from a magazine, like a ransom note. Baruch saw it and said, "Look, it's a love letter."

I woke to the peal of church bells. Baruch was rubbing my back.

THE REAL LETTER was shaped like a bullet. It said "Laura" on the outside in Arabic. Imad, the shooter's brother, held it out for me as we sat drinking tea in the shooter's bedroom. I asked my translator to take it from Imad; I did not want them to see my hands shake.

The thin sheets of paper were sealed in plastic, folded and compressed inside a small cellophane capsule, no bigger than a spitball. When I asked Imad how he had smuggled it out of prison, he smiled equivocally. Had one of them swallowed the capsule? He said something about spitting it out—a string of Arabic words that went untranslated. I was afraid to ask again.

On the bus back to Jerusalem, I unfolded the thin, crackling tissue paper. Outside I could hear the cannons firing as they did every evening during the holy month of Ramadan, to announce that Muslims could end their fast. I smoothed out the paper and held it up to the window. It was hard to decipher in the failing light. At first I thought the writing might be Arabic. Then I saw it was English. His handwriting was a miniature, intricate, light blue scrawl. He had used whiteout to correct mistakes.

> *Dear Lora;*
> *I would like first to extend my appreciation and regard for your message that I have red with interest and care. . . .*

I felt a splash of hope. If he answered with some semblance of humanity, then my revenge plan might succeed.

Then the tone changed as he turned to liberating Palestine, making Jerusalem its capital and "returning back our stolen rights through a military revolution."

> *This is not a dream, but a real fact we are seeking to incarnate on land through the long revolutional march of our revolution and in accordance with rule of justice and equality and the right of people to liberate their lands, this sacred right which was secured by the international law. We, as sons to this people, and part of its past and present, has on our shoulders the burden of holding the difficulty of the liberational road, it's our mission to let the rifles live. . . .*

The bus reached the checkpoint between Palestinian and Israeli territory. Throughout the day, the West Bank and Gaza had seen the most intense fighting in months. More than a hundred Palestinians were injured in clashes with Israeli soldiers. An Israeli soldier boarded our bus to check identity cards. Every other person on the bus was a Palestinian. He asked two young men to step off. Then he looked at me, flabbergasted. "And what's with you?"

How could I begin to explain?

> *I would like you to know that our choice to the military struggle is a legitimate choice came on a historical basis that took into account the fact that the enemy we are facing is one who stands on a Zionist ideology which is racist in its basis and fascist in its*

> *aims and means. It is an enemy based on a huge military destructive machine heigh in its ability than any other superpower state. It's an enemy that cant be faced and defeated but only by force.*

That was the end of page one. There were seven more pages.

Boy, I thought. I picked a fight with the wrong guy.

The bus let me off at Damascus Gate. Above the walls, the floodlit Dome of the Rock shone like a night sun. I continued reading the letter, stealing snatches of light as I walked between lampposts. The route took me past the New Gate, where a booby-trapped briefcase had exploded that morning, blowing off the hand of a Canadian passerby.

> *There is a huge difference, my dear, between "terror" and the right of self determination, between a criminal and a revolutionary. . . . I have noticed from your linkage between my past as being a "karate teacher" and between my choice to violent means of strugle points to a linkage which is unnecesary.*

He had been a member of the Palestinian Communist Party, he wrote. In 1982, when Israel invaded Lebanon, he joined Abu Musa, a rebel faction of the PLO, because he thought Yasir Arafat was too moderate. He was still politically active from inside prison.

> *It is hard to us, as prisoners, to accept a peace process which do not answers us all the questions that the Israeli Palestinian conflict have rised. . . . We continue our affect on what is going on outside the walls of our prisons. We are still a leading power.*

I was reading the last page of the letter as I walked down the path to my house. *At least I know he's not holding back his feelings.* I opened the door, and there was Baruch at the piano, tripping over a passage in a Chopin nocturne. He looked happy to see me.

He stood up and put his arms around me. "You don't have to hug me," he said.

I stood there stiffly. It took a minute to remember why I might not want to hug him. Prenatal vitamins. It felt like a different life.

"I just want to hug you and say I wouldn't have told you those things last night unless I wanted to work it out," he said. He held my head against his shoulder, playing with my hair.

We folded ourselves onto the couch and read the letter. The shooter seemed to think that I was conducting some kind of survey on the prisoner movement. I read the final lines:

> *Talking about prisoners case is an interesting thing, especialy for those whom their concern to this humaniterrain issue and willing to do their best for the benefit of those nobel couragause men whom are behinds the bars. . . .*
>
> *With hope to be met under the sun while being freed.*
>
> *Sincerely,*
> *Omar Kamel Al-Khatib*
>
> *P.S. Waiting to your next visite*

The *s* in sincerely was drawn as a gigantic piece of barbed wire.

"So what do you think?" I said.

"I think he hasn't seen hooters in a long time."

"Really."

"I think it's a caricature of a crazed terrorist espousing ideology."

When I read the letter to Rachel over the telephone, she was even more dismissive.

"OK, enough. It's painful to listen to," she said. "I could have written it. He sees everything in such total collective political terms, in contrast to you. Hc has such an incredibly thick wall of rhetoric and collective propaganda, the idea that anything you could do could make him react—it could never happen. He thinks of himself as a grand Arab man leader and you're a chronicler he's telling his great story to. He's so programmed and self-conscious and lecturing, you'll never be able to get him to reflect and be honest. He's living in a place where the personal is irrelevant."

Rachel and I had a habit of cutting each other off, but as I listened to her this time, I had nothing to say. *What an asinine idea—to make a fantasy real.*

"You'll never be able to shake his worldview or his interpretation of anything," she said. "His system is completely unshakable. Your first fantasy of shaking him by the collar will certainly fail. It's the fantasy of a soft, blond girl who likes to go rug shopping—she's going to throttle some big lunk of a killer. He's been tortured by the whole Israeli prison system and the army. There's no way you could top that and even if you could, that would fit into his worldview that he's a courageous, oppressed man."

As she spoke, she breathed heavily from the weight of her baby. She was shaped, she said, like a cylinder, 40-40-40.

"And your other idea will fail too," she said, "because as soon as you tell him who you are, he's going to recoil and be, like, 'You tricked me.' And then when he's free, he'll say, 'Oh, good, now I can shoot Jews again. I'll start with you—*bang.*' Either way, you'll fail."

"You're right," I said, feeling defeated.

THE NEXT MORNING, Baruch read the letter again. "Any response is a good response. He went to great lengths to write." He was straining to read the pale script. "I'm trying to figure out if he trusts you."

That was the challenge, to get him to trust me. I sat at my computer and began to write:

> *Dear Omar,*
>
> *Thanks for your letter. It was good to hear from you.*

I looked at the screen. Now what? *You're a nut case?*

He seemed so volatile. I was afraid that if I asked the wrong question, or challenged him, he would explode. I would write an affirming, flattering letter.

> *The tiny plastic packet helped me realize how difficult it must be for you to communicate with the outside world. Your English is*

impressive. Are you reading any books in English? I saw at your parents' house that you have read a lot of Shakespeare's plays. King Lear *is my favorite.*

Thanks also for the historical-political background on the Palestinian-Israeli conflict. I have written stories about the Middle East for my newspaper, but your perspective is unique and taught me many things.

Baruch read what I wrote. "It's a little too sweet for a terrorist who shot your father: 'Dear Shooter, Your English is so good! Your history lesson was so good! I admire you! I respect you!' "

"You're jealous of the shooter."

"Uh-huh," Baruch said sarcastically. He went back to the piano and started playing scales.

I continued to write.

I wonder if you can describe what it feels like to live behind walls for so many years. I cannot imagine it. What do you miss the most—what little things, and what big things?

The story of your involvement in violent struggle was interesting. You mention a distorted childhood, the rifles of occupation killing children. Did anything specific happen to you or to your family? Was anyone you care about beaten, arrested, killed, humiliated, etc.? Did Israelis do anything to you, Omar, that made you feel like hitting back?

The letter was practically groveling—*please, say something personal.* Maybe he would not bother humanizing himself for me, so I posed it as a service to the "reader." His family, I supposed, had told him what they knew about me: I was writing a book about revenge; I was collecting many stories; I was interested in Omar. How they had put it all together, I could not guess. I dared not ask.

For the purposes of my book, I would like to tell the story of your life. Not only as a prisoner, or as an ideological freedom fighter. These things are very important and true, but I want people who read this book to see you as a human being like anyone, anywhere in the world—as a man with a colorful childhood, with memories, with loves, with grudges, with plans for the future. That is why I asked about karate; it is one of the only details I know about you.

I want readers to understand who you are, and why you shot that man. How did you feel about it then, and how do you feel about it today? What has changed for you? I am sure it is a complicated story, but we have time.

Sometimes when I interview people about their lives, I tell them this: Pretend you are on a long bus journey, and you are telling your life story to a stranger who sat down next to you on the bus. What would you tell him?

I'm still curious about the poem you wrote. I wrote a poem I would like to show you.

I agree with what you wrote—I also hope that when we meet, it will be "under the sun while being freed."

Take good care,

Laura

I showed Baruch the letter. He frowned at the last sentence. "You want him to be free?"

"Not necessarily," I said.

"Then why did you end the letter that way?"

"I'd rather meet him when he's free than in jail. It's better that we meet on neutral ground—not in jail, not at his house. It seems fairer. You're not supposed to get revenge on someone weaker than you."

"You want to be fair to a terrorist?"

THE SHOOTER'S REPLY came one month later on a cheerless, drizzly morning. It was laundry day at the shooter's house. Red, green and yellow children's socks were draped on the railings outside, like Christmas lights, brightening the gray concrete.

Imad was asleep on the couch when I knocked on his door. He

wore sweatpants and a brown flannel robe. His red hair had grown out, replaced by mousy gray. He had told me that he worked as a beautician, though it seemed something had happened to his job.

"These are candies from my mother," I said, handing him a bag of Brach's cinnamon discs that my mother had brought when she visited.

"This is a letter from my brother." He handed me a brown envelope.

All I wanted to do now was turn and leave. My father's warning about *g'neyvat daat*—"stealing knowledge"—haunted me. My plan called for deceiving the shooter, but not his family. It took a bag of mental tricks even to smile when I visited them. And yet I could not simply drop off or pick up a letter as if I were at the post office. Hospitality is an important social obligation in Arab culture. It would have been insulting to reject their invitation to tea. Every time I wanted to be in touch with the shooter, I had to sit with his family for hours.

I had been visiting the family for over six months. The house that I had discovered on a fiery July afternoon was chilled with winter now. Muddy children's shoes lay by the door. A kerosene heater oiled the air.

"Omar has a court hearing next week," Imad said. He had been denied parole a few months earlier. "We're ninety percent sure he'll be released on medical grounds. He has asthma. The judge is sympathetic."

"How will you celebrate?" I asked Imad's wife, Suraya, a woman with a sleepy smile and curly black hair. She set a plate of sliced oranges in front of me.

"I'll cook him breakfast, lunch and dinner."

"What will you make—lamb?"

"He's a vegetarian," she said. "Yogurt and vegetables."

The shooter's mother came upstairs from one of her other sons' apartments. She sat on a chair beside me, warming herself under a blanket. "First thing I'll do is look for a wife for him," she said. "She should be tall with white skin and blond hair."

"He should choose a wife on his own," Imad said. "He wants to travel to France and study French, and then get married."

"Maybe he'll marry a Frenchwoman," I said.

Imad considered this. "He could marry a foreigner, a British woman or a German."

"Or a Jew," I said, the statement popping like a cork.

"No," the mother said, horrified. "No, no, no."

She told me how the Jews had come to their door at midnight to arrest Omar for the shooting. A member of Omar's cell, an informer, had turned the gang in to the police.

"I heard a noise on the staircase. I thought it was thieves. I would've killed them; I was strong then. They were looking through the peephole. I saw eyes looking in. Before Omar could even wake up, they handcuffed his wrists and ankles."

Fifteen years before that night, the Jews had taken away Imad, a member of the Popular Front for the Liberation of Palestine. He was deported to Jordan. His crime? He said he did not know.

"Maybe that's what Omar was getting revenge for," I said.

"There are many reasons," Imad said with his mysterious, unsettling smile. "His motive was a victim. He is our Martin Luther King, ringing the bell of freedom."

He launched into a political speech. For forty-five minutes, I tried to listen and take notes. I wondered if it was possible to doze off in the home of my father's shooter. I ate orange slices. I drank their dark, minty tea, playing with the cup, swirling the rainbow pattern in the surface of the liquid. A tidbit that I had read on African revenge floated into my mind: among the Nuer, feuding families were not allowed to drink or eat from each other's dishes. If they did, they believed, they would die.

Underlying the Nuer superstition, I realized, was smart strategic thinking. Once you ate with the enemy, you were likely to talk. Once you talked, you were likely to find things in common. A shared identity threatens the life of a blood feud. Revenge depends on the externalization of hate. It is something you do to others, not to your own kind. Whole cultures were built on this premise, their national identity based on avenging the other, their group made cohesive by a primary insult somewhere back in the past. I once interviewed a nine-year-old Israeli in a settlement near Hebron who embodied that spirit. Her parents had named her Nekamah, Hebrew for "revenge." When I asked her against whom her revenge was directed, she said, "All the nations that aren't us."

Revenge demands division. Us versus them. It is a simple principle that avengers understand. If they humanize the enemy, blood revenge becomes killing, which is no longer an honorable response.

Why did I call Omar "the shooter"? It turned him into the other. It simplified our roles—he was the bad guy; I was the good guy. It reduced his life to a single act, a tensed finger pulling the trigger forever.

I probably would have continued to think of him that way had I not also been a journalist. As a reporter, my most important asset was empathy. As an avenger, it was my greatest liability.

While listening to Imad recount the history of Palestinian suffering, I found myself toggling between these two roles. They were incompatible, each undermining the other. A good journalist was open and questioning; a good avenger was closed and self-righteous.

". . . no peace without justice," Imad said, winding up. "We're not the murderers. We're the ones being murdered."

Imad's wife gave me a steaming towel to wipe the orange juice from my hands. The heat made me jump.

Imad's mother took out her grandson's wedding album. Three months earlier, Imad's oldest son had gotten married. Imad did the makeup. Lama, the bride, who now lived with the family, sat next to me as we looked through the photographs. We admired the lipstick and mascara. Some of the younger children gathered around.

"France has the best makeup for beauty," Imad explained. "Chemically, Germany has the best." Imad had studied makeup artistry in Lebanon and had run a beauty shop in Jordan called Mona Lisa Palace. More recently, he said, he worked at Palestinian Television.

"Arafat is the only one who doesn't wear makeup," Imad said. "He refuses."

"What color makeup should I wear?" I said.

"Your skin is pale. You should use light brown eye shadow with yellow and beige tones. If you use blue or green shadow you'll look like someone punched you in the eye."

Aside from the obvious preposterousness of the moment, I regretted inviting Imad to look closely at my face. I joked with myself that I must never let them see me in profile. They would realize that I was a Jew. A New Yorker would instantly recognize me as Jewish. But to Imad and his family, I just looked foreign. They knew me only as "Laura," no last name, and assumed that as an American journalist I was a Christian. They wished me a Merry Christmas and, later, a Happy Easter.

Every time I saw them, I ran an obstacle course of paranoia: *Their handshakes were limp, did they figure out who I am? The way they smiled at my last question—do they know that I'm not me?*

My identity was confusing even to me. Was I an avenger posing as a journalist or a journalist posing as an avenger? Maybe I was both, or neither. I was using journalism as a magic cloak to try something I never would dare. Writing about revenge gave me the courage to live out my poem. It gave me just enough distance, enough legitimacy to do something reckless and stay on this side of sane. Without it as a cover, I never would have pursued my fantasy. Every time I walked along the edge of the gorge approaching their house, I felt dizzy with nerves. The only way I could coax myself up their cement steps was to tell myself, "This is just a story."

There were moments when the journalist in me took over, when I listened to an account from the shooter's life and was charmed. Then I would remember my father with a pang and think, But you tried to kill him.

Either way, there were ethical problems. I was breaking rules. This is one reason society views avengers as menaces. They live by their own, self-serving rules. A journalist might go undercover to write an exposé about the meatpacking industry, but I was concealing my identity to settle a family score. There was no way to defend that professionally. As for the ethics of becoming an avenger myself, I had learned from my research that Plato, Cicero, Confucius, Seneca, Thomas Aquinas, Gandhi and Martin Luther King, Jr., among others, condemned revenge.

So maybe the shooter was not the only bad guy. Maybe I was too.

"I have no soul, no guts, no insides," I wrote in my notebook, surprised myself that I was able to sustain the deception.

Imad, meanwhile, said he had decided he could trust me. He would not tell me how he smuggled the letters in and out of jail. But before I left, he confided, "When you first came, we thought you might be CIA or working for the special forces of another government."

Omar, he said, had been suspicious, too, but Imad helped convince him that I was not the government-agent type.

"The prisoners decided they believe in you. They welcome your mission. They decided you're a prophet of peace to transmit their voices to the world," Imad said. He gave me the kind of look that passes between people of like minds. "You're a prophet of love."

Dear Laura;

Thank you for your second friendly message, I'll be always on your side helping you as much as I could, and within the limites of my possibility. . . .

What you have seen at my parents house is one part of my studying memories at Bethlehem university. I have loved English litreatur, and have reading it the first years of my imprisonment; later I have dedicated my time for the reading of thearitical and philosophical books. . . . I have red the works of Tolestoy and Dostovesky. I do suggest that you read Dostovesky "Memories From The Dead House," it will help you more in the work you are conducting. . . .

The chances of being released now are so big because of my detoriorating health conditions. I'm sufering from "Azma," an illness which puts me very near to death. I'm living in unhealthy conditions, with ten of my friends in a small cold cell very full of humidity. They used to smoke, cook and do all their daily activities that brings me my hard time. You can't imagine how does it feels when you find yourself being chased even by the breath you breathe.

I don't know if the Israelians consider me as "having blood on my hands" but I do know that their is no meaning for having me at the prison after more than 13 years. The terms "blood on their hands" is a bad term I do not like to hear. It is a racist term used to fulfill some political purpose aimed to distort our picture as freedom fighters. . . .

In concern to my involvement into weapons struggle, I have been chosen to be a member into a military group that works in Jerusalem, after meeting some prisoners whom have been released within the prisoners exchange in 1985. We are ordered to plan for military attacks on some chosen military sites. We have looked for creating a state of unrest to pass the message that their will be no security and stapility on the continuation of vacating this city and its holy places. . . .

I have been so young at that time, later I have discovered that violence is something out of my personality. Maybe this is the answer for the question of why have I shot just one shot on that man despite the fact that my pistol have been very full of bullets. I have been able to shoot more, but in an unintentional manner I have shot one and left the area. . . .

The case of my hitting back, my dear Laura, is not a personal issue. I'm part of my people, part of his joy, and pain although the personal issue have also something to do with that. The family of my mother have forced to leave their home in Jaffa and cross the borders to Lebanon, after the establishing of the state of Israel. I haven't got any chance of seeing them. What I do know about them is just what have been left in the memory of my mother from stories about them. Once I have visited Jafa and went with my mother to see the runes of her lost childhood. I have smelled the faces of my grandmother, my uncles and aunts in a very beautiful imagination. I wounder how could it feel if it in a reality!

My father was born in the city of Kalkilia in the north part of the West Bank. He got married to my mother and went to live in the city of Jerusalem where I was born. I have lived the experience of this old city and faced what it has realy faced from pain and sadness. To live in the Middle East is to live in the middle heart of the history, deep in the middle heart of the world. And to live in the old city of Jerusalem is to be a saint, a profet, for the city couldn't love but only saints. . . .

This city have shaped my identity, she planted into my mind unforgetable memories. I have witnesed in it the Israelian aggression of the Six Day war. I was four years old then, but enough aware to understand what have been going on. I do remember when my mother used to hide us with the rest of our neighbours whom came to have shelter in our small room. We have been so frightened from the darkness and the sounds of the shooting of guns. Six days, and the history have entered into a new stage, the stage of the beginning of the occupation.

The resistance movement begins, and at the end of the 60s my brother was arrested and sent to prison. A new experience begins to shape itself into my mind. I have seen the painful time that my family are searching to know the fate of my brother. I do remember visiting him with my mother once or twice, but after that he have been expelled to Jordan through the desert of Wadi Arabeh. When reaching Jordan he was sent to prison there for no reason but under the pretext of crossing the borders illegaly. . . .

We are so poor family at that time, we haven't have enough mony to eat. How could it be if we need now to travel hundreds of miles to see my brother? I can't forget their journy of tierdness and pain, for I'm the one who used to accompany mother whenever she go because of my age. . . .

Do you know when it was the first time when I saw him next?! It was 25 year after. This time I'm the prisoner, and he is the visitore. After the signing of the Oslo agreement he got the chance to return to his home land. He came to visit me at Ashkelon prison. It is a very sad meeting, we both can't stop crying, I have no words to say, I have forgotten everything and felt the need of touching him, and kissing him. But no way. The fence is still between us and all along its holes I do see a tesellated picture of him.

I'm busy now learning to my examinations which will begin on the 25 of January. That why this message came to be so brief. So please excuse me and please, pray for my success.

Sincerely,
Omar

PS. I would like you to tell me if you have the possibility of translating messages from Arabic to English, for many from my side wish to write you.

AFTER I READ the shooter's second, nuanced letter, I stopped telling myself *simple justice.* Because every time I tried to simplify, things got more complicated.

9

INTERPRETATION

MUNICH, GERMANY

FROM THE WINDOWS of the train, Germany looked as I had imagined. Like photos from World War II, it appeared in black and white. I was traveling through a snowstorm from the airport to downtown Munich. Thick flakes whitened the ground and sky, leaving only the black lines of bare trees.

Hermann Raith had given me directions to his house: forty minutes to the city center, then switch trains to Wolfratshausen.

"In Solln you must jump out," he said, his German accent tilting vowels in new directions. "I will hold a badge in my hand with 'Laura.' "

We had spoken by phone, though I could tell by the depth and the heft of his voice that I was going to like Hermann. He was proud of his English and would not let me bring a translator. He would translate my interview with his wife.

"She will tell you what has happened in this accident," he said.

That was the one puzzling thing about our conversation, the word *accident.* After I hung up, I said to Baruch, "Why does he keep calling the shooting an accident?"

"He means *incident,*" Baruch said. "Maybe it was so upsetting, he can't bring himself to say *shot.*"

Hermann's wife, Isolde, was the German tourist shot in April 1986 by the same gang that attacked my father. The couple were walking on the Via Dolorosa after dinner when a young man wearing dark clothes and a furious expression fired at them. The bullet struck her an inch to the right of her spine. She was hospitalized for three days.

That much I knew from newspaper accounts. I had come to Munich to meet the Raiths because I wanted to know more. Isolde's injury was more serious than my father's, but she was the one person whose situation most resembled his. How had the Raiths reacted? Did they still talk about the shooting? Did they ever fantasize about revenge?

I was trying to figure out why some people needed to get even while others did not. Some of the traits of avengers I already had seen: people who had not only been hurt, but had been humiliated; people with long memories; people who divided the world into predators and prey; people who had a tribal, group identity; people who had simplified their view of justice.

There were other factors, of course. One of them was interpretation. It struck me as a powerful, almost magical force, while walking in Jerusalem with my father-in-law. David Weiss Halivni is a professor of religion at Columbia University in New York. He is a little man with a giant mind, quick blue eyes and hearing so keen he picks up every muttered aside at the far end of the dinner table. As a boy, he entertained adults who had stuck pins into pages of the Talmud by identifying every word on all the pages pierced by the pin. He has spent the rest of his life writing a radical interpretation of the Talmud.

One winter night, during his visit in Israel, we walked home from a late dinner. Baruch suggested we take a shortcut through a park, but my father-in-law hesitated. The park was ink-dark and deserted.

"Oh, it's OK," Baruch said.

"It could be dangerous," I said, following him toward some menacing trees.

"Yeah, we could get shot," Baruch said, making fun of me.

My father-in-law looked at us, questioning.

"My father was shot in Jerusalem," I explained, "after praying at the Wall with the Vishnitzer Hasidim." I included that detail because Baruch's family took pride in their relationship to the Vishnitzer Grand Rabbi of Romania.

Something clicked at the back of my father-in-law's eyes, as if now the world made better sense.

"So God rewarded your father," he said with authority.

"By shooting him in the head?" cracked Baruch.

"No," my father-in-law said with the knowing smile he might use to explain an Aramaic phrase. "He prayed with Vishnitzer—that's a good thing. He was shot—that's a bad thing. So God owed him and remembered him years later. God gave his daughter a great-great-grandson of the Vishnitzer rabbi for a husband."

His point of view was so unexpected it might as well have jumped out from behind one of the trees. "So *Baruch* is my father's reward for being shot in the head?" I said.

Baruch squeezed my shoulder with a teasing, smug smile.

"That's one way to interpret it," my father-in-law said earnestly.

Then he moved on to another topic. His other son was still single. Could we help him find a wife?

Meanwhile, he had helped me find a new way to resolve my problem. I had wanted revenge because my interpretation of events demanded it, though I was increasingly conflicted about it as a goal. But there might be another plausible interpretation.

And maybe one of the other victims' families had it. Three other people were ambushed by the shooter's gang—the German tourist, the Israeli businesswoman, the English pilgrim. If I could find their families, I might find a different way to interpret the event. How did they understand what had happened? Did they want revenge? Did their interpretation eliminate the need to get even?

• • •

It was hard to see out the windows at the Raiths' house. The snow was falling in a powdery veil, both protecting and obscuring.

We were having afternoon tea. The table was set with five kinds of ham and a bowl of clotted cream. The air was cozy with the smell of warm butter.

"The main change since the accident," Isolde Raith said, "was it brought the family closer."

"After the accident," Hermann said, "I call home more often on business trips."

"We had a 'second birth' of our mother," said their daughter, Birgit, who was about my age. "We had a little party, with roses and a chocolate hazelnut cake."

Hermann, with his knowledge of English, did most of the talking. He was fifty-nine years old, a computer engineer. He had fix-it hands, a reliable jaw and hair that would never thin. Isolde was all softness. She smiled a lot, in the way that people of another language do, although she might have smiled a lot anyway. Her straight blond hair flashed across her forehead. She had eyes the color of green sea glass and skin that would redden in the sun in minutes. At fifty-four, she worked as a pediatric nurse, assisting unwed mothers with their newborns. Birgit, a pharmacist, was engaged. Her younger sister was away, skiing.

I explained to them, in my precariously truthful way, that I was writing about the Abu Musa shootings from the spring of 1986. It was not until much later that I explained my personal connection to the attacks. As ashamed as I was to hear their story without telling mine, I was so fearful of the shooter learning my identity, I could not tell anyone. There was more to it, though. By now I welcomed any opportunity to escape my avenger self. Even if it was only for a few days on a trip to Munich, being a mere reporter was a relief.

That too might have been an excuse. Maybe the truth was that I was too embarrassed to tell these nice people what I was doing.

"The accident was April sixteenth," Isolde began. "That morning we were in the Dead Sea, we floated in saltwater."

Hermann got out their scrapbook. They had made an album for

every trip abroad. The trip to South Africa sat next to the Evangelical Lutheran Church Holy Land tour. They saved the itinerary, some clippings from the shooting and a fax from a friend in California: *Just heard about your misfortune on your holiday. I hope there will be no mental or physical scars.*

Hermann picked up the thread of the story. "After dinner my wife and I went for a walk. . . ."

They walked into the Old City and wandered to the first station of the cross on the Via Dolorosa.

Hermann: "I read an explanation from a sign. My wife said, 'Let's go, it's too quiet in here.' "

Isolde: "I had a bad feeling, like before a thunderstorm. He insisted on reading the history on the wall."

Then they heard a bang. At first Isolde did not recognize the sound. Hermann understood right away. His father had been a sharpshooter in the German army during World War II, and Hermann had heard him practice in the backyard.

"I felt a pinch in my back and then circles radiating, burning," Isolde said. She lifted her shirt to show me the scars. The bullet had tunneled through her rib cage, leaving two holes the size of a fingertip. The wound still ached in bad weather.

Hermann: "She said, 'I am shot.' I said, 'It could not be.' I had my arm around her. I felt blood running over my hand."

When the gun fired, they twisted around.

"I saw a young man fifteen feet away," he went on. "Unshaven, black hair, dark skin, dark eyes. A pistol in his right hand, the smoke rising from the gun. I looked at him in the eyes as you look at a wild animal, waiting. I could not read the eyes."

The gunman stood stock-still.

"He stared at us for an unbelievably long time," Isolde said. "They were cold eyes, strong, hard and crafty. If I wake up at night, sometimes I see his face. If I am downtown, and the street is very crowded and a dark man comes up suddenly, I remember his face."

The man was pointing his pistol at Hermann. For a moment

Hermann wondered if the shooting had to do with a bitter business rival in Germany.

Isolde: "I thought, The guy will shoot a second time. I tried to shield Hermann, but I couldn't move because Hermann was holding me tightly."

Then, as they stood on the Via Dolorosa, waiting for the second shot, something changed. They could see it in the gunman's expression.

"The gunman made an angry face," Isolde said. "Then he looked scared."

Hermann: "To me he looked really surprised."

Isolde: "He was really surprised we didn't speak English. He heard the German—'I am shot.' "

And the gunman ran away.

After they finished their account, we moved to the living room. The windows were opaque from the snow, blocking out the world.

I took a breath, then asked, "Do you ever think about meeting the man with the gun? What would you say to him?"

Isolde was wringing her fingers, one at a time. "I don't know."

"Would you want revenge?" I said.

"No, not really," she said. "I'd be afraid, but not angry."

"We haven't any thoughts about revenge because this man was only a tool," Hermann added. "He did it as an order from an organization. He was following their commands. The attack was supposed to be against British or Americans."

A few weeks before the shooting, America, with help from Britain, had bombed Libya.

"It was not against us. It was directed against another party," said Hermann. "He didn't know we are Germans. Germans have no complaints from Palestinians. I have some problems to understand the Israelis. The Palestinians don't have equal rights. In some cases the Israelis treat the Palestinians as the Germans treated the Jews."

"After the first shot, we spoke in German. He saw he made a mistake," Isolde said. "This saved us from death."

"From our standpoint," Hermann said, "his shooting us was an accident. There's no feelings of revenge for an accident."

An accident. That was the Raiths' interpretation. The gunman did not mean to shoot Isolde. He wanted to kill an English-speaker. This interpretation allowed the Raiths to move forward with no vindictiveness.

Months after I left Munich, the Israeli police allowed me to read a copy of the gunman's confession. A man named Fowzi Bustaan from the Jerusalem suburb of Beit Hannina gave a five-page statement.

Fowzi said that he was serving time for a family-honor killing when he met a Palestinian nationalist named Ali Mislamani. (Ali Mislamani was the third name in the DA's letter to my father.) After both men were released, Ali recruited Fowzi to join the Abu Musa cell. Ali taught Fowzi—along with Omar Khatib, my father's shooter—how to load and fire a gun. Their mission: "Shoot tourists in the Old City."

On April 16, Fowzi went to the Old City and recovered a twenty-two-millimeter Beretta, hidden in the wall near a mosque. It had a clip with nine bullets. He walked along the Via Dolorosa and spotted two tourists near the first station of the cross:

> The male tourist and female tourist were walking toward Damascus Gate. They stopped next to a church, and started to point to the church, and I'm three yards away. I took out my gun. I aimed the gun. I planned to shoot the man first, and then the woman. I fired in their direction. And the man turned and the bullet hit the woman in the shoulder. I wanted to fire again, but the gun jammed.

He could not fire the second fatal shot, hence his surprised, angry expression. There had been an accident that night, but it was not that his victims were German. His gun had jammed.

THE MAN WHO SHOT the British pilgrim was a more meticulous killer. Issam Jendal had trained on a terrorist base in Iraq and later joined the Abu Musa gang. Ali Mislamani gave him the Beretta, with eight bullets left in the gun. Issam buried it in his yard.

The day before the shooting, he scouted the area around the Old City looking for an execution site. He chose the secluded Garden Tomb, believed by Protestants to be the place of Jesus' crucifixion and burial. Issam's confession:

> I checked the area, where I would come from, where I would escape to after the murder. Then I went home and I sat by myself and I thought—what time of day is the right time for a murder?

On Sunday morning, Issam dug up the gun and wedged it in his pants, cloaking the bulge with his leather jacket. He took the bus to the Old City's Flower Gate. He checked his watch. Twelve-thirty, too early. He stopped for a glass of fresh-squeezed orange juice to waste ten more minutes.

Outside the Garden Tomb, Issam found a young man sitting next to his backpack. "How're you doing?" Issam said in English.

"Good," the young man said, looking up from under a mop of curls. He was a boyish twenty-seven, with round cheeks and believing eyes. He was holding a New Testament.

"You American?" Issam asked hopefully.

"No, I'm British," he said, raising a water bottle to his mouth.

Issam let him swallow the water and then stepped forward. He could have stretched out his arm and shaken the tourist's hand. He felt for the gun on his hip instead.

It was the gang's third shooting of a foreigner in six weeks. First my father, then Isolde Raith, and now the Englishman.

The young man fell backward, his hands at his sides, his feet splayed, in the shadow of the Garden Tomb door.

> After that, I put the gun under my sweater and walked off slowly and calmly so no one would suspect me. . . .

By the time the police arrived, the victim's lips had turned gunmetal blue. His curls were pushed back from his forehead and slicked together by blood. His head was turned slightly, as if someone had struck him on the cheek.

> I watched the news that night and heard that an English tourist was shot and killed. The name of the tourist was Paul. . . .

Who was Paul? The mastermind's family told me that Paul was "a British intelligence agent on an intelligence mission." The newspapers said Paul Appleby was a tourist from Bristol, England. He was neither, but it took a trip to England to discover the truth.

Paul had lived with an adopted family in Portishead, a town overlooking the Bristol Channel. At night, you could see the sparkle of Cardiff and, during the day, the blue-green Welsh hills. The road to Portishead meandered past sunlit meadows with nothing more threatening than the occasional sign, "Caution! Low-flying Owls."

Julian and Liz Marsh, or "Mum" and "Big Daddy," as Paul called them, were still tender with memories thirteen years after Paul's death. They welcomed me into their cottage with pink curtains and cats named Sugar and Spice. One of their three children, Sam, the eighteen-year-old, washed our plates after dinner and then snuggled on the couch next to his mother.

"Paul liked chamomile tea with a slice of lemon," Liz said in her delicate singsong. "Just the smell of it makes me cry."

"He'd ride around on our old bike with a woolen hat," Julian said with an affectionate laugh. "Liz taught him to drive. He taught our son to play cricket."

Julian was a church leader at the local charismatic Evangelical. The Marshes took in Paul, a born-again Christian, when he needed a bed for the night. He ended up staying for four years. During the summers, he went on the road with his friends who preached.

The road often led Paul to Jerusalem. He joined a prophetic ministry whose members believed they could hear the voice of God.

They lived on the Mount of Olives near the site where Jesus was prophesied to return. Paul played soccer with Palestinians and talked about religion with the Jews he met in the park.

"He was naive politically," Liz said. Mostly, what he cared about was God's acceptance.

Before he left England for the last time, Paul hesitated. He was considering giving up preaching and studying carpentry. He wanted to get married. Was it God's will that he return to Jerusalem?

"He went down to the beach, where the wind blows you back, and he gazed at the waves," said Liz. "He came back radiant and said God had said to him, 'Rise up and come to my holy city.' "

As Liz spoke, her sky-blue eyes grew radiant too. "He knew about the prophecy. He wasn't afraid of dying. He went willingly, like a lamb to the slaughter."

"What prophecy?" I said.

While preaching in California, Liz explained, Paul's Christian companions met a prophetess who told them: "The Lord spoke that the traveling companions should be chosen carefully. For there would be loss of baggage, loss of life, one would go to be with the Lord." They understood the implications.

For the Marshes' teenage son, Sam, this detail was especially moving. "Paul was so brave and faithful to go out, even though he knew one of them would die."

Soon after he settled on the Mount of Olives, Paul sent Liz and Julian a card:

> I arrived here in Israel along with Ray on the 16th of March. It was like coming home again after a long absence. . . . I hope that when and if I return to England I shall return stronger than when I left.

A month later, Paul was flown home in a coffin. His ashes were buried beneath a rosebush.

As the Marshes told their story, they conveyed their love for Paul, but no sense of injustice about his murder. As evening shaded into night and into the next morning, Julian and Liz recalled him in soft, west-country accents, their faces relaxed, their hands resting in their laps. For over a year now, I had been listening to people who had been wronged. These were the most serene victims I had seen.

"What about the man who shot him?" I said.

"We haven't thought about it," Liz said with the slightest start.

"What if you met the gunman?"

"We wouldn't be repelled," Julian said, stroking his salt-and-pepper beard. "We would touch his arm. We'd want to share Jesus with him."

"Would you forgive him?"

Again, Liz started, as if I had introduced a foreign, jarring sound. "We don't think about the gunman because Paul's dying has been linked with prophecy. The person who did the shooting was incidental. It just had to be."

It had to be. That was the Marshes' interpretation. Paul's death fulfilled a prophecy. There were no feelings of revenge because his shooting was part of God's plan.

Paul's companions from the Mount of Olives shared this view. I interviewed several separately, but their interpretations were the same. Paul's preaching partner, Raymond Keitz III, an American from Oklahoma City, identified Paul's body at the morgue. The two men had traveled the world preaching together; he was one of Paul's closest friends.

"On the one hand, you felt this deep loss, but then, wait—there was this prophecy," Ray told me over the phone from Poland, where he had moved to preach. "The prophecy gave me encouragement. It was something that was ordained."

"But what about the gunman?"

"To be honest, I wasn't interested in him. The more interesting story was the spiritual implications. Paul gets ready, he gets a white suit"—Paul had bought white clothes the weekend he died—"he's knocking on the door of the Garden Tomb and—*boom.* He's gone. It was such a fulfillment of the prophecy."

"What prophecy?"

"You see, this blood feud between the sons of Isaac and the sons of Ishmael, it goes back to Abraham. God says, 'I'm going to bless the sons of Isaac.' And God says, 'Ishmael will be a wild ass of a man and his hand will always be against his brother and his brother's children.' That's the whole Middle East story. The Arabs, Ishmael, want to be the favorite son. But Isaac is the promised son, so Ishmael wants revenge. First he gets revenge on the Saturday people, then on the Sunday people—Christians. It begins in Genesis and it's coming to a head now. The Arabs who shot Paul were used as the hand of God. It's something I have a lot of joy about."

"Even though he died a violent death?"

"Paul was a walking fulfillment of the word of the Lord," Ray said. "I can't think of any greater culmination of a life. His life came to a joyful conclusion."

RACHEL GAVE BIRTH to a six-pound boy with her black hair and David's quick eyes. Now she was at home in Providence, holding her baby in her lap, talking to me on the phone.

It was almost midnight in Jerusalem. Baruch was at the piano, doing finger exercises. I was sitting up in bed, looking out at the illuminated Old City walls. The slits in the walls above Jaffa Gate glowed. They had been cut into the stone centuries ago to pour boiling oil on invaders.

"He's sleeping with his tongue sticking out," Rachel said, cradling her baby. "He doesn't know the world is a dangerous place, and you should sleep with your tongue in your mouth."

She told me about diaper diaries and sleep deprivation. I told her about the shooter's second letter. I read her my reply:

Dear Omar,

Thanks for your wonderful letter. It was full of so many interesting details. How is your health?

I bought a copy of Dostoyevsky's "Memoirs From the House of the Dead" and have started reading it. Are you keeping a diary of prison life like the author did? If you have such a journal, I would love to read parts of it. And I'm also interested in the English text book you wrote. (By the way, we studied similar subjects—I majored in English literature in college, and have a master's degree in international relations.)

Sorry it took several weeks for me to reply. I have been traveling in Europe, interviewing more people for my book. One of the questions I am trying to answer in the book is: If a person has been hurt, what makes that person want to strike back? Why do some people choose revenge, and others forgiveness? What is your opinion? Is there anyone you hope to "get even" with, or anyone you want to tell you're sorry?

Thank you for sharing the stories about your mother's home in Jaffa and about your brother being deported. You have had to face many difficulties in life, more than I could imagine.

It is very important for me to be able to tell your story in detail, so the reader (and I) can understand your actions. I know you say that when you shot that man it wasn't personal, but I think that in the end, we're all human, and we do things for simple human reasons. Maybe because I am American, I think of things in personal, rather than ideological terms. Of course there are politics, but you are a person first, yes?

Your description of Jerusalem was great, poetic even. (Speaking of poetry—what about that poem you wrote a long time ago, "I May But I Can't"—what was that about?)

Yesterday, I was walking around the old city of Jerusalem and I thought about what you said about hiding during the 1967 war. That must have been very frightening. I also thought about what you said about only shooting one bullet even though your gun was full. It is a fascinating moment in your life. Can you describe the moment of the shooting—what you were feeling, thinking, what you saw, how you chose the target, etc. What would you like to tell this man or his family/friends if you saw them today?

Rachel snorted. "I'm sure he won't say he's sorry," she said. "He'll say, 'My cause is noble. Read Dr. Martin Luther King, chapter four, my dear.' "

I twisted the flannel of my nightgown. "You don't believe him—that he didn't want to shoot a second time?"

"I think it's ex-post rationalization, when in reality he froze. I'm sure his comrades were mad at him."

Something had started to shift inside of me since the shooter's second letter. I was hoping that Rachel was wrong.

"You sound like an ass," she said, laughing at my letter. She put on a nasal Long Island accent, satirizing what I had written: " 'We have so much in common. We studied similar subjects in school, I was part of a terrorist cell like you—I mean, I taught aerobics in college. I lost my house too when my parents sold one in Great Neck—oh, yours was destroyed by the Israeli army? Your brother was deported to Jordan? Mine was deported to Yale, Connecticut.' "

"We were both English majors," I said, clinging to the idea.

"So there are two career paths for English majors—you could become a journalist, or a pseudointellectual killer-person."

Rachel's baby woke up making hungry, sucking sounds.

"The call of the milk vampire," she said. He had to eat every hour. She and David were staggering around, bickering for the first time in their marriage.

"Having a baby is when you really slip the ring on the finger," she said. "When we had sex for the first time to conceive, I started crying because I thought it was the biggest thing I'd ever do. Four hundred sex acts later, I got pregnant. And here is a whole person lying in my lap that we made together. Once your genes twist together, you're permanently bonded. It's weaving together the essence of two people."

"That's what drives me crazy about my parents' divorce," I said.

"In some sense, your parents never did divorce," Rachel said. "They're living with other people and giving their romantic love to other people, but if marriage means a bond that lasts, then your parents are still married. Even if you get a Jacuzzi and go on cruises with someone else."

"I do feel like they're still married."

"They are. Through you. By walking around with your dad's eyes and your mom's nose and lips."

Rachel was casting one of her analytic spells and I was happily submitting. It was past midnight now. The lights shining on the Old City walls had gone out. The stones disappeared in the dark. I was in bed, wearing the same blue nightgown I had been wearing since college. The morning my mother had called to say she left my father, I wore it too. The flannel was ratty, the seams ripped. I kept it anyway, as a reminder.

"So they're married?" I said.

"Yes, because you exist."

"I believe that."

And for a moment, I did. Rachel had the right interpretation.

"Or maybe we all just like to think we're the sign of our parents' ultimate love for each other," Rachel said. "When the truth is, for some people, it's just a fuck."

"IS IT A CRIME," I asked Baruch as we walked the Via Dolorosa, "to watch a guy get shot and bleed and call for help, and just ignore him?"

"No," Baruch said. "In the United States, doing nothing is not a crime."

We turned onto David Street. The dense smell of camel leather closed around us. The dust-flecked light threw my senses into doubt. For months, I had been avoiding Tom. Now we were walking toward Jaffa Gate going home on a route that took us past Tom's shop.

Tom's car-accident story had put my revenge thoughts on pause. When he was hurt in a car crash, onlookers left him because they thought he was a Jew, exactly as Tom had done to my father. Measure for measure. How could I top that?

"Well, at the U.S. Attorney's office we don't drop charges because a guy has a traffic accident," Baruch cracked.

As we approached the store, I could see Tom on the telephone, wearing a snazzy plaid blazer and pleated pants. The pennies in his loafers shined so bright, Lincoln himself must have been squinting.

Tom saw me and winked. "Five minutes, OK?" He waved us inside. He seemed to be having some kind of intense romantic crisis. He grinned into the phone, bumping his hips against a display case filled with gold crosses and silver Jewish stars.

This was Baruch's first encounter with Tom. "What do you talk to him about?"

"At first, the incident. But last time, he said he didn't see anything."

"Why would he admit it?"

Baruch decided that he had seen enough and went home. I found a chair near some Madonna and child icons and waited.

Half an hour later, Tom dragged over a chair. He slid out a cigarette and puckered his lips.

"How are you?" I said.

"Existing."

"How's business?"

"Quiet."

"How's your wife?"

Tom crossed his legs.

"All the time I put shoes in my mouth because I don't want to speak bad of her." His words came in spurts. "I say no divorce, no divorce. If a father leaves the house, it's a table with three legs. How can a house walk with three legs?"

I told Tom that lately I had been examining the question of interpretation. I wanted to know what he thought. How did interpretation affect the way that he responded to events?

His eyes dropped to my midsection. "I can say your sweater is red. I can say your sweater is purple. I can say your sweater is pinkish too. But I cannot say your sweater is white. I can only change reality so much."

Sometimes Tom reminded me of the best and worst in fortune

cookies, at once foolish and profound. He was right, interpretation had its limits. So far I had not found an interpretation I could adopt. The Germans interpreted the shooting as an accident. The British thought it was the will of God. I could no sooner call my father's shooting an accident or the will of God than Tom could call my magenta sweater white.

An American tourist wiggled into the store. She wore a hot-pink top and heels. She seemed to have met Tom earlier.

"I love your cologne." She smiled, her mouth curling like a duck's. "What do you wear?"

"It's a secret." He winked.

She leaned over him and stroked his arm. "I'd like to buy it. It's incredible. My name is Lindy." She wrote down the name of her hotel, adding, "room 1204," and wiggled out the door.

After she left, Tom said soberly, "I don't like to give out the name of my cologne. There is an Arabic saying, 'He who gives gas and it is a bad smell, is the same who gives you perfume.' You understand the point, or you don't?"

I did not; I often did not. But I did understand that Tom's cologne worked like a tomcat's musk. It had worked on Lindy, and apparently on many others. He was cheating on his wife with his girlfriend from Alabama, and lately he was cheating on his girlfriend with a woman from Norway.

He called the two women "Alabama" and "Norway."

"Norway came into my shop with her boyfriend. When her boyfriend went to the bathroom, she said, 'I love your cologne.' I fell in love with her. I lo-o-o-ve Norway." He lay his hand on his heart. "Alabama says I've changed, that I'm nervous. Alabama is forty. Norway is twenty-seven. Alabama is home, Norway is wild!"

He spoke in a nervous, jerky voice that made every sentence sound exciting and tense. He pouted playfully; he had an idea. Norway was back in Norway with her boyfriend. Could I help him call her? In case her boyfriend picked up the phone.

Tom handed me the receiver. He said, "If a man answers, ask for . . ."

"Sally," I offered randomly, wondering how I had ended up helping Tom cheat on his wife.

The phone rang once. A woman picked up. "Hi, who's this?"

"This is, uh, Laura. Tom was just talking about you."

Tom was standing next to me, gesturing madly. "Tell her I love her."

"He loves you. He loves you so much that when he says it, he puts his hand on his heart."

Norway giggled.

Tom was beaming and mouthing the words, *More, more, more.*

"You two should be together," I said. "He loves you. You love him. True loves should never part."

I could not take it anymore, so I handed the phone to Tom. He baby-talked with Norway for a while, and then told me that he had to run to the bank.

"Can you watch my shop? The prices are all marked. If not, bargain with the customer."

Then he flew out.

I moved to the other side of the glass counter, looking over the inventory. There were watches with pictures of Jesus on the face, napkin holders shaped like Jewish stars. The store, as usual, had no customers. There was nothing to do but do nothing. I propped my elbows on the counter, my cheeks in my hands.

I am the shopkeeper.

I was supposed to be getting revenge on Tom; now I had become him? I looked out the door onto David Street, wondering about the people ambling by, wearing baseball caps and strapped with cameras.

Anyone getting shot out there?

A German couple walked in. I stood up straight and brushed the clean counter with my hand. They looked around and picked out a postcard.

"How much?" said the husband.

It was a picture of the Dome of the Rock.

"A dollar," I guessed.

"Too much," sniffed the wife.

They turned to leave.

"How much do you want to pay?" I said.

They walked out of the store. I followed them into the passage where my father had stumbled a long time ago, alone. The couple disappeared into the crowd. *How much is it worth?*

AFTER ISAAC BEN OVADIAH'S wife was shot, his daughters asked him not to remarry. He would not have, anyway. He lit a candle every day for his murdered wife. It flickered on a shelf in the dining room, burning for twenty-four hours. He bought 365 candles once a year, removing them from his kitchen cupboard one day at a time. Until he died, Isaac had vowed, her flame would not go out. Thirteen years had melted this way.

"She didn't deserve what happened to her," he said, watching the glow inside the blue glass. "Such an angel, and they came and shot her in the dirtiest and harshest way."

The gunman, Ali Mislamani—who had recruited and trained my father's shooter—did the job himself. He did not want this hit bungled.

Zehava had just arrived at her office overlooking Damascus Gate. She was fifty-nine years old, the mother of three girls. Ali walked through her door as she was settling into her chair and wordlessly removed the twenty-two-millimeter Beretta from inside his shirt. He reached across her desk.

In the window-sized photograph in Isaac's dining room, Zehava is laughing and clapping to an Arabic love song. Her head is tipped back in pleasure, a woman enjoying a party. Isaac mounted the picture in a round wooden frame and installed a bulb behind it to light up her smile.

It was the first thing that caught my attention when I entered Isaac's apartment in Bayit Vegan, Jerusalem. The rest of the room was decorated like an Arab dignitary's salon, with heavy green curtains, Persian hammered trays and Egyptian papyrus paintings. He offered me a welcoming, wrinkly handshake, his wrist banded by a pulse monitor. I lingered over his face.

Arab? Jew? He had a narrow nose, Crusader blue eyes and was dressed too much like a gentleman to be an Israeli. The neighborhood was Jewish. He spoke fluent English, his accent was Palestinian, his last name was Israeli. When a Palestinian friend called, he talked in Arabic. When his daughter called, he spoke in Hebrew.

"My daughters wanted to go to the trial," he said, sitting in his rocking chair. "The assassin didn't even try to defend himself. He said, 'I did it because I believe in it and I'm prepared to do it again.' I walked up to him after and said, 'I just want to know—why?' "

He rocked his chair forward. He held it at that angle, his body inclined and petitioning.

"The assassin said, 'Your wife is such a popular figure in Jerusalem, I was sure assassinating her would give our cause publicity.' "

Zehava was an eighth-generation Israeli, a Jew who knew Arabic. She opened a business in Arab East Jerusalem after the Israelis conquered it in 1967. In essence, she was a fixer for the Palestinians. She helped them deal with the new Israeli bureaucracy, securing permits for visits to relatives in Jordan, helping retirees collect social security. When she was killed, Musa Suss, a Palestinian neighbor, said, "Her whole life was about helping people. They should poke out the eyes of the man who did it."

"Do you ever dream about getting even?" I asked Isaac.

He let his chair rock back. "Arab clients who loved my wife said, 'Do you want us to take revenge?' A terrorist released in 1985, a man my wife did a favor for, said, 'My men will kill him in prison. You just tell me and it's done.' "

Isaac's first impulse was to say yes, though he was afraid he would get caught. His second inclination was to draw on a lesson that he had learned years before.

"My father was an Arab," Isaac said. "He saw my mother when she was a student going to school. He flirted with her. He loved her. She was a Jew." His parents married in 1920, in an era when the hatred between Arabs and Jews had not yet hardened. In 1947, when Isaac was twenty-four years old, the United Nations voted for a Jewish and an Arab state in Palestine. Arab riots broke out. Isaac's brother, an employee at the British Overseas Airways Corporation, was driving from the airport to Jerusalem with other BOAC workers. An Arab gang stopped the truck.

"They said, 'Jews on the left, Arabs on the right.' My brother went with the three Jews to the left. The five Arab employees stood on the right," Isaac said. "My brother asked the gunmen, 'Why are you dividing us? We are BOAC staff.' The gunmen said, 'We know your father is an Arab. Go stand on the Arab side. We're going to kill the Jews.' My brother told them, 'Shoot me first.' "

The Arabs shot him. Then they shot the three Jews. They hoisted their bodies onto the truck and set it on fire. He was twenty-six years old, married six months. The British police came to Isaac's home and asked his father to identify the body.

"My father came back crying, 'My son is charcoal.' " During the burial on the Mount of Olives, snipers opened fire while they were digging. There was no time to say a prayer or lay a stone.

"That night, I went out to search for an Arab to kill," Isaac said. He was wild with sorrow, tromping through a field of broken rocks and dead weeds. "I met a poor Arab walking a donkey, and he fell into my arms. I could have killed him with my hands. He said, 'Have you got a piece of bread?' "

As Isaac talked, a faint tremor shook his hands.

"That moment, I forgot that my brother was killed. I took the beggar to the gate of my house. I went inside and brought him rice and meat and my trousers and shirts."

Isaac looked down at his shoes, then at me. "I'm sure your parents taught you to do the same thing. Didn't they?"

Didn't they? A pang of shame.

Forty years after Isaac's brother died, Isaac once again had to wrestle with the impulse to take revenge. Half Arab, half Jew, he understood almost on a genetic level that revenge was self-defeating. The two people's fates were intertwined. There is a proverb in the Middle East: If you want revenge, dig two graves, one for your enemy and one for yourself.

The German tourist, the British pilgrim and my father were foreigners, and those around them—myself included—interpreted their shootings with a foreigner's sensibility. Only Isaac interpreted the shooting for what it sadly was: *It was the way things were.*

Isaac told the Palestinian man who offered to avenge his wife, no.

After mourning his wife, Isaac returned to his job as director of Arabic programs for Israel Radio. He hosted a radio call-in show that gave advice to Palestinians.

During my visit, he played a tape of an old program:

"Dear listeners, it has been a month that we did not meet through the radio because my wife passed away. Allow me to read to you a few verses of a poem I wrote to my wife:

My partner in life,
If the tomb is quiet and you feel lonely,
be not afraid.
I'll be beside you, to talk to you
and read you my poems.

If it is difficult for us to meet this spring,
then we will meet next spring.
Soon, very soon, we will meet again
and I shall see you in the blue dress I bought and you loved.
You will again be beautiful
and shine as the moon shines in a dark night . . .

The recorded voice had a deep, submerged quality, as if Isaac were broadcasting from a sunken ship. He considered himself Jewish, though he was not religious. But on the day he returned to the radio, he felt the need to say a prayer on the air: "O God, help me to be merciful and generous. If my enemy falls to the floor, do not let me take a dagger of revenge, but give me power to help him stand up. . . . O God, don't let me treat people as they treat me."

After we listened to the recording, Isaac showed me their bedroom. Everything remained just as his wife had left it thirteen years before. He touched the blue dress he had written about in his poem. He opened her bottle of perfume, White Linen, which now smelled bitter with age.

Before we left for the cemetery to water the rosebush shading Zehava's grave, I noticed a sign taped above his desk: "Love your enemies. It really gets on their nerves!"

Isaac saw me eyeing the sign. He smiled and took my hand and said, "It works."

• • •

I MAY BUT I CAN'T

By Omar Khatib

I cannot be certain, (though I know that I may),
Of all of the things that I'm wanting to say.
They tell me I may but I'm not sure I can,
Solve this problem I'm facing again and again.

"You can but you may not" my mom likes to say,
To my question of "can I go out now and play?"
When I ask "can I help you?" Dad often will chant
"You're allowed but not able, you may but you can't."

Well they try to correct me each time I am wrong,
And they tell me the same things I've known all along.
I know what they mean when they tell me I may,
They mean that I can, it's as plain as the day.
So when they tell me to talk right, it makes them all rant,
And I tell them quite simply, "I may but I can't."

THE SHOOTER wrote two more letters. They began, "Dear friend Laura."

I raced through the pages looking for personal revelations, but they were about the mechanics of prison life. I had asked him about conditions; I regretted it now. Two smuggled letters wasted. At any time—if he was caught by the guards, if his family no longer wanted to take the risk, if he grew tired of my prying—our contact could end. And I would not have what I needed.

He described the physical layout of the prison, the prisoners' political hierarchy and the factions of freedom fighters. He complained about bad food, crowded cells and the four-hour time limit in the exercise yard.

His main joy, it seemed, was taking university classes through a correspondence school that, coincidentally, my father's cousin helped run. He had learned French and Hebrew. He wrote a grammar book for the prisoners he called "The Practicle Use of English Structure." He had six courses left to complete his BA.

> *My exams are going so well, I got 90 at the course "democratics and dictatorships on the 20th century." I'm preparing now for another two exames on the "foreign policy of the USSR" and on the "basis of administrating the public institutions." I hope passing them well. I'm keeping my study at night from 12–5AM and do wake up at 9am every day.*
>
> *I have no table to study on, so I have made my special one from an empty pakets of cigarettes and covered it with cartons. It is about 70x40. They have refused allowing me have a lamp, but I petitioned to the court, and when the time came for the discussion they allow me have a lamp on the condition I drop the case. . . .*
>
> *I have considered writing a special autobiography, but things are not as you may imagine. Written materials from this kind may be disclosed to the "other side" through their security inspections, and that could endanger for us many information may be revealed about us to them. My position gets me to know many secret, and puts me to be in the depth of the developing political movement outside the prison. . . .*
>
> *We the prisoners used to correspondent by poetry, so that if for any reason our letters reached wrongly or fell under the hands of our enemy, it will be hard for them to understand. The story of my poem in "I May But I Can't" is a different thing.*

Finally, the shooter was going to explain his poem. His mother had shown it to me months before, when we were going through his papers. All along, I had interpreted the poem as a sign of his anger at his parents. It made me think he shot my father out of displaced revenge. He dared not confront his parents. So he directed his rage at a more suitable enemy—a Jew.

> *When I began presenting my subject at the university, I presented this poem as an exercise.*

He then wrote out the first verse of the poem for me. He drew a circle around all the words "can" and "may." The poem that I had interpreted as the key to the shooter's soul was a grammar exercise for an English class. A native English-speaker had helped him write the poem, he said. The content had nothing to do with him.

I should have known.

Then he went on to talk about his health:

> *My health is so bad, I'm taking a course of "prednsone 60 ml" and I'll be having an xray on the main clinic of the prisons authority. Beside that, I'm working for the sake of my release on the basis of my bad medical situation. We are waiting for the session of the central court. I hope it will be very soon. . . .*
>
> *Many may think that being in prison is being out of natural life. It is not the case of us. The true meaning of life comes only when you realy suffer and strive for this decent desired life. To be a prisoner means to be free and alive, not a dead moving body accepting to be deprived from his rights. Those who deprived themselves from their basic human natural rights are undeserved to belong to human being. . . .*
>
> *I'll stop here, it's 4 am and tomorrow is my family visit. Forgive me for not being able to continue.*
>
> *I'm thirsty for asleep. . . .*
>
> *Yours, Omar*

The letters were compelling, though not what I was after. Somehow, I had to get closer to him. So on Friday, when Baruch wheeled his bike through our front door with eight bunches of carnations and said, "I just want you to know, I've noticed how nice you've been to me lately and I appreciate it," I kissed the inside of his elbow and said, "Let's go to Ashkelon."

We both could use a romantic weekend at the beach, I said. We could celebrate his good news: Baruch had just received word from the States that he had been picked to become a criminal judge, a life's dream achieved. And I had been filling in for the *Washington Post's* Jerusalem bureau chief and was looking forward to a break, I said. The most recent news story that I had written began: "Israel launched a military offensive against Hezbollah targets in Lebanon, vowing to attack the Shiite Muslim group by air, sea and land in retaliation for a bombing this afternoon that killed four Israelis. . . ."

It was the latest in a seemingly endless chase of predator and prey. It reminded me that in the cycle of world violence, my father's injury hardly registered.

Halfway through my pitch to Baruch, he went off to look for his sunblock. We borrowed a friend's car and drove to Ashkelon.

The next morning, while we were lying in bed in our hotel room by the sea, I mentioned that the next day was March 7, the anniversary of the shooting. If I could not confront the shooter, I said, at least we could frolic near his prison. Baruch rolled his eyes.

"What a Kotzaleh," he said, using my nickname, "little thorn."

He fell back on his pillow and pulled me closer.

An hour later, I nuzzled his shoulder and smiled. "Remember . . . ?"

"How can you reminisce about things we did five minutes ago?"

"I like remembering. Remember when you—"

"Shh, shh, shh." He kissed me quiet. "You don't always have to remember."

Later still, we went for a walk on the beach. The waves were weak, hitting the shore in small splashes. The light was so strong, it bowed our heads. I looked for seashells and picked wildflowers, marveling that the shooter could live so near and never see these things.

"What are you doing?" Baruch said as I tucked some shells and flowers into my shorts' pocket.

"Pocketing the moment."

In Israel, moments were often twinned, a simultaneous time of past and present. We passed the thirteenth-century tomb of a holy man, Sheik Awad. A Palestinian family sat in its shade, slaughtering a black goat, the blood of an ancient rite dribbling into the sea. Later, we passed a snack bar, the Delilah Cafe, named for the biblical vixen who brought Samson of Ashkelon to his knees. Delilah was the reason I loved the Samson story. A song was playing in the cafe, *"All you have to do is follow your heart . . ."*

"Did you follow your heart?" Baruch said.

His question surprised me. It was not like him to wonder.

"What do you think?" I said.

"I think you followed your daddy's heart," Baruch said. My father was awed by Baruch's father, by his interpretation of the Talmud. "Your daddy told you to marry me, so you did."

"No." I had my own silly reason. The lifeguard crush. "I followed my imagination."

He said something next that sounded rehearsed, as if he had been repeating the words inside his head, but only now had found the courage to say them: "It's not easy being the object of your imagination. I'm afraid you're always going to be disappointed with me."

His mouth crumpled a little. His eyes had that vulnerable, peeled-back look. It was a look, I realized then, that I would remember when we were eighty and still married.

We went back to our hotel room and took a bath. Baruch sat behind me and I leaned my head on his chest and felt the steam drift around us.

"So," Baruch said tentatively. "What do you think about starting to take prenatal vitamins?"

I could not see his face. I listened for his heart, trying to hear if it was beating fast. Mine was.

I listened. His was steady.

That evening, before we drove onto the highway leaving Ashkelon, I asked Baruch to indulge me and turn left at the grain silo.

The boulevard had not changed since I had been there the previous summer with the mastermind's family. The tall palms, the fortresslike walls rising above everything else. The street was dark and empty.

"What do you think?" I said to Baruch.

"It looks like a prison."

"Slow down. Isn't it weird to know the shooter's in there?"

"It's comforting, not weird. That's where he belongs." Baruch shifted the car into neutral. We sat below the prison walls, Baruch looking straight toward the highway, and me looking up. There were no sounds except for the idling of our engine.

Then the guard dogs began to bark. A prison guard in black, posted on the tower, yelled something at us through a megaphone.

I opened my window. Black ocean air rushed in.

"What?" I said in English.

The guard yelled again. Unintelligible, but angrier. He turned on a searchlight and swiveled it toward our car, training it on our faces. The dark street was suddenly blinding with light. The guard dogs were howling. The guard kept yelling, the same indistinct words.

"What?" I opened the car door and started to step out.

"GET—OUT—OF—HERE!"

"Oh."

Baruch drove us away.

"I find it really hard to believe someone could be kept for so long in so small a space," I said, hugging my knees. "Is thirteen years a lot of jail for shooting someone and injuring him?"

"Don't forget he was part of a conspiracy that committed two murders," Baruch said. "And if your dad were an inch taller, he'd be dead."

"But he didn't take a second shot."

"Those are arguments his attorney would make. He's guilty of murder."

"What would you sentence someone who shot and grazed a guy's head?" I said. Now that Baruch was going to be a criminal judge, he would be hearing murder cases.

"A guy shoots a gun— Was it intended to kill? Was it intended to scare? Was it intended to harm? The same act, depending on intent, can have widely different penalties. I'd need a lot more information. Does he express regret? Does the court believe him? Does he accept responsibility?"

"Does he?" I said. "You read the letters too."

Baruch shrugged.

I wondered.

We slowed at an intersection. I stared absently at the red taillights on the car ahead of us. It occurred to me that I was approaching interpretation from the wrong end. I had it backward. It did not matter how I interpreted the shooting. Who cared? That was a game people played inside their heads. When I told Baruch about interpretation, he said, "more like self-deception."

The only interpretation that mattered was the shooter's. How did he interpret the event? Was it one that merited revenge?

I WROTE ANOTHER LETTER to the shooter.

> *As I mentioned in my last letter, one central question I am trying to answer in my book is about justice: If a person has been hurt, what makes that person want to strike back, like an eye for an eye. When do you choose revenge, and when do you forgive? I have interviewed many different kinds of people on this subject.*
>
> *What about you—is there anyone you hope to "get even" with, or anyone you want to tell you're sorry?*
>
> *Also, back to the shooting incident. I know it must be a hard moment for you to revisit. But I was intrigued by what you said about choosing to shoot only one bullet even though your gun was full. You said this man was a military target, but how did you*

> *choose him? If you saw him today, or met his friends/family, what would you like to tell them?*

I knew it was a lot to expect for him to repent his crime. His act, in a sense, justified his existence. The shooter had told me to read Dostoyevsky's *Notes From the House of the Dead.* In the book's descriptions of prison life, I picked out sentences, imagining that they were clues. One, on page 21, stood out: "There was hardly a man among them who would admit his crime to himself."

Meanwhile, I continued to look for ways to see the shooter. The court would be holding a medical hearing, his family said. Every court date that had been set had been postponed. I also went to the American consulate in Jerusalem to apply for a passport with Baruch's last name, Weiss—if I ever managed to arrange a prison visit, I did not want to register as "Blumenfeld." The shooter, I suspected, would remember his victim's last name.

"Hello, Mrs. *Weiss,*" Baruch taunted when I came home with my new passport. He was in the kitchen, making dinner. "Now I'm your lord and master."

"I didn't change my name for you," I teased back. "I changed it for him." Although, it did make me wonder. "Do you feel like we're a family?"

"I thought we were. I mean, we're married."

"I don't mean a document. I mean a feeling, an identity."

That kind of mush was too abstract for Baruch. "I'm going back to work." He was writing about the mental state of criminal accomplices. A defendant could be declared guilty or innocent, depending on his intent. Baruch was trying to define intent.

While I was trying to determine intent.

A FEW DAYS LATER, I brought my letter to the shooter's family. Imad slid it under a ceramic pitcher. I was surprised to find him wearing the jacket from a green military uniform. He had told me that he was a beautician.

Who was Imad? He said he had been deported to Jordan for his "activities" in the PFLP, where he was jailed for three years. Once he said that in Jordan, in the 1970s, "the PFLP hijacked airplanes, and gave speeches to the foreign passengers about Palestine. It was how we made public relations."

Was he talking about himself? I never knew what he meant by "activities." Talking with Imad felt like running in sand, pleasant and warm, though always shifting beneath me. Another time, he mentioned Fayez Jabar, the head hijacker from Entebbe, the one whose picture I had shown to Benjamin Netanyahu. Imad said he met Fayez Jabar in Jordan. He called him "a good man."

Was I drinking tea with a hairstylist, or a retired hijacker, or both? Or maybe because I was an impostor, I assumed everyone else was too. In any event, I was afraid to press him further. His wife, Suraya, sat opposite me, her arms folded across her chest, her legs crossed, too.

Arms folded. Legs crossed. Unfriendly body language. That was enough to set off a spiral of worry. *Did they figure out who I am?*

In many ways, we were having a typical visit. When I walked along the rim of the gorge toward their house, I watched their children throwing rocks at the rusted frame of a refrigerator. "Will my uncle Omar be free?" one of them asked. A stitch of guilt threaded my side. The German shepherd barked and leaped, straining his chain.

Imad talked politics. He said there was no justice in the world, now that the Soviet Union had dissolved. There was no justice in his own life either, thanks to Israel.

"So don't you want to do something to get justice?" I said.

"A person can't stand before a state and fight it."

"Omar tried."

"My goal in life is my children more than justice," he said.

Looking for ways to fill the hours while we drank tea, I told Imad and Suraya that I had been to Germany to interview people for my book. Suraya livened up. She had an uncle in Germany. She would give me his address the next time I went there. She started to tell me about her other relatives. She and Imad, it turned out, were first cousins.

"It's not logical to marry a person you're not related to," Imad said. "The most important thing is family ties. We don't think it's important to have love and know each other. People marry without love and have a happy life. And people marry with love and get divorced."

"Was yours a marriage of love?" I asked. He had painted the living room wall with a green and red mural. Twin hearts, pierced by an arrow, with the words in English: LOVE FOR EVER.

"My marriage was traditional," he said. "We have lived together twenty-five years."

Suraya shifted on the couch. "Love comes after marriage."

"I just got married a year ago; what's your advice?"

"Don't have a lot of children," Suraya said without hesitation.

"How many?"

"Two. Maximum." Suraya was my age. She had married at age fifteen and had seven children. Her eldest son was going to be a father soon. It would be her first grandchild, the newest member of the Khatib family.

As we talked about family, I almost started to feel comfortable. For the first time, they asked where I lived in Jerusalem. They asked about my husband's work. I said that he was going to be a criminal judge; we would return to live in America in June, in time for his confirmation hearing. That might be before Omar was released, I said. I would be sorry if I had to leave before meeting him.

"We're going to keep our connection with you, even after you leave," Imad said. He smiled warmly. "You're part of our family now."

I was sure that I had misheard him.

"You're one of us," Imad said. "Laura is not just Laura. Laura is family."

I had to hide my face. Too many conflicting emotions were running across it. I bent over my notebook, scribbling random notes:

> The door is gray metal. Over the entrance to Omar's bedroom, a string of peach, plastic flowers. From his window, a view of forever.

For more than a year, I had been pursuing revenge, trying to assert my identity as a Blumenfeld. I wanted to prove to my father that he had a family that cared about him. In the process, I had driven my new husband into keeping a daily record of his "insufferable and intolerable" marriage. And for no reason other than the revenge effort, I had changed my passport to Weiss. After all that—I was a *Khatib?*

Suraya slipped the ring off her finger. It was silver, with a black center stone.

"For you." She held it out for me.

My face felt hot, crisscrossed with emotion. Suraya misunderstood my confusion for disapproval.

"It's real silver," she said, as if that were the problem.

I took it from her hand. "I love black," I stammered. "It—matches my jacket." The jacket my mother had bought me so that we could be twins. "Thank you."

I put her ring on my finger, next to my wedding band.

10

ACKNOWLEDGMENT

JERUSALEM

BARUCH WAS SITTING on the roof with my father, their voices drifting through a kitchen window.

"Her neck is too thin, that's the problem," my father said.

"Maybe she could wear a necktie," said Baruch.

"Or a scarf. And a black trench coat. She'll look less suspicious in a coat."

"Most men don't have two breasts sticking through their trench coat."

The two of them were discussing how to sneak me into the men-only section of the Western Wall. A tall, metal barricade runs down the middle of the wall, separating men and women. The best chance I had, they decided, was to go disguised as a Hasidic boy.

My father's favorite example of "constructive revenge" took place inside a passageway off the men's section of the Wall and he wanted to show it to me. He was hoping to persuade me that constructive revenge—self-improvement—was the best revenge.

The last time I had visited the wall, Conservative and Reform Jews, men and women together, had been praying at the far end of the plaza. Hasidic men were pitching dirty diapers at them, and a ring of police had to hold back the mob. Other times, when women tried to sing and dance like the men, Hasids had hurled chairs. Even though I was covering the clash as a journalist, the violence had offended me.

Late that evening Baruch, my father and I walked through the metal detectors at the entrance to the Western Wall plaza. I had borrowed a black raincoat and a scarf from my father-in-law, an Orthodox rabbi, who was about my size, and was visiting Jerusalem. ("Don't ask what it's for," I said to him.)

Once we passed the guards, I tucked my hair into a black fedora. My father handed me his large, gold aviator glasses. The prescription was weak and the bifocals cut every blurry image in two. The wall was lit up, white against the night; above it, the Al-Aksa mosque glowed green.

Baruch and my father stood on either side of me, looking around nervously. The night before, I overheard my father saying to him, "Don't force religion on Laura. I made that mistake with her mother." Maybe that explained why Baruch was willing to come along.

At that hour, the only people at the wall were Hasidic men, dressed in white shirts and black suits. We stood out, an odd, uncertain trio: an older American man in a brown sports coat, a younger man in a bomber jacket with his collar flipped up and an effeminate, pencil-necked Hasidic boy. I tried to lumber from side to side like my father. We were tense, arguing in whispers.

"You have girl lips," Baruch said to me. "Put the scarf around your mouth."

"Take that scarf off your mouth," my father ordered. "You look like a crazy person."

"Let's put a note in the wall," I said to my father. "What should we wish for?"

"Don't even try," Baruch said. He was a traditionalist, and was conflicted about what we were doing. "If they see you're a woman, they'll throw rocks at you and beat you up."

"We don't need you coming along and ruining things," I said.

"I'm not ruining things. I just don't want anyone to hit my wife in the head with a chair. I'd like a wife with her head intact."

"I'm going to pray too," I said.

"On the women's side," Baruch said.

"No, on the men's side."

"It's the same wall, the same stones," Baruch said. "Other than being pigheaded, why do you want to pray there?"

"You pray at the wall next to your dad. I want to pray next to mine."

We stepped into the men's section. A hive of Hasids. We were surrounded by buzzing, swaying men.

What am I doing here?

In the home I grew up in, women counted as equal partners in religion. But Baruch came from a home with more traditional, men-only customs. When we were engaged, we often quarreled about whether I "counted," about whether our daughters would "count" if they wanted to be practicing Jews. What hurt was the lack of acknowledgment.

Acknowledgment, for many people, is the emotional goal of revenge, more than the desire to hurt. They want the other person to acknowledge his mistake, to acknowledge the legitimacy of their pain.

"The only substitute for revenge is acknowledgment," said Hanoch Yerushalmi, a psychologist at Hebrew University. "Acknowledgment is more than regret, it's accepting responsibility. It's when you 'own your guilt.' "

Yerushalmi told me that he encouraged acknowledgment in family therapy. But he also thought it could play a role in Middle East politics.

"On a national level, the most therapeutic thing for the Israelis and Palestinians would be to acknowledge they did something wrong and to acknowledge each other's legitimacy."

The power of acknowledgment should not be underestimated, he said: "Acknowledgment establishes a new reality."

That was what I was looking for with the shooter—a new reality. The snaky, coiled feeling I had been carrying inside of me was wearing me down. I could not forgive the shooter. But I was willing to consider giving up on revenge. If only he would acknowledge that he was wrong.

My father's shooting and the violence of the Hasids toward the women at the wall were hardly comparable. Yet both cases came down to acknowledgment. With the Hasids, it was their lack of acknowledgment, a kind of disrespect, that made me want to act disrespectful back. But sneaking into the men's section was also a way to test my nerve. As the date for our return to America approached, so did the moment when I would have to drop the journalist's cloak—and act. After all my research and preparation, I was still scared.

Led by my father, flanked by my husband, I brushed along the black-coated men. The world looked different through an impostor's eyes. The images moved at an irregular speed, like footage from a shaky, hand-held camera. Beneath the surge of adrenaline, at my core, I felt strangely safe. Not so much because my father and my husband were protecting me, but because they were standing by me. Counting me.

We entered the mouth of the passageway. The tunnel brought us into a cool, domed hall. My father pointed up. "There it is."

Tall black letters were nailed across a white wall. Deuteronomy 32:43: "O nations, Acclaim His people, for He will avenge the blood of His servants, render vengeance on His foes."

Below it, men were seated at tables, studying Talmud. Their shadows bobbed against the biblical verse. They were arguing over texts, their voices multiplying in the arches of the ceiling.

My father described these men as a vivid example of constructive revenge. By studying Jewish books, they were getting revenge against all those who had tried to destroy their people. They were reading the same words that the Nazis had burned in bonfires. They were dedicated to recovering what had been lost while improving their own lives.

"This is the most powerful form of revenge," my father said.

He handed a prayer book to me. "Here, hold this over your face."

I peered over the book at the hundreds and hundreds of people with facial hair.

If this room blasted off into space I would be their only hope to continue the human race.

A man approached us. He needed ten men to make a quorum for a prayer service. Were we available? Then he took a second look, a question forming in his eyes. He called over another man. Baruch caught my trench coat at the elbow and steered me toward the exit. Outside, I shook off Baruch and darted through the crowd of praying men, toward the blocks of stone.

"Dear God," I scribbled on a piece of paper.

Then I wrote one word. What I wanted most from the shooter.

"Hurry," Baruch said standing behind me. He jammed his hands in his pockets, bulking his chest and lifting his shoulders, doing his best to look big. More and more men had doubled back to look at the delicate Hasidic boy and were starting to murmur.

"Hurry."

I kissed my note and crammed it into a crack in the wall. Then we turned around and ran.

"My God," my father said, clutching his heart as we left the plaza. "We could have gotten clobbered."

"Happy?" Baruch said.

I tipped my fedora at him.

"Now you got revenge on the Orthodox," he said.

"Wearing your father's coat." I smiled.

WEARING SURAYA'S SILVER RING, I rounded the corner to the shooter's house. His reply to my letter had arrived.

The German shepherd looked at me and yawned. He was lying next to another dog and their litter of puppies.

Before I left for the shooter's house, I had called Rachel. "I just want him to regret it."

"Zero chance," she said.

I climbed the stairs to Imad and Suraya's apartment. Green graffiti stretched across a wall: "The Glory is for the Martyrs of the Al-Aksa Mosque."

I was excited to get the shooter's letter, but I was apprehensive about reading it. As long as I did not read it, I could imagine he had written an expression of acknowledgment.

Where did my revenge go? Exhaustion. Cowardice. Empathy.

Over the months, as I got friendlier with the shooter's family, I worried how they would react when they learned the truth. The fraud was gnawing at me and I rented a post office box, hoping the shooter and I could mail each other letters. That way I would not involve his family. The shooter said no, too risky.

Suraya welcomed me with a plate of date cookies that she and Lama, her daughter-in-law, had baked. Lama was four months pregnant and was starting to show. She was seventeen years old.

Imad had Omar's letter, Suraya said. He was late coming home from work.

"Cutting hair?" I said.

Suraya laughed. "He left the hairdressing business a while ago."

Imad was a colonel in the Palestinian National Security Services, she said. He worked as a military assistant to Sheik Jamal, one of the speakers at the Al-Aksa mosque, above the Western Wall. Before that, Imad was a member of Force 17, the Palestinian militia, along with Saed, his older brother. No wonder he had given me a weird look a few months earlier when I brought him a can of American hair spray and an issue of *Vogue.*

While we waited for him, I admired Lama's wedding jewelry, her gold bangles and earrings. Suraya packed a bucket of cookies for me. The younger children brought me outside to play with the German shepherd's puppies. Their fur was nearly white, soft against my cheek. I could feel their small, panting ribs in my hands. One of them licked my nose. At moments like these, I was so caught up in pretending, I was not entirely pretending.

When I went back into the house, Suraya glanced at the clock. She ran worried fingers through her hair. "Imad is late," she said. "Maybe a Jew shot him."

Then I remembered who I was and who they were.

"I'm afraid of Jews," she went on. "I'm afraid for Imad to work there. Jews shoot people in the Old City."

"Oh, no, don't worry," I said stiffly.

There was a silence.

"Eat another cookie," Suraya said.

Lama brought me another cup of tea. Her hand was resting on her belly.

"My brother is having a baby in a few weeks," I said. "They don't know if it's a boy or a girl."

"Neither do we," Suraya said. "If she has a boy, we'll name him Imad."

"That's nice."

"If she has a girl, we'll name her Laura."

Suraya saw my confused expression and said to her daughter-in-law, "I don't think she understands."

I understood.

"I don't like the name Suraya," Suraya said, as if that explained everything.

I felt sick. Was she serious? She sounded sincere. Half of me was touched. Her gesture meant many things, among them that my bedtime-story revenge plan was working. The other half of me was more darkly calculating. Laura Khatib. Unwittingly named for the daughter of Omar's victim. Not bad for revenge.

Imad walked in, escorted by two official-looking men. I said good-bye to my mother. His manner was more brusque than usual. It made me feel shaky.

Somehow it came out that Suraya had told me about Imad's work. Imad said something to her in rapid, annoyed Arabic.

"Are you alone?" Imad said to me.

"Yes."

"All alone?"

I had mentioned to Imad that my father was visiting me.

"I want to meet your father," he said.

"Yes. It would be good." When I got rattled, I started to sound like a robot.

"What is your father doing here?"

"Tourism."

Imad pulled his brother's letter from his shirt pocket. It was the size and shape of a bullet.

I stood up, edging toward the door.

"Stay for tea?"

"Thank you. I really have to go." Three hours of this was more than I could take.

Imad walked me to my taxi. He told me about the latest date for Omar's medical parole hearing. The hearing would take place in a court, in the southern city of Beersheba. I would travel there with the family. I was part of the family now, he said.

"Don't forget the date," he said as I got into the taxi.

"I won't."

Imad lay his hands on the driver's window. He bent his head level with the driver's. "You must take care of her."

As soon as I got home, I ran up to the roof. Usually, I skimmed the letters on the bus back to Jerusalem. This one was too important. I needed a quiet place where I could concentrate. This letter, I thought, would decide everything.

Let him say he's sorry. Please make it be true.

I broke the seal of the plastic capsule. Unwound the thread that bound the letter. Rubbed the string between my fingers and sniffed. Day-old spit. There were three pieces of tissue paper folded twenty times. The writing made my eyeballs ache. Each character was a tiny, pale freckle.

His note began with a warning. Prison guards were cracking down. We had to watch what we wrote, he said. I should "stay far from the main subject." I wondered what he thought our main subject was.

Then his tone relaxed:

> *It is a great news, dear Laura, that you visited the sea of Ashkelon, and you have enjoyed a good time. I wounder how the sea looks like now. I haven't seen it more than 15 years. But I do feel its presence, mostly when I do stand out at the coridor looking at the old city of Ashkelon and smelling the breeze coming out of*

the sea. I used to close my eyes for seconds and dive into imagination, while the taste of the sea are being smelled by my weak lungs. How great is the feeling that gets me escape out of the prison far away from the darkness for few seconds.

On the coming dayes, I'll be travelling to Barzili hospital at Ashkelon to have some medical tests for my lungs. I hope passing near the sea that I could see it. Concerning my health, still things are going so bad to a degree of touching the different faces of death many times. I have felt how beautiful is life and how great are its meanings. I do believe that life is fighting for me. It doesn't want to ignor me, or turn its back on me. I'm her great present, how could she leave me!?

I have many things to do if I do win getting back to life. I have learned many things through this long journey of mine. I have learned to believe in my princibles, and to respect the holyness of others lives.

People are so different when you get to know them from near.

That last line jumped from the page. *Exactly!* I thought. That, more or less, was my philosophy of journalism, if not of life. We were all more alike than different.

I've known some people from near, and discovered how different they are especially when you feel, and understand their hopes, and needs, their true humanity. We need to believe in peace between peoples. We need to give and forgive to find ourselves living a true life.

At this stage, I'm working so hard to finish my studies, so when I do get released, I could find my place of work at the field of diplomacy where I could work for the benefit of introducing mutual international issues such as the universal peace issues and the introducement of economical co-operation between peoples of the world. I hope I could take part in shapping the new history of the Middle East. . . .

Everything he had written so far looked promising. *He will apologize. He must. Even if he doesn't mean it, I'll believe it because I want to.* If for no other reason than that, I did not know what to do next.

> *For the sake of answering your questions, I've told you, what I've done is not personal. You have to see it as part of our leagal military conduct against the occupation. Occupation knows no justice. We learned it to be a duty to fight the aggresor. Land, in our believes, is a holy main thing we are ready to die for.*
>
> *If the Israelian people could forget and forgive the Nazis for what they done for them, we could forgive them for the occupation to our land—a thing that can't be imagined. . . .*
>
> *With concern to "David Bloomingfield"—*

My eyes had skipped over the line about the Nazis to my father's name. The shooter had never mentioned my father's name before. No one in his family had.

> *—"David Bloomingfield"—I hope he could understand the reasons behind my act. If I were him I will. I have thought a lot of meeting him one day. We have been in a state of war and now we are passing through a new stage of historical reconciliation where there are no place for hatred and detestation. Under this new era and atmosphere, he is welcome to be my guest in Jerusalem.*
>
> *I hope, Laura, you too could be there. You could believe that God loves us both. Me for leading my act and having me shoot him just one shoot, and him for having his injured lightly. We are both children of God, and he probably knew how to take care of us.*
>
> *Dear Laura, feel free to ask any questions you want. You are not overwhelming me with your queries. The fact is that I've little time to concentrate on what I write you. . . . Time passes so fast, I hope the day will not end, so that I could work and work.*
>
> *My family do love you and keep on telling me about you*

on their visits to me. Feel free and open when you're with them. . . .

with my best wishes to you,

Omar

My eyes misted. *Yes! He's sorry.* He acknowledged his wrongdoing. He accepted responsibility for his act. There was no longer a need for revenge.

I called Rachel and read her the letter, looking forward to gloating.

"I had a chill," she said when I finished the last line. "He sounds like you. It's a UNICEF letter. Maybe this whole thing is a joke on you. He's saying what you want to hear. Maybe he's like, 'Ugh, this journalist is writing me again.' He's telling his cellmates, 'You write the first page and I'll write the third page.' "

Rachel was voicing one of my unspoken fears. Maybe he was playing with me. Tricking the trickster.

"Still, he says he's sorry," I said.

"He's *not* sorry. He's worse than not sorry. He thinks there's nothing to be sorry about." She quoted his letter back to me: " 'I hope he could understand the reasons behind my act. If I were him I will.' "

As she spoke, I was thinking about the downside of having smart friends.

"He's saying"—she said a little too loudly—"I don't owe him an apology because what I did was OK. That's a more extreme form of not being sorry. Ha! I was right. He's not sorry at all."

Rachel was right. I had misread his letter.

"You don't think he believes in peace?" I said.

"He's saying 'peace,' but that's pragmatic, not a change of heart. There's a peace song playing now, so he's an asthmatic, poet, philosopher-politician who believes in humanity. But if the music changes and peace negotiations fail, he'll become a lion-warrior again. It's that tribal thing, that Mafia thing, 'it's nothing personal.' Then *bang*—he shoots you."

"Shoots an innocent man?"

"It's disingenuous to say your father was just walking in the market, minding his own business. He's a Jew; his collective group is guilty."

"I don't believe in that. I believe in reconciling individuals."

"That's so American. Everyone doesn't have to be friends."

"But that's the whole point of me: 'Let's all be friends.' "

"Then you shouldn't be playing in the Middle East. In the Middle East people just look across fences and grimace. People aren't friends in the rest of the world. It's sort of cute that you believe the whole world works that way. It's all brave men and pretty women, and good triumphs. It's a joke."

My head was aching. I hoped that she was wrong; I feared that she was right.

"This is not about the heart of an individual," she said.

"I'm going to prove you're wrong."

Baruch had come home and climbed to the roof.

"You OK?" he said.

I shook my head no.

He mouthed the words *I love you,* and retreated.

I said to Rachel, "Can't the personal overcome the collective?"

"So what, then—you'll see the shooter in court, and you'll fall in love and you'll have intertribal children? And he'll say, 'Did you take prenatal vitamins?' "

I could not keep up with her when she was on a tear.

"You know," I said, hoping to slow the fight, "we're trying to make him more like ourselves. We're projecting onto him, as if he's a figment of our imagination. I want him to be a dreamy idiot. And you want him to be like you—a tribal cynic."

"But I'm the one in touch with reality. He doesn't regret shooting your father, and he never will. How are you going to deal with it?"

I decided to stop calling Rachel.

INSTEAD I WENT looking for acknowledgment to see how it worked. I watched a *sulha,* an Arab reconciliation ceremony. In its origins, in the desert, the two clans would meet under a white flag. The killer would arrive wearing a red cloth around his neck. After his family acknowledged his act, the clans would reconcile and the killer could remove the red collar.

In Bethlehem, the two families met in the basement of the victim's mother. The offense was not murder, but a car accident: A woman in a silver BMW was driving her daughters to school. A taxi driver rear-ended her. The woman, Nahid Harum, was a Christian from Bethlehem. The taxi driver, Suhil Karaje, was a Muslim from Hebron, Bethlehem's rival city to the south. The taxi driver opened the woman's car door and tried to grab her car keys. He waved a metal club, cursing, "You are an adulteress, your father is a pimp." He compared her mother to a part of the female anatomy.

The taxi driver was arrested by the Palestinian police and jailed for assault. The woman's family was not satisfied. The taxi driver's family had ignored the custom of calling to apologize within three days. The woman's brothers grew agitated. A mediator arranged for a *sulha* to preempt revenge. All the taxi driver's family had to do was acknowledge the wrongdoing. The ceremony would take fifteen minutes.

Seventeen of Nahid's male relatives sat in a half circle of chairs, facing a half circle of empty chairs. Nahid's uncle was warming them up, in a kind of pre-*sulha* pep rally.

"The car accident isn't our issue. More important things are at stake." His voiced filled the room. "He insulted her honor. That's the main issue. Let me role-play. Let's say I am the person coming here and I admit only the accident; are we going to give him a cup of coffee?" That was how the parties sealed an agreement. "Who is the driver to say an abusive word to her? Their son dishonored our daughter!"

Now, as her honor was being defended, Nahid stood in a nearby room, listening through the door, wearing a neck brace, clenching her fists. Her daughters and her mother stood with her. Women are not permitted at *sulhas,* although I was allowed to watch as a journalist.

Nahid's husband, Gabi, sat with the other men, twiddling his thumbs, his round face looking vaguely mortified.

"I'm a Christian," Gabi had told me earlier. "I was going to forgive him and be done with it." Nahid's brothers said no, the driver had to learn a lesson. Gabi's mustache frowned over his words, "These are our traditions."

The other men in the room were getting heated up.

"They will admit it!"

"They have to admit it."

"It's our right!"

"Our justice!"

"If he doesn't admit it, we'll *make* him remember."

"Sh, sh, sh. Here they come."

The Bethlehem men stood up. The members of the Hebron clan clunked down the stairs wearing nervous, frozen grins. Nahid peeked through a crack in the door, looking for the driver. She kept the driver's name on a piece of paper in her wallet. Nahid's daughter held on to her sleeve and whispered, "I'll karate-chop him." But the driver was not there. He was in jail.

"Peace be upon you," the Hebron men greeted the Bethlehem men.

"And upon you. Welcome."

They began to rapidly fill nine ashtrays.

After a traditional moment of silence, an old man in a white kaffiyeh, the leader of the Hebron family, spoke. "We don't know what happened. In the name of Allah, will you please tell us?"

This was part of the ceremony. It reminded me of other reconciliation sessions, from couples' forgiveness therapy in America to hostage negotiations in Nigeria. They begin by giving the aggrieved party a chance to air his complaint.

Nahid's uncle began, "There was a car accident."

"A car accident?"

"Yes, but the accident was not the problem. The injury was slight. It's the psychological pain."

The man in the white kaffiyeh turned to a relative and said, "What do you think?"

"I think they're trapping us. The woman is in good health. If there's any damage to the car, we'll pay. That's all."

The man in the white kaffiyeh said to Nahid's uncle, "Let's not look at all aspects of the issue now. There's an Arabic saying, 'If you examine bread too closely, you'll never eat.' "

The uncle raised his voice. "But a lady was dishonored. Your son insulted our daughter."

The white-kaffiyeh man raised his voice a notch higher: "You don't trust me? I know nothing of the insult! You're trying to make the issue bigger than it is."

"Don't twist the facts," the uncle said, his back arching. "Did you come here to admit what you did? Will you admit it? Will you? Admit it!"

The Hebron leader pushed back in his chair, staring at a spot in the middle of the floor. He pressed his lips together.

The uncle stormed up the stairs. The *sulha* collapsed.

"We are one family," the mediator shouted above the noise. He addressed the Hebron side of the room. "We are all Palestinians. But if you make a mistake, you must correct it. They're not trying to trap you. You're from the mountains of Hebron. You know the tradition—you must admit it."

When the clamor subsided, the mediator persuaded the two families to agree to a truce. During a truce, there is no revenge. The Hebron men left, promising to check the facts. They would return when tempers cooled.

The Bethlehem men loitered afterward.

"They pretended not to know."

"They were arrogant."

"Uncivilized."

"Hebron people drive too fast."

"They just came here to get free coffee."

I went home disheartened. How was I going to extract acknowledgment from the shooter? Even when acknowledgment is ritualized, as in a *sulha,* it goes against human instinct. The impulse to justify behavior runs deep, even when a person knows he is wrong.

Countries do it too. Leading the news around that time was NATO's accidental bombing of the Chinese embassy in Belgrade. It was a terrible mistake that killed three Chinese and wounded twenty. Tens of thousands of Chinese students marched outside the U.S. embassy in Beijing, shouting, "Kill the big noses!" and carrying signs, "Blood for Blood."

American officials issued a statement, printed in the newspaper. "We regret any loss of civilian life or other unintended damage." It should have stopped there. Instead, it went on: "But there is no such thing as a risk-free military operation."

I drew a red circle around the word *but.* As soon as someone justifies, excuses or tries to explain, an apology is no longer an apology.

Done well, public acknowledgment can help. In South Africa, the Truth and Reconciliation Commission found that acknowledgment by the enforcers of apartheid sometimes helped victims forgo revenge. Acknowledgment works better than asking for forgiveness because it does not presume the offense is forgivable. It does not ask the victim for anything. It gives the victim a sense of control, which is often all he wants. In murder cases, in traditional reconciliation ceremonies around the world, the killer presents himself to the victim's family with his hands bound, his face covered or his body naked, as a gesture of vulnerability.

In his own way, the taxi driver looked vulnerable when the *sulha* reconvened two weeks later in Bethlehem. Just out of jail, he sloped his shoulders and walked with a humbled shuffle, his father at his side.

Nahid's uncle boycotted the meeting, and Nahid was too nervous to listen through the door. She stayed upstairs, playing pinochle.

The driver's father opened the discussion. "The devil pushed us toward evil and whatever you want, we'll pay you."

A man named Odeh Bisharah spoke for the victim's family: "We can conclude from your words you've come to give us our right. There was an accident, but our main issue is the insult. In our tradition, we cut off the hand of the man who insults a lady who isn't his wife. You have to buy back his hand if you don't want us to cut it off. We live in a forgiving society. I don't say two million for his hand, or one million. All we ask is half a million Jordanian dinar."

While the taxi driver's relatives grumbled among themselves, Odeh whispered to a friend, "I said half a million to let his heart work a little quicker, to make him feel like he did something wrong."

Then the bargaining started. This was part of the ritual.

The taxi driver's father said, "For the sake of Jesus Christ, can you lower the sum?"

The victim's family agreed.

"For the sake of Mohammed the prophet, will you lower the sum?"

They agreed.

"For the sake of Yasir Arafat?"

The price dropped to three hundred JD.

The driver's father handed a stack of bills to Nahid's husband, Gabi. He counted the three hundred dinar and returned it, as prescribed by custom: "Because you came and showed your faces we give you back the money."

"This house is a house of generosity!"

"Coffee! Bring the coffee!"

Nahid's brother passed out tiny cups from a silver tray. The coffee had to be drunk, closing the deal, before it turned cold.

The driver's father drained his cup and said, "Your daughter is my daughter."

"Sitting here together we benefit because we meet new people."

"Come and visit us in Hebron."

"We will tighten the bond between our two cities."

They all shook hands. The Hebron men left.

Nahid's brother went upstairs looking for her. He sounded demoralized. "If the insulted lady was a Muslim, they would have paid more. She was a Christian, so they lowered the price."

He found Nahid playing cards. When he told her what happened, her eyes flamed. "That's *it*?"

He nodded.

The card table wobbled under her angry elbows. "I don't accept this," Nahid said, scattering her cards. She removed the piece of paper with the driver's name from her wallet, ripped it and threw it in the wastebasket. "I'm against these Arab traditions. They don't satisfy a person. They wouldn't satisfy a baby. Whenever men are talking, there's no resolution. It's empty words. Empty."

"I'm not satisfied either," her brother said. "But there's no alternative."

She walked out to the balcony, complaining about her husband. "I told Gabi not to forgive him, but he doesn't like problems. He said Jesus would forgive." She threw up her arms. "I'm not Jesus."

She looked across her courtyard. The view reached over the rooftops of Bethlehem to the Church of the Nativity.

"I want justice," she said.

"But how?" the brother asked.

She said nothing.

"How?"

She turned to face him. "Chop off his hand."

ACKNOWLEDGMENT, PERHAPS, was overrated. At that point though, it would have satisfied me.

There were other routes I was considering, forgiveness the most gracious of them. All year, I had tried to avoid any message of forgiveness. Then I met Paul Appleby's adopted family in England. Their spirit of generosity had stayed with me, though I tried to put it aside. Forgiveness was the one thing I could not allow myself to feel because I had some points that I was trying to make. From the beginning, they were complex. One had to do with what the shooter represented to me. I was trying to prove that it was possible to transform evil. The other point had to do with my feelings for my father. I was trying to prove to him how much I cared. If I failed at revenge, I was ready to fail. But I could not forgive the shooter. Even hearing the word *forgiveness* felt like a threat. I still had too much to prove.

I would take another shot at acknowledgment. One thing the *sulha* underlined for me was the importance of meeting face-to-face, perpetrator and victim. The men from Hebron and Bethlehem sat and drank coffee together. They became humans, flawed but real. It was, perhaps, one reason Nahid was not satisfied. She did not witness the acknowledgment firsthand. The shooter had never seen "David Bloomingfield" as a man. He kept calling my father a "chosen military target." Maybe if I described my father to the shooter, he would acknowledge that trying to kill him was wrong.

Dear Omar,

Another amazing letter from you, thank you. Did you see the sea on your way to the hospital? I loved what you said about imagining you are somewhere else. I do that too. When I feel sad, I think back to my childhood home and remember sitting with my best friend on our front steps, watching the rain, feeling safe and loved. The house is sold, long gone. (The view from your house, by the way, is beautiful.)

*I also found what you wrote about reconciliation heartening. As you know, much of my book is about revenge. But lately I am also interested in reconciliation. As part of my research, I went to see a "*sulha*" ceremony in Bethlehem. It was fascinating to watch the ritual, how the wrongdoer apologizes, and then each side forgives the other.*

*Anyway, what you wrote about meeting David Blumenfeld one day in Jerusalem made me think of the "*sulha*." That would be great if it could happen. I would like to be there too.*

Also, I agree with what you wrote, that "people are so different when you get to know them from near." There are many interesting things I've learned about David Blumenfeld you might like to know: He is not with the military. He is not even an Israeli. He is an American, lives in New York, was just visiting for a week. He was here trying to learn more about how to build a museum. His grandparents were killed in the Holocaust and he was helping to build a memorial in New York to honor their memory.

He has visited Israel many times, and the irony is—he supports and likes Palestinians. He taught this to his children. His son is a neurologist. His daughter graduated from college a year after the shooting incident, and she decided to come here for a year, to live in a Palestinian village. She taught English to Palestinian high school students, and organized recreational outings for Palestinians to meet Israeli children so they could have fun together.

I had to explain how I knew about David. I told him that I had interviewed David in New York by the telephone. Which, like many things I did that year, was both true and a deception.

Obviously, David hasn't had a chance to get to know you or your kind family, or to understand where you're coming from. But this is what he said: He thinks you have been wronged by Israel in your life. He believes that you went through hell, as did your brother, Imad, and your parents. He does not feel vindictive towards you. He respects your ideology and does not want to argue politics. He wouldn't mind if you were free tomorrow.

But he has one question: Would you ever use violence against anyone (innocent or not so innocent) again? That is his one concern, whether you would endanger a life again for your ideology. This might be a difficult question, because I know your beliefs are strongly held.

He talked about the idea of "constructive revenge," how a person can channel his anger and pain into building something up rather than lashing out. At first I thought it was a silly idea, but maybe he has a point. I told him about your interest in diplomacy and he was very impressed. That would be a way to show your love for your family, and to build your homeland. That is what he was trying to do with the New York Holocaust museum.

Again, sorry this letter is so blunt and rushed. I am leaving the country soon and want to help, if I can. I hope all your medical tests went well. What were the results? Looking forward to hearing from you. Take care of yourself!!

All best,

Laura

• • •

DURING MY FATHER'S VISIT, I read him my letters. I tried to read the shooter's letters too, but he sometimes lost interest.

One blustery afternoon, we walked around the Old City. I showed him where the shooter's gang had ambushed the other tourists. As we walked through the Arab market, I told him about the families I had met in Germany and England, and about Isaac Ben Ovadiah, who lit a memorial candle for his wife each day.

"Mommy wouldn't have done that for me," my father muttered.

Why did he always have to change the subject? My steps fell harder. "I'm trying to get the shooter to regret what he did. Or at least to say he's sorry."

"I don't care if he says he's sorry. I'm not here to forgive him. I just don't want him to do it again."

"So why do I want revenge?"

"I don't know. You've got to ask yourself that question."

"But you raised me—"

A patrol of Israeli soldiers broke around my father like a wave. When we reconnected, I found him by a pastry stand. "Mmm, those prune Danishes look good, man."

I took him through an alley, a dim passageway redolent with the smell of lamb fat. This was where the shooter had lain in wait.

We reached David Street and the souvenir shop where Tom sat on a stool playing desultory rummy. Fast-moving clouds flew overhead. The wind rattled the metal overhang.

"How are you?" I said to Tom.

"Still living."

With a swallow, I introduced my father to him. They exchanged perfunctory hellos. Each looked as if he were dropping the other's name straight into the recycle pile. We continued down David Street.

"That guy is gorgeous. Who is he? He looks just like Baruch."

"Dad." I stopped and touched his arm. "That's the shopkeeper."

"Oh, give me a break. Get out of here."

"He said he doesn't know you."

"He doesn't. You got the wrong guy."

The sound inside my head was of cat claws on a roof. As if a cat had lost his footing and was scrabbling against gravity, trying not to fall.

"Look," my father said, trying to set me straight. "I'm walking up here and this guy comes around the corner and *pow.* He drops the gun. I'm stumbling and I begin to yell, and I look to my left and there are two guys, sitting on stools. And they look me in the eye and turn away."

"You looked to your *left*?"

Tom's shop was on the right.

"The stores on the right weren't even open."

The year before, when I first asked Tom if he had witnessed the shooting, he said, "Maybe," and winked. I took that for a yes. Now, with a nauseating jolt it occurred to me: Tom always winked.

"You said he was in the corner shop," I said, trying to argue away the facts before they settled into place.

"Wrong corner. Good try. My guy was a short, fat, dumpy shlub who hadn't shaved. He had jowly cheeks. Tom is a gorgeous movie star." My father was upset, but he was having a good laugh, too. "Jeez, is that what you did all year? An American girl sits talking with this gorgeous guy? Oh, brother. Now you're going to have to stay another year."

I took my hand off his arm. He saw that my palms were damp.

"Why are you sweating?"

"Because I just spent a year trying to think of a way to get revenge on him. And when he had a car accident, and no one helped him, I thought it was his fate for not helping you."

"Let me show you the store," my father said. "I was around here somewhere. I'm not sure . . ."

We were back to where we had started the year before, wandering the maze, trying to remember. My father led the way through the gloomy light. I felt angry and stupid and more than a little ineffectual. Beneath that, though, I was relieved. Happy, even. I was allowed to like Tom.

"I was coming up over here, past the embroidered dresses and the drums," my father said, "and—this—is—the store."

I looked up at the archway. Hebrew graffiti: "Death to the Arabs."

"I'm almost positive now. I even remember the floor, these shiny black tiles."

My father entered the souvenir store. He reached for a trinket on a shelf.

"What's this?" he asked the shopkeeper.

"The evil eye."

The shopkeeper's name was Abed. He had long, tapered fingers and cynical eyes. "Where are you from?" he asked.

"The United States."

"What do you do?"

"I manufacture office supplies," my father said. "I make paper clips."

Whenever our family went on vacation, my father would tell people that he made paper clips. That way he could escape the stereotypes of being a clergyman. It was a sneaky thing to do, hiding his identity. But he liked the feeling of people getting to know him for who he really was.

"Would you like a drink? I offer you hospitality. Orange soda?"

"No, thank you. My stomach is feeling unsettled," my father said, looking around. "You've had this store a long time?"

"It was my father's." Abed's father had retired and moved to America.

"I was here thirteen years ago. Was your father short?"

"Yes, and he was heavy. He had a full face. Did you speak with him?"

"He was sitting on a stool."

"And you spoke with him?"

"Yes, I was looking for . . ."

"Leather sandals?" the shopkeeper said. "Was he nice to you?"

My father nodded to me. "This is the place. I'm a hundred percent sure now."

My father picked a small, olive-wood plaque off the shelf. It dangled from a chain. It said *Shalom,* the Hebrew word for peace. "Do you think there will be peace?"

"I don't think so," the shopkeeper said with a snigger.

"How much do you charge for these things?"

"Sixty-seven dollars."

"No way."

The trinket was worth a dollar or two.

"My true brother," the shopkeeper said, "look what I'll do for you. Forty-eight dollars."

Later it occurred to me that 1967 and 1948 were the years of major Arab military defeats.

My father put the trinket back. He was halfway out the door when the shopkeeper caught up with him and grabbed his arm. He breathed into his ear, "You are really a very, very hard man, but I like you."

Uncertain of how to extract himself, my father tried for a joke. "How come you like me, you don't even know me?"

"Give me twenty dollars. Then you can leave, my true friend."

The flesh on his arm was being squeezed. It was not clear if my father was shopping or being mugged. He looked to me: "What should I do?"

I did not know, but I could not stand to see him humiliated.

With one arm still in the shopkeeper's grip, my father took out a twenty-dollar bill. Later, he told me that as he paid him, he was thinking, What the heck am I buying a peace symbol from him for? His father was a rat-fink who turned his back on me.

My father said to him, "I'll hang up this *Shalom* to remember this city." Before we left the market, the chain broke.

I never went looking for the shopkeeper again. I was afraid of the real one's son, and embarrassed to see Tom. Late one evening as Baruch and I were walking home, we saw the silhouette of a man with his arm around a woman.

"Look," Baruch whispered. "He's working his hand toward her breasts."

The man was giving the woman a moonlit tour of our neighborhood. He spoke in a familiar voice so deep it seemed to come from his feet. The woman sounded impressed. She sounded Australian. The man tipped his face toward the moon. There was the unmistakable dimple, the frame of black curls. I wondered whether Alabama and Norway knew that Tom had a new woman named Australia.

I took half a step forward, to say hello, and to tell Tom the story of my father and mistaken identity. But he was caught up in Australia; the subject was romance not revenge.

• • •

Dear friend Laura;

I'm so sorry to write you while I'm in bad conditions at Ramla hospital. I have thought a lot about writing to you in spite of my bad health. To my big sorrow, I haven't got the chance of seeing the sea. But I have imagined myself travelling into a deep big sea of a different kind, seeing all different amazing creatures and sites from the small window of my submarine. It was a very interesting film to see the people walking, the children playing, the trees, and the flowers smilling.

I guessed by "submarine" he meant the prison van that transferred him to the hospital.

When I landed from my submarine in front of Ramla hospital, it was as if I'm an alien from another world. Each one of my "body guards" took his place around my vehicle. Guns are ready for use. The door was opened, and all around me I see people looking with strangeness. I landed peacefully with slow steps while my hands and legs are tied. I got deep breath and looked to the sky feeling the need to fly. And with half-smile I moved while being surrounded by guards towards the hospital. And all the people looking at me with pity and wounder because of my weak apperance.

They led me to the elevator to the main section of the test. We waited till a very beautiful Morrocan girl came to lead us to the room of the examination. I did introduce myself to her and spoke

> *with her a little about the prison while she is conducting the test for 3 times. She was shocked to see the bad results of the test. I do thanked her, and we went back again to my submarine.*
>
> *And again the same film starts to show me itself once more while getting to my "Galaxi," Ashkelon Prison. . . .*

When Baruch read this part of the letter, he said, "He writes better than I do."

The shooter still was the monster in my closet, but he had become, over six months of writing letters, a perverse kind of companion. As I got to know him, I found myself minimizing his flaws. He wrote that when he visited his mother's home in Jaffa, it was rubble. Destroyed by the Israeli army. His mother, meanwhile, told me the house was intact. They had not returned to Jaffa because they would have to pay back taxes. In another letter, he wrote that he shot the American on March 30 because it was Land Day, a day of protest against Israeli confiscation of Palestinian land. That sounded romantic, but it was not true. He had shot my father three weeks earlier, on March 7.

His half-truths would not have mattered if I were not weighing the next step of my plan. It involved helping him. Not out of goodness, entirely, and not out of charity. But first, I had to figure out if he was telling the truth about his health.

"Do you think he's really sick?" I said to Baruch as he practiced a Chopin mazurka.

"It's not a question of whether I believe he's sick," he said. "One's opinion is not a substitute for proof. He has every motive not to tell the truth. As a judge, I wouldn't give it any credence."

Once Baruch handled a case at the U.S. Attorney's office against a leader of the Hamas militant group. The prisoner was a diabetic. His lawyers claimed that his blood sugar levels were dangerously high and that he should be released on bail. Later, the government discovered that the prisoner was buying jars of honey at the prison commissary. He was consuming huge quantities of it to drive up his blood sugar to support his phony claim.

"You never know with these guys," Baruch said. "They have every incentive to exaggerate, especially to a journalist."

"Well, I believe him," I said. "I've come to know him."

"Come on. You've 'come to know him'?" He trilled two notes on the piano with his fingers. "You didn't even know me when we got married. You bought me an antique toothbrush for a wedding gift."

He stood up. "You have no idea what the prosecutors have on this guy. They could have intercepted conversations between him and fellow prisoners, planning countless bombings. I'm afraid you're going to become the unwitting pawn of a man who is far more dangerous than you could imagine."

"You think I'm being naive?"

Baruch kissed me on the forehead. "Extraordinarily."

Dear Laura,

What you have said about remembering your childhood led me to remember a poem of one of my American friends when she wrote me on Christmas eve to let me remember when I used to celebrate with them Christmas at Bethlehem. She wrote:

In my mind I see a far-away place
where the sun is alwayes shining
Little flowers weave gently in the breeze
and there's the sound of children singing.
There is no pain and sorrow there
This place knows only peace
And I can run as far as I want
For I have angel's wings.

—"dedicated to Omar by Tristie Dec. '87"

I used to have many American friends whom come here to visite the holy land. So my duty was to let them visit the Palestinian camps, in order to have a real knowledge about people, not just about stones and places. . . .

Allow me, Laura, to be with total disagreement with you in the point that comes; I don't find any place of metaphor between "sulha" *and the historical political process of reconciliation between the Palestinians and the Israelians. We couldn't speak about the conflict between the two people by using terms like* "sulha." *Reconcilation between peoples could be done on the basis of mutual admitance of each other's rights and on the basis of international normes and rules.*

It is within the context of the ongoing peace process that I do allowed myself to think a lot of meeting David one day. And because what has been done is part of the past, when hatred and alienation ruled the minds then on the two sides; Today we are living in a new phase where there is a place to think of being friends not enemies.

When talking about the subject of your work, you are taking cases and presenting your ideas through these cases. The most important thing to do, in my opinion, is not to separate these cases from their political, social, economical background. You shouldn't look at each case from the personal level of analysis and ignore the other levels. . . .

In the case of the Palestinian-Israeli conflict, if we do try to make "sulhas" *to solve this dispute, think how many hundreds of thousands of* "sulhas" *we need to hold.*

I was disappointed by his tone. It reminded me of Rachel's: Too much politics, not enough humanity. There were long blocks of text about principles and accepted norms of international rights and justice. He had ignored everything I had written about David Blumenfeld. My attempt to humanize my father had failed. Although he did answer my father's question: "Would you ever use violence against anyone (innocent or not so innocent) again?"

Back to David, I do admire his talk to you and appreciate his understanding, his support and like to my people. If these are realy from the depth of his heart, this may contribute a lot to our friendship. Of course, my answer to his question is NO.

True, my beliefs are strongly held as you said. This is because I do believe in the well of my people. You don't suppose me, Laura, to be an Israelian, nor you may suppose any Israelian to be a Palestinian. Each side has his own dreams, hopes and aspirations. We are moving now toward our national freed land as a first step towards the establishment of our full independent state. . . .

The idea of "constructive revenge" as introduced by David is a very well known biblical idea to me. I have got a chance of studying a comparative course of religion. You may find a great deal of ideas at the same spirit all over the holy books. One of the reasons for me being so creative in my life in prison refers to my reading these books.

I'm sorry for this quick letter. I hope I could feel well so that I could write you well. Sincerely

No signature.

I tried to shelve my disappointment. I waited a few days to call my father, who had returned to New York. We would be going home soon too, for Baruch's judgeship confirmation hearing. I had one more chance to write to the shooter. In the end, whatever I did had to be OK with my father. I could not disappoint him.

"Hiya, honey," he said, answering the phone. "I'm outside, pruning the roses. How are you?"

I told him about the shooter's house. How sometimes there was no running water. How once when I wanted to use the bathroom, a girl had to go next door with a bleach container to ask the neighbors for water.

"Maybe he needs our help," I said.

"I'm not sure."

"He says he's changed."

"Not exactly. He said times have changed. But is he genuinely a changed person?"

We started arguing, our sentences chasing each other.

"OK, but he said there's peace now."

"What if the peace breaks down?" My father was yelling. "You know what the Middle East is like. A few months of quiet, then the violence explodes. How old is he?"

"Thirty-five or thirty-six," I said.

"He's still a young person who could fall back into violent ways, and it isn't as though he's finished what he's done. If he was really sick, I would have compassion on him. But I don't want to be a fool."

He stopped yelling for a moment and said, "You know I'm not really mad. We're just discussing this. I'm just worried when you get into an ideology," he said. "Look at Algeria. Fundamentalists are slitting children's throats while they sleep. I don't hear him renouncing violence."

"His family has been so nice."

Now his voice got very gentle, all the way down to a bedtime daddy. "There's something that happens when you get to know people. We're inclined to like people. No one wants to be mean and vindictive. What's happening with you is natural. You're a wonderful child who grew up with innocence and love. We taught you all these optimistic, utopian feelings. All these things we taught you—you want life to be that way."

I remembered a home movie my father took of my mother as she fluttered down our hallway in a negligee and a crown. The tooth fairy. As I slept, he filmed her tucking a quarter in an envelope under my pillow. The cat, who was sleeping next to me, woke up and her eyes gleamed into the camera. The next morning, he filmed me dancing around my pink bedroom, waving an envelope, missing a tooth, enchanted.

"I'm more cynical than you. I'm a rabbi." His voice began to ratchet up again. "I've dealt with people. The letters could be bullshit. I bet Baruch thinks so too. Ole Judge Baruch knows better. Men are not so innocent. I grew up in Newark. We had gang wars. I got beat up for all kinds of reasons. You don't know anything about that world. You grew up in a hootsy-tootsy-cutesy neighborhood in the suburbs."

"But, Daddy, what if he's really sick and dying?"

"Why don't you ask your friend Rabinowitz?"

"Rubenstein," I said. Israel's attorney general. Baruch's friend from law school. "Baruch doesn't want me to drag him into it."

"Look, if there's medical evidence that he's really, really sick, then I'd write a statement he should be released. If he's paid his debt to society, and he's been rehabilitated, it would be nice to help straighten him out. I want him to go home to his family. Their son suffered, and it's enough already. But I don't know the guy well enough to know if he's totally bullshitting his medical situation."

He was quiet for a moment. I could hear a lawn mower in the background. "I'm not close enough to the situation," he said. "You are. But, of course, you're gullible."

Dear Omar,

Hi, how have you been? I am so sorry you are in the hospital. I hope you are feeling better.

I loved the submarine description of your trip to Ramle Hospital. Too bad you didn't see the sea. When I went to the Ashkelon beach in March, I picked up a couple of shells for you. So what are your days/nights like in the hospital? Have you seen the Moroccan girl again?

I also enjoyed the poem by Tristie. If you'd like, I could interview her. I liked her poem because it was about building a happy, imaginary world. My older brother wrote in his high school yearbook: "we must ignore reality in order to live." I didn't understand what he was talking about then, but now I see he's right.

Speaking of my brother, his wife had a baby boy last week. I'm going home to the U.S. to meet him. It's the first grandson for my parents.

The research for my book is almost complete. Here's my main journalistic question for this letter: What satisfaction do you think a person needs to stop feeling like he wants revenge? Does he have to actually take revenge, or are fantasies enough, or if the offender expresses regret and apologizes does that suffice?

All year I have been interviewing people who were wronged somehow and wanted to get even. What does your life experience tell you—what is the best way to respond? When you were angry or hurt deeply by someone, how did you deal with that impulse towards vengeance?

Or, what if someone hurt a member of your family, how would you react? And what about David, does he have the right to seek revenge?

Before I could decide about helping him, I had to gather more facts. The medical review board found that Omar Khatib did have asthma. But the prisoner was not so sick, they determined, that staying in jail endangered his life. He was appealing the decision.

The new hearing was set for July, after our departure. I would return to Israel, briefly, for it. For months, Imad had been promising me access to Omar's medical file, but he kept coming up with excuses. I was running out of time. I decided to ask the shooter directly.

I spoke to my editor last week and told him about your story. When he asked basic questions like what you were charged with, or about your medical condition, I couldn't supply him with the facts. He said that in order to write a responsible book, I must have the public records relating to your case, like the court file, medical reports, etc. I know that privacy is important, but would it be possible for you to ask either your family or your attorney to let me see the relevant documents?

As for the sulha, *OK, I guess we disagree. I think thousands of* sulhas *wouldn't be such a bad idea.*

You wrote that the shooting took place in a certain political context, when "hatred and alienation ruled the minds then on two sides." But what does David have to do with a war between two nations? He was just some guy from New Jersey, walking down the street. He says he has never hated Palestinians.

In fact, when I told him about your condition, he said that if you are so sick, and if you will never endanger another person's life again, he would not mind if you were free. He thought people should have compassion for your family.

I remember what you wrote to me once, that "people are so different when you get to know them from near." If you want, you could write a letter to David. I'll forward it to him in the United States.

Finally, I just want to tell you that your family has been amazingly nice to me all these months. I feel bad that I don't speak Arabic well enough to really communicate with them. Please pass on my gratitude for their hospitality and their help. It has been fun getting to know them. Soon you will be a great-uncle too—from your niece Lama, "inshallah."

That's it for now—feel well. I look forward to hearing from you.

All best,

Laura

BEFORE I LEFT ISRAEL, I wanted to check up on the other people I had interviewed. They too meant more to me than I had let on. I watched Zevadia—the short young man from Ethiopia who had been picked on by tall kids—wing across the finish line of the Jerusalem Marathon, in first place.

Father Edward of Gethsemane, who sensed the Evil One hovering over the Holy Land, left the country for New York City.

The Holocaust Avengers were still being pursued by the past. German prosecutors were considering filing charges against them for attempted murder by poisoning. Neo-Nazi groups offered to cover the costs of any former SS officers who would come forward to testify.

Jamal, the taxi driver, whose wife withheld sex because he withheld love, was now romancing his wife with roses and dinners at Burger King: "But I get the last revenge because when we make love, I think about my ex-girlfriend."

I went back to say good-bye to the feuding fifth-grade girls, whose parents had decided to separate them for middle school. Their story and the others had become a part of my own search and pointed oblique arrows toward a solution.

One of the avengers I followed closely was Mahdi, the Druze teenager who had strangled his sister to avenge his family honor. His trial was held on scattered dates throughout the year. Summer, winter, Mahdi wore the heavy black hiking boots that his sister had bought him the week he killed her.

"I lost control," he testified. His leather jacket hung limply on him. "I never felt so horrible. My blood was boiling in my brain."

The court clerk translated his Arabic to Hebrew as he stood at a lectern, holding the neck of the microphone. "I strangled her with my hands, then I kissed her and said, 'Forgive me, sister.' "

The prosecutor leered skeptically. "Did you know she died a virgin?"

"To my great dismay, I now know."

"So why did you kill her?"

He gripped the neck of the microphone. "I didn't know she was a virgin."

Mahdi's brother told me that when Mahdi read in the autopsy report that she was a virgin, he tried to hang himself with a sheet. His sister had run away with a boy from high school for twelve hours and he had assumed the worst. He was wrong.

"And you strangled her with this," the prosecutor said, holding up the computer mouse cord. "You strangled her, and she tried to resist, and you kept strangling until she stopped moving."

He looked beaten down. "That's what happened."

"Honor is very important to you, yes? That's what you told the police."

"Yes."

"Is honor still important to you?"

"No. It took my sister's life, my sister who I love very much. I'm very sorry."

"But you love your honor more. You had to choose between your sister and honor. You chose honor."

Mahdi said nothing. The veins in his forehead stood out.

"Before your sister ran away, she wrote a letter to the one person in the world who she wanted to explain her actions to, because she loved him so much."

In the letter she had written to Mahdi, she asked him to forgive her for running away. She could not endure life with her stepmother.

"Read it," the prosecutor said. "I'm showing it to you. Here, it's in Arabic."

He read the letter to himself. He wavered for a moment, glancing around for a chair. He looked like he might collapse.

"What did she write?" the prosecutor said.

His voice was choked off. He stepped back from the lectern and with slow, precise steps walked across the courtroom to the defendant's bench. He sat down.

The prosecutor went after him, striding as she spoke. "You murdered your sister in cold blood, for no good reason, because your honor is the most important thing to be a man. Why aren't you man enough to stand up and tell the court?"

"I don't know," he croaked. He folded his arms, crossed his legs, hunching over, shriveling like a spider swept up in a dustpan.

The next witness was Mahdi's older sister.

As she testified, the rest of the family was crying, everybody except for Mahdi. As the witness spoke, Mahdi unfolded his limbs and took off his leather jacket. He clasped his hands in front of him and reached for the floor, as if he were stretching. When he sat up, he looked like he was feeling better. Almost proud.

"Who's Nibal?" the prosecutor asked the witness.

"My sister."

Nibal was the youngest girl in the family. She had testified earlier.

"Is Nibal a good girl?" the prosecutor asked.

The court translator clarified the question. "She means, 'Is Nibal an honest child?' Not is she sexually loose with boys."

But it was too late. The prosecutor had shamed Mahdi and then questioned his sister's honor. Mahdi had slipped off his hiking boot and hurled it with all his might. It hit the prosecutor in the head.

The prosecutor stumbled backward.

"Clear the courtroom!" cried the judge.

Mahdi was put in ankle chains and dragged out. He wore a look of satisfaction that stayed with me.

The other avenger who intrigued me was Smitt, the burglar. With each person I had interviewed about revenge, I withheld the fact that I was one of them. Except Smitt. I felt comfortable enough to drop the pretense.

Smitt divided the world into predators and prey. Essentially though, he was a nice guy. Once he suggested that I demand restitution. "What he did to your father, it's worth a kilo of coke, or half a kilo of heroin. Five kilos if he had died."

During the final weeks of my newlywed year, we sat on the curb outside the methadone clinic and watched the ant trails in the gutter. Smitt said he wanted to get back at his ex-wife for keeping their son. He talked about burning down her house. "It's like someone oversalted my food, a burning thirst," he said. I knew he would not do it. By then I recognized the line between the desire for real, violent revenge, and fantasizing about violence.

Smitt gulped his shot glass of methadone. "Tastes like a kiss," he said, rubbing his mouth. "Wipes over you like a wet rag."

While the methadone washed through him, I told him how, lately, I was looking for acknowledgment. How could I get the shooter to acknowledge his deed?

Smitt perked up. "We call it 'Little Red Riding Hood revenge.' You act nice, but you really want to drink their blood. The wolf acted nice. He dressed up as a grandma and then he ate Little Red Riding Hood."

I bit my thumbnail, waiting to see where his fairy tale was going.

"You could go to the guy who tried to kill your dad. You get close to him because he thinks you're his friend. Then you put a gun to his head and say, 'I could kill you now. Was it worth it?' I think at that moment he would say he was sorry."

I kicked a pebble. Why was it that whenever I said "revenge," everyone assumed I meant guns?

"What if I don't have a gun?"

Smitt was very relaxed now. The methadone had spread a smile up and down and across his face. "OK. The best revenge is to be very, very nice to him. Nicer than you really are. Then he'll say, 'Listen, I'm sorry. I didn't know the family. If I had known the family, I wouldn't have shot your father.' If he isn't stupid, he'll realize he made a mistake."

Smitt told me a story to prove his plan would work: "This pimp I know took a girl and made her a whore. Her brothers wanted revenge. The pimp said, 'Hey, I didn't know she came from a good family.' He paid them restitution and she went home."

I liked the gist of what Smitt was saying.

"But is it manly to be really, really nice for revenge?" I said.

"Of course. It means you're strong. If you make him feel regret, it restores the honor of your family."

I liked that even more.

"And that's the best revenge?"

Smitt lay back on the sidewalk. He was woozy now, talking to the sky. "He tried to spill your blood. Now you put honey in his blood. It'll stick in his veins."

BUT FIRST I needed to see the shooter's medical report. My father said he would help him if he was seriously ill. Since his family would not let me see the file, I would have to ask his lawyer.

All along, I had avoided his lawyer, Leah Zemel, who was one of the toughest defense attorneys in the country. She was also one of a few Jews willing to represent Palestinian militants. A visit to her East Jerusalem office would end badly, I thought. In her years of experience with foreign journalists, she understood and recognized their ironic detachment. I could not fake it with her.

Yet I had to try. I made an appointment for Friday, two days before we were scheduled to leave the country.

In the meantime, I slipped into a more comfortable role, the reporter. Israel was about to choose a prime minister and I was helping out with the coverage for the *Washington Post.* The election, like others before it, hinged on one issue—the conflict with the Arabs. The choice was not as simple as turn the other cheek, or an eye for an eye. But boiled down, it was something close: peace or security.

The peace camp was led by Ehud Barak, the most decorated military man in Israel. Like his mentor Yitzhak Rabin, he believed that Israel had to take risks that would make it vulnerable, if it wanted to end the cycle of predator and prey. Netanyahu, the incumbent, believed that in the jungle of the Middle East, those who took risks for peace were eaten. The voters tended to swing back and forth in every election. They put a peace man in office for one term. The next term, often after a spate of violence, they voted for a hawk. The two choices, like forgiveness and revenge, competed in a ceaseless rivalry.

In the days leading up to the election, I wrote an article about Rabin's assassin. Yigal Amir saw himself as a human instrument of divine revenge. He was serving a life sentence in solitary confinement and was barred from talking to journalists or to anyone outside his family. For months, I had been asking his mother, Geula, if I could interview him. One evening she finally agreed and told me to come over. I brought a list of questions to their white stucco home in a suburb north of Tel Aviv.

Soon after I arrived at his house, the phone began to ring. Geula bolted up the stairs to Yigal's bedroom, holding her nutmeg-colored wig in place. "You're *killing* me. Wait a minute!" she shouted at the ringing phone.

A prison guard confirmed that the voice on the line was Geula's. Then he transferred the call and another guard handed the receiver through a slot in the metal door of Yigal's windowless chamber. In fifteen minutes, a bell would ring, signaling the end of the conversation.

The assassin sounded depressed.

"So who are you voting for?" his mother asked.

I listened in on the speakerphone, recording the conversation.

"I don't know. What does it matter?" he said. "Both are keeping the peace agreements, continuing on Rabin's path."

"The left will celebrate if Barak wins. And you'll be seen as a big failure."

"Ach, Mom," said the man who killed a prime minister, "you take politics too personally."

I went home and typed out my story. I looked at the words I had chosen. Yigal Amir "admitted this week that although he killed one of Israel's most famous peacemakers, he has failed to kill the peace process." *At least I got* someone *to admit his act of violence was a failure.*

A few days later, Barak beat Netanyahu.

"Today you chose hope, not fear," Barak told thousands of supporters on election night in the plaza where Amir had shot Rabin.

There was a sense of euphoria in the crowd. Their worldview, they believed, would be vindicated. Politically, they were the opposite of the realists, the cynics and the hawks who lived in a world of predator and prey. They believed true peace was possible, not just chilly deterrence. They laughed and smashed wine bottles and hugged strangers. A man waved a pink placard, "Peace Avenges Rabin's Blood." The spirit was infectious.

TWO DAYS BEFORE our flight home, men came and took away the rented piano. Our long, embroiled honeymoon was over. I dug out the brass balance that I had buried in the closet, the left pan still heavier than the right. It reminded me of what I had to do.

Late that afternoon, I walked to East Jerusalem for my appointment with the shooter's lawyer. I was apprehensive, but Leah Zemel had the facts and I had to have them if I was going to help him. Otherwise, as Baruch and my father had warned, I could get duped. In the reception room, I ripped my list of questions from my notebook, holding it in front of me like a paper shield.

—did he plead guilty?

—medical condition?

—one crime or multiple crimes?

—public record?

—prognosis?

—July 7 hearing?

—why a 25-year sentence?

I introduced myself to the secretary as Laura Weiss. She looked at me coldly and said, "Omar sent us an emergency fax. He said not to tell you anything."

My ears grew warm.

Leah Zemel ushered me into her office. She had a small face, a tight red ponytail and green eyes that narrowed to slits when she smoked. Her chin came to a point like a fox's. She wore a dress incongruously covered with pink and green daisies.

My voice came out too high. "Did something happen? Why won't he let me see the medical file?"

"I don't know." Leah shrugged. "Maybe he likes his privacy."

It was a reasonable answer, but my thoughts were racing well past reason.

"Can I have the Khatib file?" Leah said to the secretary.

The secretary frowned. "But they said not to show it to her."

"I know," Leah snapped.

She went to get it herself.

He's figured out who I am. But how? Then it clicked. The Israeli papers had reprinted my article on Rabin's assassin, along with my name. A picture of the front page of the *Post* with my byline, "Laura Blumenfeld," had led the evening news. The shooter diligently followed the news.

Leah returned to her desk with the Khatib file. If the shooter was suspicious, she was not.

She removed the charge sheet, skimmed it and said, "He shot and wounded a tourist in the Old City. He was part of a larger group that caused other different actions. They were a group that decided to shoot tourists in revenge for America attacking Libya." Her mouth crimped around her cigarette. She blew her smoke at me. "So that's it."

I should have let it go.

"But the strike on Libya wasn't until April," I said. "He shot the American in the beginning of March. It couldn't have been revenge."

Now she looked alarmed. "How did you know *that*?"

"Because I did research," I said, ruing my big mouth. "I'm looking at a cluster of events at that time."

She closed the file. End of interview. She pointed a hand toward the door.

"Should I ask the family about the records?" I stammered as I started to get up.

"If they'll talk to you. Do you have a business card?"

I rustled around in my wallet. I did have a card. It said "Laura Blumenfeld." I made a big show of pulling out other cards.

"I see you've been shopping at all the right stores," she said with an arched eyebrow.

"Yes, well. I'll come back another day and bring my card. Thanks for your help."

Without saying good-bye, she walked to a bookcase and bent over with her back to me.

I followed her and said, "Thank you. Good-bye."

She did not respond.

"Good-bye, thanks," I said. I waited a minute, then two, then I realized that she was never going to turn around. So, making eye contact with the green and pink daisies on her behind, I said, "Bye-bye."

Back home, Baruch was lying on the couch, studying books on American criminal law.

I told him what had happened. With Leah Zemel, I felt I had a head of glass, my thoughts running naked back and forth.

"Are you sure she suspected you?" he said. "Israelis are capable of monumental rudeness."

I was not sure. But I was sure that the shooter had figured out who I was. We were leaving the country in forty-eight hours and I was beginning to fall apart.

"I just feel like I have to come clean. I can't keep lying and pretending."

My friendship with Imad and his family might have been phoney, but I thought I owed them something. An explanation. An apology. We all had been pretending, in a sense. They had to be nice to me, following their custom of Arab hospitality. I had to be nice to them, as part of my plan. Yet somehow all the make-believe had led to something real.

On Sunday, Imad was going to visit the shooter. I wanted to tell him who I was before the shooter did. A preemptive confession.

The impulse to confess was barely stronger than the urge to flee. Saturday I woke with a start at 4 A.M. My palms were imprinted with three pink crescent moons. I must have been digging my nails into my hands while I slept. I sat at my desk in my nightgown and wrote the shooter a final note. I wanted him, more than anyone, to understand my motives.

> *Dear Omar,*
>
> *I hope this letter finds you well. I am sorry you have been in the hospital so long. I am leaving for the U.S. in two days, and I thought I should explain a few things before I go.*

This was not how it was supposed to end. In my father's bedtime stories, revenge led to enlightenment. It led to redemption. That was what I was hoping for, for all of us, in my own revenge story.

And now when I was close—I could feel my plan succeeding—the whole thing was unraveling. Now I was the one on the defensive, apologizing, feeling guilty, proving nothing except that I was reckless.

I opened a window to a dry night wind. It carried voices across the valley from Mount Zion. It was Shavuoth, the Jewish holiday that commemorates the giving of the Ten Commandments. Thousands of people were streaming through the dark, serpentining up the path to the Old City. They had studied the Bible all night and would pray at the Western Wall at dawn.

I stared at the slumbering city walls. I had spent a year of my life staring at them. If only I could see through the wall, inside the shooter. What was he thinking?

> *Usually, I ask you questions; in this letter I am going to give you answers. A year ago, I came here to find you. I wasn't entirely sure what I wanted. But I wanted to know you, and I wanted you to know me.*
>
> *You have told me that the shooting wasn't personal. For me it was personal. . . .*

I told him who I was. Why I went undercover. What I was trying to achieve. How surprised I was to learn that he was in prison. What happened over the months as I got to know his family. And then I told him about my poem.

> *What else do you want to know? Shall I tell you a hundred stories about my gentle father? I'm not sure what the point would be. I've met your father several times. Once I gave him a ride in my taxi from Kalandia to Jerusalem. He is a kind man. You love your father. I love mine. I don't need to burden you with guilt.*
>
> *My father taught me many things as a child, but he didn't teach me how to cope with this. I am so happy you didn't take a second shot. You have no idea. When I write this, I can't help crying. It is a funny thing to thank the man who shot your father. But there you are—thank you, Omar (or to quote you again, "We should all thank God.") . . .*

As I wrote, a blur of tears separated me from the words. I kept on typing. It was the longest letter I had written to him. I ended it by saying that I expected he would be angry at first and that I understood why. Then I said:

I was always glad that you wrote "Dear friend Laura," even if it was based on an illusion. Is it true, that we are friends?

THAT NIGHT a desert wind pulled our geraniums from their stems. Orange, pink and red petals blew under our balcony door. In the morning, they dappled the white bedroom floor.

Baruch was lying awake when I opened my eyes. His arms were wrapped around me.

"Kotzaleh," he said softly, "we have to do this in a safe fashion."

A drowsy moment passed before I realized he meant the confession.

"I want my mother," I whispered into his side, as if I were Eve burrowing back into Adam's rib. "Are you ever sad or afraid and you just really want your mother?"

Somewhere I had read about a brave revolutionary or vicious criminal, I could not remember which. When they took him out to the prison yard to execute him, the last word that welled from his lungs was *"Mamma!"*

"No," Baruch said. "When I'm under pressure, I imagine myself out in the middle of the lake at camp, sitting in a kayak by myself."

We got out of bed. It was Shabbat, the Jewish Sabbath, and the holiday of Shavuoth. Baruch went to synagogue to hear the story of the giving of the Ten Commandments. I stayed home and printed out my letter to the shooter.

After fidgeting through a farewell lunch with friends, I got ready to see Imad; his wife, Suraya; and the rest of the family. I put a picture of Baruch in an envelope and one of my father and my mother walking me down the aisle at my wedding. Finally, the shooter's family was going to meet mine.

"Is there any way to meet them outside their house?" Baruch said. "In a public place, a hotel lobby?"

"No, there's no time. I keep calling them, and no one answers. I just have to show up."

For the first time, he hesitated to let me go. He could not drive with me to Imad's house because driving on Shabbat, even being driven, would violate the fourth of the Ten Commandments: "Remember the Sabbath day and keep it holy." Baruch was faithful to the law—federal, state and Jewish. I had come to expect and accept that.

A backup, to an extent that I had any, was a high school friend, a pilot we called the Iceman. He was the only person I knew who owned a gun. In a rush of panic, I had confided in him and he agreed to stand by. His number was punched into my cell phone. If I pressed *send,* like pushing a panic button, he would be there in half an hour. It was feeble, bordering on the absurd.

Before I left, Baruch tried one last time to talk me out of it. "Maybe you have the need to confess, so you've convinced yourself the shooter knows. I've seen criminals do that, they just turn themselves in."

"No, no, I'm telling you, he knows."

Baruch walked me to the road. Families were spread out on blankets, eating Shavuoth picnics. I flagged a taxi and got inside.

Before I could close the door, Baruch caught the handle. His face was so tense and serious, I had to look away.

"I don't want to violate Shabbat," he said. "But I can't send you there by yourself."

He slid onto the seat beside me.

"The road to Ramallah," I told the driver. I reached over and squeezed Baruch's hand.

The taxi passed Damascus Gate, reminding me of the Israeli businesswoman Zehava Ben Ovadiah. We passed the Garden Tomb, and I thought of the British pilgrim Paul Appleby. This was about my father, but over the months, my messy and chaotic effort had come to include them too.

In my lap I held a glass plaque embossed with an English poem about friendship. One of the "simple justice" avengers—the employee who unplugged her boss's meat freezers—had given it to me. She was a Palestinian woman. We had become friends through my interviews. As Baruch and I were leaving the house, I took her plaque from a shelf.

We drove north of the city. Baruch bit the hair off the back of his knuckles. We really were a couple now, I thought: he was worrying, so I did not have to. We sat quietly, holding hands, looking out opposite windows. I had made my decision and I was resigned.

Then we came to the tattered black flag strung up on the electric wires. The turnoff to the shooter's house. My stomach began to ache in my throat.

"Don't be rash," Baruch said as the car bumped down their broken road. "Don't do anything that's irreversible."

Baruch was going to wait in the cab while I went inside. A sheen of sweat glazed his face. A wrinkle, shaped like a dagger, dug between his brows. The car stopped at the rim of the ravine. The house loomed above.

"Position yourself by the stairs so you can just run out if you can't scream," he said.

"But it's a twisting, cement staircase," I said, opening the car door, thinking, *And I'm wearing dumb, smooth-soled shoes.*

Baruch put his hand on the small of my back. "You're my brave wife. I love you very, very much."

I walked up the cement stairs to Imad's door. I had made it up these steps before by telling myself, "This is just a story."

Then why am I so afraid?

I knocked.

Imad was not home.

"Sit, drink something cold, orange soda," said Suraya. "He'll be back soon."

We dragged red plastic chairs onto the landing, overlooking the ravine. A dozen or so relatives stood around us. From where I sat, I could see Baruch's elbow sticking out of the window in the taxi below.

Miners were blasting in the ravine, looking for phosphates, sending up plumes of white dust.

At first, everything felt OK. We drank orange soda. I took out the confession letter to the shooter, ready to give it to Imad. I gave Suraya the glass plaque:

> There's a miracle of Friendship that dwells within the heart
> and you don't know how it happens or where it gets its start.
> But the happiness it brings you always gives a special lift
> and you realize that Friendship is God's most precious gift.

She did not understand the words, she said, but the flowers were pretty. "It's for me a reminder of Laura."

Our conversation was sluggish in the heat. Someone brought up the subject of foreign languages.

"My skills are weak," I said in broken Arabic.

"Do you speak Hebrew?" Suraya asked. They understood Hebrew.

I lied. "No."

"When are you leaving?"

"Tomorrow night." I shifted around on the hot, plastic chair. Sweat evaporated from my stomach and rose from the crooks of my arms.

Where's Imad?

As soon as Imad arrived, I would tell him who I really was. He, more than anyone, had been my pretend friend. His smile might have been cryptic, but I had come to almost like it.

A blast of dynamite threw up another cloud in the quarry, turning bedrock into air. I checked for Baruch's elbow. It was still there below, poking out of the taxi window.

Lama, the daughter-in-law, leaned back on the railing, her stomach butting through her orange smock.

"How was your doctor's appointment?" I said to her.

"The baby is a boy," she said.

There would be no Laura Khatib.

I thought I detected a strain of defiance in her tone. The red pencil outlining her orange lipstick, I noticed, made her look harsh. I tried showing them the photographs of my parents and Baruch. They flicked through, scarcely interested. A different tint began to wash over the scene. Suraya looked me sharply up and down, in what felt like a reprimand. Their house took on a precarious tilt, as if one push would send it into the abyss.

I checked my watch. More than an hour had passed.

"Where are the puppies?" I asked, glancing around for the German shepherd and the puppies I had played with.

"Oh, a neighbor stoned them."

They chuckled.

It reminded me of something.

"The puppies all died," a cousin said offhandedly. "The father howled so much, we got rid of him."

And then I remembered my first visit here when they chuckled about the American man shot in the market.

I looked at their faces melting in the sun, Lama's orange lipstick sliding from her lips, Suraya's sweating eyes, and my own face melting, slipping away. I had a bad feeling just then. As if this whole love and understanding thing I had thought was there—was not. Was it?

Where the hell is Imad?

Dynamite exploded in the ravine again, sending tremors through my legs.

11

TRANSFORMATION

NEW HAVEN, CONNECTICUT

I DID NOT SAY A WORD. The sound of my own voice, I thought, might wake me from this quiet dream. It was summer, a Saturday afternoon. I was sitting at the kitchen table, watching my father and mother bustle around with domestic intimacy. He was making her his specialty: Swiss cheese sandwich. Thick, irregular slices of tomato. Globs of mayonnaise. Cheese hanging over the edges of the bread.

The three of us were alone in the house. There were toys on the floor, coloring books on the table.

My mother was trying to open a bottle of apple juice.

"Here, Dave, can you get it?" She smiled deferentially.

My father lay down the knife, making a point to put it in the sink. It annoyed her when he left the mayonnaise knife on the counter.

He rapped on the apple juice lid with the back of the spoon. "You used to hate it when I did that." He laughed.

"You dented all our silverware," she said, though she looked like she did not mind anymore.

They sat down and ate their sandwiches.

"You lost weight," my mother said.

"A little." He looked pleased. "You lost weight too."

The dreamlike feeling began to retreat, leaving me to reality. Several weeks had passed since Baruch and I had returned from Israel. We were visiting my brother for the weekend.

Baruch and Hal had gone running. Hal's wife had taken my niece and my newborn nephew for a walk. Fran was in Ohio, making her annual visit to her first husband's grave. My mother had driven up for the afternoon from Long Island.

My parents had always been pleasant to each other. The conversation now was pleasant too. They talked in a way that was both familiar and stiff, like old, comfortable shoes left out in the rain.

"Boy, I could use a cheese Danish," my father said, smacking his lips as he finished his sandwich.

"I brought some Spa wafers," my mother offered.

"What are Spa wafers?"

"From our trip to Hungary." She and Bernie had just come back from a tour of Eastern Europe. "Want one?"

She opened a box of chocolate cream–filled wafers.

My father bit one in two. "Mmm, delicious. Chocolatey."

Oh, God. Chocolate wafers?

In the end, I had not achieved much revenge beyond the wafer caper. My final hours in Jerusalem were an overheated sequence of misunderstandings and missteps. Imad never came home that afternoon I wanted to confess. He had decided to sleep at his parents' house in the Old City and to visit his brother in jail the next day. I waited into the evening, flinching as the dynamite blasted the ravine. Convinced that he and the shooter had figured out who I was, I canceled our flight home. How could I leave? Baruch and I sat around our empty apartment for a week. I called Imad, asking little hinting questions, until finally he said with an exasperated laugh, "Laura, I don't know what you keep asking about. Your Arabic isn't very good."

They knew nothing. The drama was in my head.

I did not send the confession letter to the shooter. Instead, I sent him the seashells and the wildflowers that I had gathered at the beach in Ashkelon. The shooter sent me a farewell letter. "It seems that our long bus journey is coming to a station," he began. Then he continued to justify shooting David. My description of my father as "some guy from New Jersey," who was helping build a Holocaust museum as a gesture to his Polish grandparents, did not have its intended effect.

> *I hope David do believe that Israel is a state of occupation and not the state of the jewish people all over the world as they used to define it. You may know that the jews in the diaspora represents the outskirts of the center—in accordance to the theory of center and outskirts. Israel plays the roles of controlling the human and material resource, whereas the jewish populations in the diaspora playes the role of supporting the center moraly, financialy, ideologicaly. . . .*
>
> *The idea of the Holocaust has been ideologically occupied in the support and justification of the presence of Israel and its occupation to Palestine. It is not their promised land of God, and this was done on the expense of the pain and vagrancy of my people. Working on an idea like the one of David, is strengthening of these ideas. People will continue to be directed by the propiganda of seeing Israel as a leagal state and it won't be seen in its true image as an imperialistic project in the middle heart of the Arab world. . . .*

He also wrote a few paragraphs evaluating my performance as a journalist.

> *I would say that you are highly professionalized. You know how to direct your questions, and know the points you want to get to. You are able to ignore those that you doesn't want to.*
>
> *The terms you have used in directing your questions seems to be irrelevent to cases of political dimention, and so I admit facing some difficulty in putting the answers. This is the dark side of the unjust wars of occupations and aggressions that do in some situations justifies hitting the crowded areas. . . .*

He had reduced my father to a "crowded area." More than ever, I wanted to shake up Omar Khatib.

If my last month in Jerusalem had been filled with promise, my first month back in America was filled with petulance. The new reality I had been reaching for was overtaken by an old one. Baruch and I were staying at my mother and Bernie's house while we looked for a place of our own. Bernie welcomed us with a seven-page memo—twenty-seven helpful hints on how to run the house while they were away on vacation. My father refused to call me there. He complained that I spent more time with my mother than with him. I had grown so sensitive and guilty about slights to him that in New Haven, when he made a cup of coffee for my mother and she said, "Tastes like dishwater," I burned with indignation.

I drove over the Whitestone Bridge between my mother's house on Long Island and my father's in Westchester, thinking about my failure as an avenger. The Albanians had told me that when a son failed to avenge his father, even for the smallest slight, his clansmen rebuked him by passing a glass of raki to him behind their backs. The gesture was meant to humiliate him.

It was hard to look my father in the eye. I wondered if I was failing for a reason.

One morning at breakfast with my mother, I mentioned that I would be returning to Israel for a brief visit. Baruch was staying behind. His judgeship confirmation was expected any day.

"Oh, no," my mother said to me. "I'll miss you too much. Don't go away again. Ever."

"I have to. There's someone I have to see."

The shooter's medical hearing would be my last chance to confront him. I still had two competing inclinations, although the angrier one dominated my thoughts these days. If his soul was unshakable and my bedtime-story revenge unworkable, I would revert to my other plan: tell him who I was. Then shake the son of a bitch by the collar. It was as close as I could come to hitting somebody.

"OK," my mother said, unaware of my relationship with the shooter. "Then I'll come with you."

It was impossible to imagine my mother and the shooter in the same room. He was always brooding. She had told her new doctor in a patient history that she suffered from "chronic cheerfulness."

"It'll be an adventure," she said. "Like when we went to Sinai, looking for that Bedouin fellow."

"It's not that kind of adventure."

"We'll be in it together."

All year, I had been looking for a partner. Hal, Baruch, Rachel and even my father had made it clear that they wanted no part in revenge. My mother had always been my friend and my co-conspirator. Maybe she would conspire with me now.

"What are we doing?" my mother said as she booked her plane reservation.

"You'll see when we get there."

WE TOOK OFF on the Fourth of July. Red, yellow and green bouquets of light bloomed over Manhattan, below our airplane. I would be happy to come home to America when this was over.

In Jerusalem, we settled into a short-term rental, down the block from where Baruch and I had lived. I peeked through our old honeymoon window and saw a gray-haired couple sitting stolidly on the couch.

I did not call Imad nor anyone else in the shooter's family. Seeing Imad might weaken my resolve.

After lunch, my mother found a cozy chair in the living room and said, "So what are you doing? I can't believe you'd do anything I don't know about. We talk every day. I thought you tell me everything."

She thought that we might be going to the trial of Mahdi, the Druze teenager who had strangled his sister to avenge his family's honor. "That's the scariest thing you've been doing all year," she said.

I led her into it slowly, step by step.

"You know I'm researching revenge," I began.

I started by telling her a simple story. A boy named Eli was molested by his neighbor for years. "He was very hairy and fat," Eli had told me. "Sometimes he lay on me, and his stomach was bigger than all of me." When Eli grew up, he and his friends knocked on the neighbor's door, grabbed him, pulled down his pants in front of his wife and children and slammed his testicles in a drawer.

"Good for him," my mother said.

Then I told her how I got caught up in my own reporting. In Sicily, I did more than research stories; I absorbed the Sicilian bravado. I even applied it in the Iranian bazaar, when the hundredth rug merchant tried to cheat me. He swore on his father's soul that the carpet I was about to buy was an antique. Tired of being preyed on, I said, "If you lie to me, my husband will kill you. He's in the Mafia." The merchant got down on his knees and reexamined the rug. "Because I like my life, I must tell you, miss, I see now this rug is new."

My mother liked that story somewhat less.

Finally, I told her about my search for the shooter. I told her everything, about my father's pain, my need to ease it. She interrupted once, when I got to the part about collective punishment.

"You mean you were actually thinking of doing something to his family?" She struck her forehead with the heel of her hand, horrified.

I kept talking. I talked for hours. She sank deeper into her armchair. I ended by telling her how I had become friendly with the shooter's family.

"So that's it. Tomorrow I'm going to meet him, finally," I said.

For a few moments, she said nothing. The chair had grown around her as she shrank down into it. Her body was still except for her right index finger, tapping like a telegraph operator's on a torpedoed ship.

"Sounds like the revenge issue with him is over," she said. "You like him. You've sort of gotten over this guy."

"I still want to stand up and say, 'Don't fuck with the Blumenfelds.' "

She nodded cautiously, then said, "Sounds like you want to stand up to me"—her voice broke—"more than to the shooter."

I talked past her comment. I was not prepared to hear it, and I could not begin to respond. "I wanted to do a nice thing for Daddy."

"Hurting that fellow in a prison in Ashkelon isn't doing a nice thing for Daddy. I think he triggered all these angry thoughts in you and he was a vehicle to get your feelings out. Daddy being so hurt by the divorce. And you feeling guilty about being a part of it because I confided in you."

Her thoughts were too sudden, and too precise. I bent forward, with my elbows on my knees, hanging my head.

"I feel terrible that I involved you in the divorce," she said. "I shouldn't have confided in you when the marriage was ending—why I wanted to leave. Now I think you want revenge on me."

"No." I looked up at her. Revenge on my mother? She was my life's companion. She and I had made plans to meet in the afterlife. Revenge was personal, but not that personal. "Definitely not," I said, even as I understood that the answer might be yes. "No, that's too scary and too horrible."

"Here." She stood up. "I'll close my eyes and you can punch me." Her eyelids trembled. "Once."

I looked at my mother, bracing for my blow. I had hardly seen her in over a year. Her face was still lovely, but the lines cut deep. Standing before me now, she looked almost withered.

"Sit down," I whispered. "Please."

"OK."

She sat down. I wondered which one of us felt worse.

Then she started to speak, trying to find a way out for us both. "Maybe the important thing is you and I together do something that shows we respect Daddy—"

"—and that we care about him," I cut in. "That if he died, we would care."

"Is there some question about it?"

"Yes."

"He felt that we wouldn't care?"

"That you wouldn't."

"Oh, my God." She turned pale. "I've triggered this insane act on your part and clearly I caused a lot more pain to Daddy than I could have imagined. It didn't dawn on me that a phone call to him in Israel wasn't enough. I did call. Didn't I? I think I called. I mean, the shooter only grazed his head."

"But your not caring pierced his heart."

The quivering at the corners of her mouth drew me out of my chair. I wanted to hug her and make her feel better as she had done for me all of my life. It is a terrible thing to make your mother cry.

"I'm sorry I'm the one to tell you," I said. I went to the bathroom to bring her tissues.

"Maybe for him, it was the moment that he realized the marriage was over," she said, sniffling into a tissue. "My God, we spent six months talking to a divorce mediator. I kept going over the same things, over and over, like why we can't save the marriage and why it's too late. Finally the mediator said to him, 'You know, David, it looks like unless someone hits you over the head with it, you're not going to be able to accept that the marriage is over.' Maybe the shooter's bullet was getting hit in the head. He finally realized that I was going to go back to the pool to Bernie, and not fly to Israel to be with him. It was finally clear—it was over."

"I wish you could be sorry."

"I'm sorry that I hurt him. But I don't have a single regret that the divorce happened." She blew her nose. "Laura, look at me—you can't undo that moment, the moment you're trying to undo."

Which moment—with her and my father? With the shooter and my father? I was confused. She was right about my anger, though only up to a point. This was not only about her. I still had something to prove to the shooter. Even when the hate burns out, revenge is a commitment. Like a marriage, after the love is gone.

"So what do we do with the shooter?" I said.

"I think we have to do something that's very much about the future, that doesn't have to do with the past."

"I don't know where to go, except to the past."

She smiled through her tears. "You know what you need?"

"What?"

"No. You'll get mad at me if I tell you. You're going to get hurt."

I thought she was going to tell me to forgive the shooter.

"You need to have a baby," she said. "That baby is going to be the unity that you're sad to leave. You look at the divorce as failure and punishment, but your child is going to think of it as 'Yay! I have six grandparents and they have treats in their pockets for me.' And that's going to be your healing. That's not going to be a broken world to your child, that's going to be a beautiful world. A good, whole, loving world, as happy and as sweet as your childhood."

When she finished, she let out a long, exhausted breath.

"What time is it in New York?" she said, glancing at her watch.

"Seven-thirty A.M."

"Too early to call Bernie." She stared at the hour hand, willing it forward. "God, I miss him so much."

AT 5:44 A.M., the telephone rang.

"This is your wake-up call."

It was Baruch. I was lying in bed awake.

I had been tossing around, churning with expectation, worse than on the night before our wedding. The air was so still, I could hear individual leaves rustle outside my window. I listened to the rusty wingbeat of a night beetle. I had gone into the other room to look in on my sleeping mother, wondering if she was afraid of me that night. And I lay back down, waiting for the day on which, ready or not, I would have to act.

"I only slept two hours," I said.

"Don't worry," he said. "If I was meeting the guy who shot at my father I would only sleep two hours too."

"Someone shot at your father?"

"A lot of someones. Nazis shot at my father. At my mother too."

How did he cope with that?

"I never met evil before," I said. "What if he's evil?"

"He's not evil. He's complicated."

There was a loud gasp from the other room.

"You OK?" I called to my mother.

"Yeah, I stubbed my toe," she said.

She came into the room and smiled when she saw me. The church bells began to ring. My mother and I dressed quickly and caught an early bus to Beersheba. We talked about my father the whole way south. At the bottom of my purse, I found Suraya's ring and slipped it on my finger.

In Beersheba, prison vans lined the curb outside the district court. I peered through the caged windows, searching for the shooter. We went inside the court building and found his prison ID number first on a list of prisoners to be judged that day. It was early and the lights were still off in the hallways. We sat on a bench outside the chief justice's office. I held the top half of my body still, jiggling my feet beneath the bench.

"You don't want to approach him in anger, right?" my mother said.

"I didn't. But in the last month I got bitter. He's so committed to violence. I'm going to ask him if he's sorry, then I'll tell him who I am. That's all. I hope it hurts."

"If you really want revenge, you should testify against him. In the United States, at parole hearings, they give the victim's family the opportunity to testify. That carries a lot of weight. But that's not relevant in this case."

This was not a parole hearing. It was an appeal of a lower court's refusal to release the shooter on health grounds. There would be no witnesses, no testimony. Baruch had explained to me that the lawyers would argue about the existing record. It was a pure matter of law. No new facts.

The lights turned on in the hallway. My mother nodded toward the stairs. "Maybe that's them. I see some Arabs. How do you say hello in Arabic?"

I stood up, forgetting all my Arabic. Imad's lanky form came toward us. Eleven relatives followed close behind, dressed formally. Imad had put on a tie. The women wore traditional black robes and scarves. The shooter's father had on a lemon-yellow blazer.

Imad broke into a friendly smile and said to my mother, "Laura, she is a sister. She is welcome in our home." The women patted my arms and held my hand. Their skin felt soft.

"Marhaba," I greeted them, the Arabic lobe of my brain resuscitating.

"Merry-hay-bah," my mother said with her Kansas City accent.

"Why didn't you call?" said Imad, a little put off.

Because I'm trying to hate you. "Because I knew I'd see you here."

I introduced my mother to Imad, and mentioned that she was a tax attorney. I introduced him to my mother, and mentioned that he had been marched across the desert into Jordan.

"Why did they deport you?" my mother said.

"I'll tell you later," he said, shifting his eyes.

An awkward pause.

"Uh, you both just had your first grandsons," I said. "I mean, Imad's son will have a baby in two months."

Imad was used to my getting flustered. "Did you finish your book?"

"Not yet. Almost."

"I have a title for it: *Candle on the Road for Peace.*"

The rest of the family had gone into the courtroom. My mother and Imad chatted for a while. Before he joined his family, he looked at me, then at my mother and said, "You have the same face."

My mother and I sat back on the bench, our shoulders touching. My head felt out of order. My thoughts were being slapped by cross-currents. All these years, I had held on to a promise made in a poem, *This hand will find you/I am his daughter.* Finally I had my chance. But something inside of me was uncoiling.

"I'm having a change of heart," I said, barely audible.

I turned toward my mother. "Am I crazy? Am I naive?" I looked into her face for the answer. "I don't want to be a fool. I want to believe the shooter's good because I want the world to be that way."

She sounded sad, though her words were the most hopeful I will ever hear:

"Well, that's all we really have in life."

• • •

WHEN MY MOTHER said those words, I knew what I had to do. But how?

"Go to the judge," my mother said.

I knocked on the office door of the chief justice, pushing it open before anyone could answer.

"Hi, my name is Laura Weiss," I said to the secretary. "I'm a journalist. Can I talk to the judge about a case he's hearing today?"

"Are you here professionally or personally?"

"Both. It's complicated."

The secretary disappeared into the judge's chambers, then reappeared ten seconds later. "He says talk to the prosecutor."

I found her inside the courtroom. She shooed me away. I tried to explain, but in my state of agitation, I must have come across as a gadfly or a loon.

Meanwhile, the courtroom had filled with lawyers, defendants, relatives and friends. Israelis and Palestinians were packed together on the benches. A pile of case files were stacked on the judges' bench. Drug offenses, robberies, murders, political crimes. A panel of three judges would mow through them by midafternoon.

My mother and I squeezed onto a bench in the front row directly in front of the shooter's family. A Palestinian boy from another family sat next to me. I could feel the heat rising off his arms.

My mother handed me a cinnamon candy and chattered, trying to keep me calm. I had made my decision, mostly, but was vacillating again.

"Last trial I went to," she said, "was Don King, and before that, Adolf Eichmann."

She started to tell me about going to the Eichmann trial with my father when they lived in Jerusalem.

Her words caught in her throat. "Here he is."

A pair of feet chained together at the ankles stumbled into my line of vision. I hesitated to look up. I knew that if I looked up, the shooter would no longer be a disembodied act of violence, but a person.

First he kissed his sister. She started to cry. Then his mother kissed him on the neck, next to a pulsing vein. When she picked up her head, stepping away from their embrace, her scarf drew back like a curtain from his face. He had big—no, huge—frail, brown eyes. His skin stretched taut around his skull. There was an odd swelling around his mouth. His cheekbones backed into his ears and cast skeletal shadows under his eyes. His arms were hairless, the color of cardboard. A police officer held on to them firmly.

Imad ruffled his brother's hair, which was black, cut short, and bristly. Then Imad said to him, "Laura is here."

"Laura!" Omar said, turning toward me.

His bottom lip was trembling. "I hoped to meet you one day, but not in this setting. When did you get here?"

"Yesterday."

"Welcome. How is America? I wish I was there. It's hot here."

"Yes, it's very hot." *We're talking about the weather.*

"Are you in the hospital?" I said, summoning a friendly voice. We spoke in English. "How is your health?"

"I went back to the Ashkelon prison to take my college examinations."

Say something, do it now. Don't be a coward. This is your moment.

"This is your mother?" Omar said. "She is prettier than my mother. My mother looks old."

"I'm old too. I'm sixty," my mother said with a laugh.

"Yes? My mother is sixty."

Omar shuffled around toward us, bringing with him the officer and the convict he was shackled to, who was hugging a carton of cigarettes. Omar bent over, close to my face. I wondered if he could smell my cinnamon candy. I looked at his brown shirt. A T-shirt. No collar to grab.

"Let's go," the police officer said, tugging Omar's arm. "Your lawyer's late. They're delaying your case. Back to the cell."

I looked Omar in the eye. The friendliness fell away. "I need to know if you're sorry."

"I will write David a long letter."

"No. I need to know now."

The officer was pulling on him.

"Let her finish," my mother said to the officer. "This is very important. Give them a moment."

"Are you sorry?"

I looked into the dark part of his eyes.

His eyes moved sideways.

"Yes?" I prodded, though I suspected the answer was no.

The officer insisted, and dragged him toward the door. Omar called back to me, an afterthought, "Yes. Yes, yes . . ."

I looked at my mother. Her gaze bore into Omar's back.

"Why were you looking at him like that?" I said when Omar had gone.

"I was thinking, my God, he's electric with potential. What a waste of a beautiful life. He walked in with his head up, not like a prisoner, but like a hero. Not like one of those poor, beat-up little animals that came in earlier with their heads down. This is an extremely sensitive young man, very bright and precious, who acted out as an adolescent and got carried away."

She hugged herself, holding on to her elbows. "Or is he a beautiful, slim, and cunning, poisonous snake who's trapping my daughter?"

While we spoke, the three judges ambled into the room. They skipped Omar's case, which had been scheduled to go first. Omar's attorney, Leah Zemel, had not shown up. The family went outside and paced the halls. My mother and I watched the proceedings, a wife-beating case.

"String him up," my mother muttered. "They get off too easily for domestic violence."

The defense attorney was trying to persuade the judge that the defendant's wife did not want her husband imprisoned: "She says, 'Sometimes you love someone, and you're willing to forgive.' "

My mother took out a pad and scribbled a note: "Forgive him. Forgive me."

I glanced away.

She underlined the words and elbowed me. "Forgive him. Forgive me."

"Come on," I said, getting up. "We can't just sit here."

I realized that I would not have another chance to talk to Omar in the courtroom. The officers would hustle him in and out. If I was going to confront him, it would have to be now, in his holding cell.

My mother and I wandered down the stairs, stopping to ask the guards for the holding facility. We found a windowless shack surrounded by blue metal bars. An Israeli woman was waving a box of cigarettes through the bars, yelling the name of a prisoner, "Gideon Hershkovitz!"

A guard brought her husband outside. He took the cigarettes from her. Easy enough.

I copied her, and stuck my hands through the bars, waving my fingers, yelling, "Omar Khatib!"

A skinny cop sauntered over. "And who are you?"

"From the family. Can I talk to Omar?"

"That one can't come out."

"Please, then, can I come inside?"

"No. Talk to him in court. This area is restricted to lawyers."

"I'm a lawyer," my mother said, excited.

"I need to see ID."

My mother dug around in her purse and plucked out a plastic card: New York State Bar Association Major Medical Insurance Program.

He took it from her and examined it closely. "This is an American lawyer ID. We only allow Israeli lawyers."

"But I'm a Jewish lawyer."

"You have to be Israeli."

"But I'm *Jewish!*"

"Mazel tov."

And he walked away.

Two more hours passed. We went to the canteen to buy water, sat at a table near the stench of the bathrooms, under a reluctant fan. My shirt was sticking to my back.

"This is nerve-racking," I said.

"Imagine how his family feels," my mother said. "So vulnerable and in the control of an alien government."

Omar's brother Saed and his son sat at the next table, bouncing their knees, talking nervously. It was noon and Leah Zemel was four hours late. She was on another case, in another city. The court had recessed for lunch.

Imad and his family entered the canteen and invited us to join them. Imad brought me and my mother cheese sandwiches with pickles and sauerkraut. My mother and his mother sat next to each other, puckering their faces at the pickles, and smiling.

I looked at my watch. Five A.M. in New York. I turned off my cellular phone. Whatever I would do, if anything, would be on impulse. If Baruch called me now, he would try to reign me in. "You can't ambush the criminal justice system," Baruch had told me many times. That afternoon I was going to try.

My mother looked at the Palestinian sitting beside me. It was Omar's father, in his yellow jacket. He was smoking with one hand and drinking black coffee with the other. He had not touched his sandwich. He stared despondently outside, into the glare. His lips were moving with unspoken anxiety.

"Is he part of our group?" my mother whispered.

If I had been an Albanian avenger, he would have been my target.

I leaned into her ear. "He's the one I was supposed to shoot."

"ALL RISE!"

The judges filed into the courtroom. My mother and I stood up, next to Omar's family. The court reconvened with a drug case.

Leah Zemel was at the defense table, the slashes between her eyebrows deepening as she opened Omar's file. It was 1 P.M. Omar was the forty-third Palestinian she would represent that day. Her copper ponytail was pulled so tight that the tension was visible along the hairline. She was the most intimidating woman I had ever met, seeringly indifferent to niceties.

Even so, I had to talk to her. The chief justice and the prosecutor had brushed me off. If I was going to pull off my revenge, Leah was my last hope.

I ran over to her.

"Hi, excuse me, remember me?"

She glanced up, then looked down at her papers.

"I have something to say about Omar," I said.

She did not look up again. "Talk to me after the hearing."

"No, no. I have to talk to you now. I can make a difference."

She was preparing her statement. Her eyes were down, negative, tight. "Look, I'm busy."

"I have to say something at the hearing."

"You should have submitted it in writing two weeks ago. Why didn't you write to me?"

"Because I just got here yesterday."

"Well, it's too late," she said, her pen point scurrying across the page. "You should have come to me earlier."

A picture came to mind—Leah's behind as I said good-bye to the pink and green daisies. "I tried to, but you weren't very helpful."

She looked up, almost hissing: "Go sit down."

I went back to my mother on the bench, despondent.

While I had been pleading with Leah, Omar was brought into the courtroom. His entrance was triumphant. He stopped to shake hands with the other prisoners, slapping them on the back. His smile was so wide, it stamped crow's-feet around his eyes. He flashed a confident thumbs-up to his family.

This worried me because I was still unsure. His shoulders relaxed as he sat down, the skin on the back of his neck rippling. He had changed into black clothes, reminding me that he had worn a karate black belt during his trial. I could not peg his looks, which made it harder. They were neither robustly sinister nor pitifully sick. And he looked the wrong age for his age. Too young. As if being held away from life all those years had slowed his maturation. He was not as I had imagined him to be.

His sister handed me a note from Omar.

Dear Laura, Hello,

****It is a surprise to see you today and your kind mother. You are exactly as I have imagined you to be.*

****I'm sitting now at a very small cell, so small and uncleand and all my mind is nothing other than this visite of you, and the long awaited opportunity of seeing all my family and having the chance to kiss them and hug for me it is a dream. . . .*

I tore through the letter. It was three pages long, written that morning while we had waited for Leah. There was nothing new or important in it. I refolded the pages, and started to stick it into my notebook. Then I noticed some Hebrew print on the back. He must have had no paper inside his cell and used the only paper that he had. A photocopy of his medical report. I had been trying to get my hands on it for months; my father said we needed it to make sure we were not being duped. I looked at the Hebrew stamp: "Dr. Alexander Kahany, General Practitioner, Prison Authority." There were five options to choose from at the bottom. The doctor had checked the box for: "Recommend that prisoner be sent to the medical release committee because of chronic illness."

I looked up. Leah Zemel was waving me back to her table. I ran to her.

"You're awfully desperate," she said. "Tell me what you want to say, and I'll say it for you."

"No. I have to say it."

"Who do you think you are?" Her voice was rich with scorn. "Who are you to judge, just because you're white and you think you're so superior and smart?"

I sucked in a breath. "No, it's because I've spent over a year with them."

"Well, they think you're a pain in the ass."

That stung. Because that was believable. My own husband called me Kotzaleh—"little thorn." It explained, perhaps, why they did not want me snooping in Omar's files.

"I couldn't tell them who I am," I said. "I've spoken to the victim."

She pursed her lips, as thin as an incision. "Did you meet the victim face-to-face, or did you speak to him on the phone?"

"Both. Please, I have to speak at the trial."

"This is an appeal, not a trial," she snapped. "There are no witnesses. Why are your hands shaking? Who are you?"

"I can't tell you."

"Then I can't recommend that you speak. There's no procedure for this. You have no standing in the courtroom."

A rush of thoughts clambered to get out. About my father, about my uncertainty of the right path to take, and about whether the world was good or evil. But there were too many thoughts, and they were too unruly, so instead I said: "You have to promise to keep my confidence. Omar doesn't know who I am." I nodded toward Imad and his parents. "They don't know who I am. I don't want them to know. I know you're Omar's lawyer, but I need you to promise."

"I won't tell."

When I told her who I was, Leah's green eyes sparkled. Her nostrils flickered like a fox sniffing something small and delicious.

"I'll do my best," she said, her tight face loosening. "I've been a lawyer for twenty-seven years. This breaks all the rules of procedure."

When I sat back down, Leah rose to defend another Palestinian. The prisoner was inclining toward Omar, laughing at something Omar was telling him. He had been arrested for shooting an Israeli in his car.

"He didn't do it for ideological reasons," Leah said.

My mother looked at the other prisoner and said, "He looks like a nice boy too."

While Leah talked, Omar kept turning his head, trying to meet my gaze. The last man who caught my eye across a courtroom was Baruch, at the Don King trial, mouthing the words *I love you.* I would not make eye contact with Omar until I was through.

The judges were slouching, swiveling in their chairs. One of them said, "The prisons are full of people like him. Why should we make an exception?"

"Because he's sorry," said Leah.

"Yeah, well, tell it to the parole committee. We'll send this one back to the committee. Let's dispense with Omar Khatib the same way."

Leah objected, "Omar Khatib has health reasons for being released."

A judge said, "He gets better health care in an Israeli prison that he would get on the outside. It's not like he's going to die."

"His condition is deteriorating. *Wakef,*" Leah said to Omar, Arabic for "stand up."

Omar rose, displaying his bony frame. His hand covered his mouth, concealing all but the corners of his frown.

"He hasn't even served two thirds of his term," a judge said. "The medical report says it's hazardous for him to stay in prison, but it doesn't specify why. Send it back to the parole committee. Next."

Leah stepped toward the judges. "One more thing before I finish. It's a special request. A young girl has come from abroad who wants to comment."

The judge straightened up. "Just some young girl?"

"No. She's known the family for a year."

"On what terms will she speak?"

My hands would not stop shaking.

Leah said, "No one is allowed to know."

The prosecutor stood up. "Not even me?"

The judge: "Or me?"

The chief justice said to the prosecutor sarcastically, "We're not important. You're not important."

The prosecutor strode toward the defense, her hand extended. "Leah, you can't do this."

"This is unheard of," said a judge.

Omar looked troubled by her request too. Imad and the family were murmuring among themselves.

For fifteen minutes, the three judges argued, with Leah and with each other, going back and forth. While they debated, I wrote a hasty note to Omar.

"You can't call a witness," a judge was saying.

"This isn't really a character witness. It's someone who knows the guilty family and has ties to the victim too," Leah said. "She came all the way from abroad with her mother. Just give her three minutes."

"One minute." I stood up. "That's all I need." The tension had lifted my shoulders to my ears.

"Who is she?"

"Why should we let her talk?"

"Let her speak," said Leah. "And you'll see."

Finally, the judges voted, 2–1.

"Call her up," the chief justice said. "For the record, we'll call her 'anonymous.' "

I asked my mother to move to the back of the courtroom. I did not want her sitting near Omar's family. Maybe they would be so angry, they would try to hit her. She passed my note to Omar, then changed seats.

> *Hi Omar,*
>
> *I am very disappointed that I couldn't speak to you longer face-to-face. I have something I wanted to tell you in person. I hope you understand the reason I am here. It is because I believe every life is precious and we have to learn that lesson—more important than anything. Please keep your promise. Let us both believe in good. I hope you understand why I did what I did.*

Then I added a line along the bottom, quoting from one of his letters:

> *"People are so different when you know them up close."*

The judges directed me to stand at the front of the courtroom, on a raised platform. My back was to the spectators, my face toward the judges. I stood with my feet together. The muscles in the small of my back were clenched so tight, I stooped forward slightly.

"Your Honors," the prosecutor said, protesting, "she's breaking all the rules of evidence."

Leah folded her arms. "This young girl is a good reason to break the rules of everything."

Standing there as a woman named "anonymous" felt like the defining moment of my life. If this worked then the world would be as I wished. Queen Esther, as my father had told me when he tucked me in at night, hid her identity. When her people were about to be destroyed by royal decree, she revealed her faith to her husband, the king. The political became personal. His love for her saved the day. I hoped, with all my irregular heart, that this story was true.

Transformation was the word I had written on the scrap of paper and tucked into the Western Wall the night I had dressed as a Hasidic boy. Transformation was my wish. If I could be a boy, then the shooter—my symbol of evil—could be good. I could make him sorry. But it would take a radical act, something impossibly optimistic, to transform him. That act would leave me vulnerable, and possibly the fool. It would be riskier than anything I had done so far, but my mother's faith in the goodness of people gave me the courage to try.

THE CHIEF JUSTICE looked benignly down at me, signaling with his hand that I could begin. He said to me in English, "It's OK, you can speak in English."

"I prefer to speak in Hebrew," I said in seamless Hebrew.

Omar's family knew Hebrew, not English, and I wanted them to understand.

Omar jumped up. "Leah, what's she doing?" He lurched forward, alarmed, his Adam's apple bulging. The Christian American journalist was not the person she had seemed to be. She knew Hebrew. "What's going on?"

"Sit down," Leah said. "Just listen."

"My name is Laura," I continued in Hebrew. "I come from the United States."

In the back of the courtroom, my mother was stifling a little cry, thinking, Laura, don't break down. Be in control. Be strong.

I concentrated on the judges' faces and spoke as if in a trance.

"As a journalist, I have gotten to know the Khatib family over the past year, and through them, to know Omar. I don't know all the facts in this case. But I can tell you after a year of knowing him, I think he is truly sorry for what happened, and he has promised never to endanger anyone again. He has promised to find a nonviolent way to promote his political beliefs. I have spoken many times to the victim, David Blumenfeld—"

The judges scowled and began interrupting. "This is classic hearsay. We can't admit this."

"Let me finish," I said.

"There are people a lot more qualified than you to talk."

"Young lady, it's time to sit down."

"Your time is up."

I kept going, talking over their protests. "And David Blumenfeld feels that, thank God he didn't die—"

"You can thank God, but don't thank Omar," the chief justice cut in. "He wanted to kill him."

I rolled on, "And David Blumenfeld is OK, but Omar has been sitting in jail for thirteen years. David Blumenfeld feels that if Omar is truly sick, let him go home. Enough punishment."

The judge on the right glowered at me. " 'Enough punishment'? This is ridiculous!" He threw up his arm.

The judge on the left said, "Make her sit down. She has no right."

"Let me *finish,*" I argued, wondering how bad it was to talk back to three judges.

"We've heard enough," the chief justice said, leaning forward on his elbows, gathering his brows in a punctuating knot. "You have no right to speak."

"I do have the right to speak."

"No, you don't."

"Yes, I do."

"Why?"

The words trembled off the edge of my lips.

"I am his daughter."

No one spoke for a thin second.

"Laura Blumenfeld," I said.

There was the sound of crying behind me. Men and women crying. It started with one gasp and then rolled through the crowd. I did not look back. I would not look Omar in the eye until I was done.

The judges' eyebrows jumped. All three fell back in their chairs. Leah Zemel broke down. The prosecutor was walking in small, penned circles, seething. Omar's mother, who did not understand my Hebrew, looked around the room, bewildered, and said, "Why are my children in tears?"

"How did you present yourself to the family?" the chief justice said, still trying to grasp what was happening in his courtroom.

"As a journalist."

"How long did you keep up this front?"

"A year."

"Why did you do this?"

Finally, I could explain: "I wanted them to know me as an individual, and for me to know them. I didn't want them to think of me as a Jew, or as a victim. Just Laura. And I wanted to understand who they were, without them feeling defensive or accused. I wanted to see what we had in common."

"Why did you do such a dangerous thing?"

"You have to take a chance for peace. You have to believe it's possible."

I pivoted to face Omar, locked eyes with him. My voice was hard, unforgiving. "And you promised me you would never hurt anyone again."

Omar looked flabbergasted. A little scared, happy, but shocked. He looked, simply, shaken.

The judge said, "What? He didn't know before?" He asked Omar, "When did you find out who she was?"

Omar leapt up, stamped his foot, pointing at the ceiling. "Right now." He pointed at the floor. "Right now." Again at the ceiling. "Right now."

"And you promised me, Omar." I held on to his eyes, angry, firm, hoping that he felt ashamed. "This is on your honor. Between the Khatib family and the Blumenfeld family."

A woman stood up at the back of the courtroom. She blurted out in English, in a loud, shaking voice, "I forgive Omar for what he did!"

Forgive? It was my mother. Why did she use that word? This was not about forgiveness. I was not forgiving him. Didn't she understand? This was my *revenge.*

"And if the Blumenfeld family can forgive Omar," my mother continued, "then it's time for the state of Israel to forgive him."

The chief justice mopped his brow. Another judge let out a little whoop and said to Leah, "You're very, very good."

"Are you kidding?" Leah said. "I tried to blow Laura off. I thought she was a pain in the ass."

The third judge, I had noticed, spoke Hebrew with an American accent. He said to me, "It's not my place to judge or to comment on victims, but I think it took a lot of guts to do what you did."

"I did it for one reason." My voice, for the first time, quavered. "Because I love my father very much, and I wanted them to know—he is a good man, with a good family." I took a breath, regaining my composure. "I wanted them to understand, this conflict is between human beings, and not disembodied Arabs and Jews. And we're people. Not 'military targets.' We're people with families. And you can't just kill us."

The American-born judge smiled warmly and said, "I know."

I stepped down from the platform. Without stopping to speak to Omar or to his family, I walked to the back of the courtroom to my mother. I held on to her arm. "Let's get out of here."

"Are you OK?" she said as we rushed down the hall. "I've never seen you so emotionally connected to an idea in your life. I've never seen you so deeply feeling."

"But what did we do for Daddy?"

"You showed that he raised you to be a good human being. That's the biggest tribute to a parent." She put her arm around me. "Now you really have to forgive me."

"Laura!"

We turned around. Imad and his sister were running after us, crying.

Imad's sister and my mother fell into an embrace. Imad opened his arms. Were we going to hug? I was a married woman. He was a married man. It would be a huge breach of Arab custom.

"You helped me a lot, thank you," I said to him, feeling timid again. Without Imad, I never could have written to Omar.

"No, you helped me. I should thank you." His eyelids were red.

We stepped into a brief, clumsy hug.

"I'm sorry I tricked you," I said.

Saed came over and joined us. "Please, come back to the courtroom," he said. "Omar asked me to get you."

Back in the courtroom, the family were still crying, crumpling tissues in their fists and throwing their arms around one another. A crowd surrounded Omar.

His mother took my mother's hand and said, "We are two mothers, one family. And we are both the same."

I hung back, away from the tears and the hugs.

Omar worked his way through the crowd, toward my mother, dragging his ankle chains. He said to her, "Please, send my best regards to David."

There was a sweet flash as I realized that he thought the Blumenfelds were still a family. And then a second, terrible flash as I watched him reach for her. The shooter and my mother were kissing.

EPILOGUE: EVER AFTER

Dear Laura,

A week has passed since that day of the hearing at the court, and all what in my mind and imagination nothing except the picture of your stand in front of the court, and the echo of your voice.

You get me feel so stupide that once I was the cause of your and your kind mother's pain.

Sorry and please understand.

Of course I was shocked to know that you are David's daughter. I'm still holding my hand your last message, thinking again and again in the meanings it has. I didn't sleep for almost two dayes I went on reading again all your precious letters trying to re-arrange the whole puzzle again. I have succeeded in part.

Dear Laura, while writing you this letter, I passed through a very hard breath attack that left me unable to continue until so late this night. I had many attacks before. I don't know why it is so different this time . . .

Soon after I returned to America, my father received a letter from Omar. "God is good to me that he gets me know your Laura," he wrote. "She was the mirror that made me see your face as a human person deserved to be admired and respected. I apologize for not understanding her message early from the beginning."

That, in the end, was my revenge. Neither an eye for an eye, nor turn the other cheek, I had found a third way: Transformation. Revenge does not have to be about destroying your enemy, it can mean transforming him, or yourself.

"Laura chose a positive way of getting revenge from me," Omar said. "And she succeeded."

Along with his apology Omar sent my father a gold necklace with the name "Omar." "If I have learned something from you, it is to be constructive," he wrote to my father. "I do agree with Laura that you really have a point. And you, David, if God helps and I get to be released, I hope you accept my invitation to be my guest in the holy city of peace Jerusalem."

But one year passed, then two, and Omar was not released, and Jerusalem, more than ever, became a city of war. The Middle East, indeed the world, swung heavily toward an eye for an eye. The Palestinians and the Israelis exchanged some of their bloodiest, ugliest blows. On September 11, 2001, as my father walked to work in New York City, a plane flew low overhead. The woman next to him clapped a hand over her scream. Baruch, biking down the Hudson River to work, saw a second plane tear into the World Trade Center. The terror that we had seen in faraway places had come home. Now the question of revenge was before us all.

Following the attack, our president spoke of the need for "revenge" until an aide urged him to call it "justice." News channels adopted the slogan "America Strikes Back." American bombs dropped on Afghanistan were covered with payback messages: "WTC" and "Remember NYPD." Yet as the first bombers roared off the flight deck of the USS *Enterprise,* the captain told the crew, "Don't think of this as revenge. Revenge only belongs to God."

Like so many Americans, I was groping for a response. And like many, I wavered between hope and despair. More than ever peace seemed elusive, and my story felt dreamlike, even to me. When I thought about my newlywed year, I shook my head in disbelief. Some days I felt proud of the stand I took at Omar's hearing. Other times, I wanted to hide under a blanket. My father said, "It was a great heroic moment. You were brave standing up like that, saying 'I am his daughter.' " My friend Rachel said, "It was utterly ridiculous. You were a jackass." One thing I learned that heady day in court was how thin the line is between a hero and a fool.

Then my father and I returned to Jerusalem, at a time when each day was described as the bloodiest ever. We traveled in a bulletproof van to the Khatibs' house. So much had happened in the three years since I had seen them, so much hatred and violence had touched our lives. I was afraid the visit would be strained if not hostile.

At first I did not recognize Imad, waiting for us beside the road. His hair had turned white and his jacket flapped about his lanky frame. His father had died and his mother was close to death. He stepped toward my father. He kissed my father's shoulder three times. While we sat inside their house, eating bananas, and admiring photos from the weddings I had missed, Palestinian snipers patrolled the streets. Omar's sister smoked a hookah pipe with my father. Down the road, an Israeli tank fired a missile at a militant's pickup truck.

"It's good that Laura didn't say who she was the first time she came to us," Suraya said. "We would have closed the door to her, and closed our hearts."

Before we left, my father sent a pen to Omar, inscribed "For Omar, from David," along with a note: "Continue your studies. You're still a young man, you can do something good."

At dusk, Imad hugged my father good-bye.

• • •

BUT WAS IT REAL? Could this tale be true, a bedtime story in a darkened world? I asked the question out loud when I finally spoke to Omar. After serving two thirds of his sentence, he was released on medical grounds and for good behavior.

"It *is* a true story." Omar sounded perplexed by my doubt. "A rare story like ours. In every public session I tell people about you. It brings hope to the heart of the people. It's the hope which brings me the freedom again."

We spoke by telephone. I was in Washington, where Baruch had taken a job with the government seizing and freezing terrorist assets. I had dialed Omar's number, feeling the familiar pinch in my stomach.

"I'm in Kalandia now, where you were years ago," Omar said. "They are showing me where you sat, where you drank tea, where you played with the children." His voice was friendly, surprised, energized. I felt so uncomfortable, I could barely speak.

"How is your mother? How is David?" he said.

My mother, in fact, had invited my father to lunch, and apologized for causing him so much pain.

"They're good," I said.

"What are you doing now?" he asked.

Baruch and I had settled into a happy marriage.

"I had a baby. And another baby," I said. "What are your plans?"

"I am preparing for a job that may suit my qualifications."

I tried to imagine what that might be.

"Diplomat," he said. "International relations. I will support the peace process and continue to move forward beyond the violence. Violence is not a way to gain our rights. I need to build my family. I need to build my home. To do all the things my mother wanted."

"Something constructive."

"It is my promise—to you and to David." In his breast pocket he kept the pen from my father as a reminder. "It is so funny you called me now. There is a girl from Kalandia. Intelligent, very beautiful, a cosmetician. In one hour I am going to ask for her hand."

"Are you nervous?"

"No. I met her once, we talked for two hours." He laughed. He had to go. The family was waiting. "Say hello to your father and your mother. And to the small child."

I hung up thinking back to the first time I saw his house. The gunman was not home. His brother dismissed my father's shooting as "nothing personal." Now it was Omar—not a gunman—who had come home.

It was personal for me. And it was personal for him.

It gave me a bit of hope.

Several weeks after Omar's release from prison, he appeared on the cover of Israel's weekend Hebrew-language magazine under the headline SORRY I SHOT YOU, MR. BLUMENFELD. Photographed in the Arab marketplace on the spot where he ambushed my father, Omar renounced violence and said, "It is only through personal contact that Israelis and Palestinians will reach an understanding." When my father read Omar's interview, he said, "With all the killing going on right now, isn't it dangerous for him to be speaking about peace? I hope he doesn't get shot."

ACKNOWLEDGMENTS

THE PECULIAR THING about this project is that I owe perhaps as many people apologies as I do acknowledgments. Most of the people I interviewed did not know that there was a personal aspect to my interest in revenge. Some, justifiably, will feel betrayed. Others may understand my circumstances. I wish to thank those who helped me and to note that they are not responsible for my actions. After I revealed my identity to the Khatib family in the courtroom, they gave me their blessing for this book.

Karen Armstrong, Neil Belton, Yaron Ezrachi, Meron Benvenisti, Moshe Greenberg, Danny Rubenstein, Ari Weiss, Itamar Rabinovitch, Gadi Baltiansky, Yossi Klein Halevi, Edna Arbel and David Hartman generously shared their insights and knowledge with me. I am indebted, in particular, to Moshe Halbertal, the wise man of Israel. Philip Graubart and Susan Freeman guided me through the subject of collective punishment. Ben Plesser arranged key interviews on divine vengeance. George Davis sent me his astute paper on the psychology of revenge. Noam Haas introduced me to Smitt. Sarah Sofer, a dear friend, told me about Anez Abu Salim. Clinton Bailey, Israel's foremost expert on the Bedouin, offered his expertise and his brilliant translations of Bedouin poetry from his book, *Bedouin Poetry from Sinai and the Negev: Mirror of a Culture.* Susan Jacoby's *Wild Justice: The Evolution of Revenge* gave me the best background on the subject.

I worked with several translators in several countries. None were as hardworking as my friend Mohammed Najib, who translated Arabic to English. In Germany, I owe a special debt to Regine Wosnitza; in England, to Roger Gilbert. Karen Avrich performed indispensable library research. Maralee Schwartz was a treasured companion on walks through the Old City. My colleagues and friends Lisa Dallos, Ilyse Ehrenkranz, Eric Weiner, Sharon Moshavi and Flore De Preneuf were generous and supportive. From the beginning, Jonathan Freedland and Gene Weingarten offered me invaluable advice and encouragement. David, Tziporah, Shai, Diane and Ephraim Halivni embraced me with love. My grandmother Ann Gale taught me that anything is possible.

The *Washington Post* has been blessed with three outstanding Jerusalem bureau chiefs, all of whom contributed immeasurably to my book: Glenn Frankel, Barton Gellman, Lee Hockstader. The *New York Times*'s incomparable Thomas L. Friedman gave me my best sources and was a source himself—of inspiration. I wish to thank Leonard Downie, Steve Coll and Tom Wilkinson of the *Washington Post* for sending me on book leave with their blessings.

The names of all the characters in this book are real with two exceptions. The mastermind's brother asked me not to name his children. My father asked me to change the name of his professional nemesis to "Jake Shain." He did not want to shame him publicly.

During the writing process, a cherished group of friends read my manuscript and improved it dramatically: Michael Abramowitz, Geraldine Brooks, Lisa Chase, Glenn Cohen, Mary Hadar, Steven Goldstein, Laurie Goodstein, Peter Grand, Richard Leiby, William Powers, Jonathan Rosen, Rene Sanchez, Leonora Shaw, Martha Sherrill, Tom Shroder, Kara Swisher, Melanie Thernstrom, Alona Wartofsky, David Weil.

I also wish to thank my agent, the awe-inspiring Esther Newberg. For her intelligence and enthusiasm, I thank my editor Greer Hendricks. For her resourcefulness and good cheer, I thank Suzanne O'Neill. I am grateful to David Rosenthal, godfather of this creation. The Simon & Schuster public relations team, Victoria Meyer and Aileen Boyle, were a writer's dream. Seale Ballenger was a champion of the paperback.

Most of all, I wish to thank the subjects of this book, who welcomed me into their lives and trusted me with their stories. Rachel is a prized friend and adviser. Fran and Bernie contributed grace and good humor. Hal and Michelle pitched in on every level, from suggesting topics to research to critiquing early drafts of the manuscript. Anyone who has read this book knows what Baruch endured during our newlywed year. I thank him for his stubborn, unshakable love. He will always be my hero. Finally, I thank my beloved mother and father, where the story begins and ends.

INDEX

EDWARD MARRIOTT

The Plague Race

A Tale of Fear, Science and Heroism

PICADOR

As he heaved his bags off the jetty, and stood looking out across the deserted dock, Yersin must have felt his initial excitement flagging. He was prepared for an entrance into epidemic territory, but the complete absence of any kind of reception party mystified him. By now, he felt sure, the French consul would have received the despatch announcing his arrival in Hong Kong: why, then, was there no one to welcome him? With the wind getting up and the rain beginning to sting his face, he shouted to his helpers, and together they hauled the cases to the lee of the customs house.

The Plague Race is the story of how one brave scientist unlocked the mystery at the heart of this most feared of diseases. This discovery was made in Hong Kong 100 years ago, during an outbreak that threatened to decimate the island and, from there, the world. A tense and frightening race was run in appalling conditions by two rival scientists: Alexandre Yersin – rigorous, solitary, cerebral – and the suave Kitasako, unscrupulous, enigmatic, careless.

Spiced with anecdotes, facts and chilling reconstructions, this book is an enthralling work of narrative history. And Marriott's investigations into plague in the modern world bring some disturbing facts to light . . .

WILLIAM FIENNES

The Snow Geese

PICADOR

Shortlisted for the Samuel Johnson Prize 2002

Snow geese spend their summers in the Canadian Arctic, on the tundra. Each autumn they migrate south, to Delaware, California and the Gulf of Mexico, and in the spring they fly north again. One year, William Fiennes decided to go with them and to write about his travels. The result is a mesmerizing and extraordinary journey, a moving story about the joy of being alive, of being on the move and – above all – of returning home.

'A profoundly moving account of joy returning, of one man's rediscovery of the world'
Sunday Times

'A terrific book . . . *The Snow Geese* is a delight'
Spectator

'The descriptions of the geese and their environment are jaw-droppingly beautiful. But Fiennes's most remarkable talent is for describing the quotidian with such freshness that it is like seeing the world for the first time'
Mail on Sunday

'With William Fiennes an unmistakably gifted new writer appears on the scene'
The Times

PAUL COLLINS

Banvard's Folly

Thirteen Tales of Renowned Obscurity, Famous Anonymity, and Rotten Luck

PICADOR

History will long remember the Edisons, Einsteins and Darwins: they succeeded in changing the world, and the world has repaid them by enshrining their names. But what of those others with similarly revolutionary and groundbreaking ideas who plummeted into oblivion? They are gone and forgotten . . . until now.

'Failure is generally a lot more interesting than success . . . Failure's coming home; we should all support it by buying Paul Collins' wonderful book'
Mail on Sunday

'Here's a wonderful corrective for a culture obsessed with profile, celebrity, fame, spin and blah. *Banvard's Folly* consists of thirteen discrete and minatory tales, complete with digressions and curiosities, each one the length of the average attack of seasonal anomie, and offering enough Schadenfreude to soothe even the most bilious stomach'
Daily Telegraph

'Drawing heavily on the riches of the nineteenth century – that golden age of miraculous invention, mass communication and epidemic credulity – Collins delivers a beguiling parade of ill-fated flights of fancy whose pioneers have been long forgotten'
Scotsman